P9-CDW-984

CASTLES

A SIEGE OF THE FIFTEENTH CENTURY

From a manuscript belonging to Edward IV., now in Sir John Soane's Museum.

The walls, having been breached by artillery, are being stormed through the breaches; the stormers are covered by the fire of hand-gun-men, crossbowmen and archers.

CASTLES

by

CHARLES OMAN, K. B. E.
M.A., All Souls College, Chichele Professor
of Modern History in the University of
Oxford; Member of Parliament for the
University; Hon. LL.D. (Edin.) and
Fellow of the British Academy, etc.

Illustrated

BEEKMAN HOUSE
NEW YORK

Half-crown of Charles I. of the Civil War Mint of Weymouth-Sandsfoot.

Special material copyright © MCMLXXVIII by
Crown Publishers, Inc.
All rights reserved.

This edition is published by Beekman House,
a division of Crown Publishers, Inc.

e f g h

BEEKMAN HOUSE 1978 PRINTING
Manufactured in the United States of America

Library of Congress Cataloging in Publication Data

Oman, Charles William Chadwick, Sir, 1860-1946.
  Castles.

  1. Castles—England—Guide-books. 2. Castles—
Wales—Guide-books. 3. Great Britain—History, Local.
4. Wales—History, Local. I. Title.
DA660.046 1978   942   78-9930
ISBN 0-517-26196-0

Foreword to the 1978 Edition

The great castles of Britain have long been symbols of mystery and romance to many, but few people know much about the realities of these legendary buildings—their architecture, fascinating stories, or the beautiful and history-laden lands in which they sit. This book offers the reader a unique opportunity to see these magnificent structures through the eyes of a man who studied the military, political, and architectural history of castles throughout his life.

Professor Oman takes us on a tour of all the castles of Southern England and Wales, giving us a detailed description of each one. Before he embarks on this journey, however, he provides a comprehensive history of the castle, from the simple *motte*-and-Bailey structures (inner mounds with outer enclosures) of the eleventh century to the large stone-fortified dwellings built during the next three hundred years. He traces the evolution of the castle over the centuries from a purely military stronghold to a seat of political and social power.

Professor Charles W.C. Oman was one of the foremost military historians of his day. Educated at Oxford under the noted historian Bishop William Stubbs, he became professor of modern history at Oxford and had great influence on the next generation of historians. He was knighted in 1920 and represented Oxford University in Parliament from 1919 to 1935. Extremely prolific throughout his long career, he wrote on many subjects, from ancient Greece to the Napoleonic Wars, and many of his works became standards in their fields. They include *The History of the Art of War in the Middle Ages, The History of the Art of War in the Sixteenth Century, The History of the Peninsular War* in seven volumes, *The History of Greece, Wellington's Army, Napoleonic Studies, Warwick the Kingmaker*, and *The Great Revolt of 1881.*

GAIL ALLAN

PREFACE

THIS book is the result of two most interesting, if rather laborious, journeys, devoted to castle-seeking, one in 1924, covering Wales and the English counties along the Welsh border; the other in 1925, devoted to Somerset, Devon and Cornwall. I was accompanied throughout by my son and his camera, to which about half the illustrations, large and small, in the volume are due. Of eighty castles described in full, all but six were carefully inspected, and recorded by my own note-book and my son's photographs. Tempestuous weather and indisposition are responsible for the fact that the remaining six had to be left unvisited—four of them lie in rather inaccessible corners of the Welsh Marches. In addition to the eighty castles thus described, we looked over some dozens of others, where we found that the buildings had entirely or almost entirely disappeared, so that comment and photography were alike unprofitable. The object of this book is to explain the historical and architectural interest of each castle, so that the visitor may appreciate its meaning. If in some cases I may have missed facts recently elucidated in the Proceedings of some County Archæological Journal, and followed an obsolete theory, I must plead in excuse that local antiquities are discussed in scores of publications hard to find, and often practically inaccessible. In regard to the Welsh section, I ought to express my indebtedness to two most admirable books—Professor John Lloyds' *History of Wales*, and Mr. J. E. Morris's *Welsh Wars of Edward I.*

In conclusion, I must make an appeal to the archæological traveller. There are four classes of castles from the tourist's point of view. (1) Those which lie open and exposed, generally on windswept hills or little-trodden valleys, like Caer Cynan, Dinas Bran, or Tretower. (II.) Those which are ruinous, but in custody of the State, or of an owner who exacts a fee and keeps the place in order, like Chepstow, Raglan, or Kenilworth. (III.) Those which are inhabited, but opened to the public at certain hours and under certain conditions, like Windsor or Warwick. (IV.) Those which are inhabited, but only accessible by the specially obtained leave of the resident owner. The tourist must not drop in casually at places such as these last, and expect to view them at his leisure. He must write beforehand, and submit his convenience to that of the owner. Permission to view at reasonable hours and for proper purposes is seldom or never refused. I have to acknowledge much kindness and courtesy shown me by many castle-dwellers. It would obviously be intolerable to the resident owner if unannounced archæologists kept presenting themselves when he was giving a garden party, holding a political meeting, or offering a lunch to his tenants. In all such places previous correspondence is absolutely necessary.

C. W. C. OMAN.

CONTENTS

PART I

English Castles

PART II

Castles of Wales, and of the Marches

ILLUSTRATIONS

PLATES

ix

PLATES—*continued*

x

PEN AND INK SKETCHES

PLANS

MAP

Usk Castle

INTRODUCTION

The Definition of a Castle

WHAT is a Castle? Probably every person to whom this simple query is propounded thinks for a moment that the answer is easy. But a little reflection, concerning the widely divergent structures to which the name is applied in daily conversation, will suffice to show him that a definition is not so readily to be found as he had expected. The word "castle" is linked to all manner of things, from prehistoric earthworks down to preposterous erections of the twentieth century, with mock battlements and sham drawbridges, built for misguided lovers of the romantic or for ostentatious profiteers.

To take an example of the first class—everyone has heard of "Maiden Castle," the vast ringed series of banks and ditches, three miles outside Dorchester, which probably served several successive British tribes as a stronghold long ere the Romans came to this Island. Certainly nothing could be more unlike a castle, as generally conceived, than this complicated structure, which is represented in the first illustration of this book. Yet "Castle" it has been called for at least eight hundred years, though it has none of the features which we associate with the name, save that it was once a place of defence— a fortress of the days that knew not of brick or of hewn stone. And, oddly enough, we know that the Romans called these British hill-forts *castella*. Juvenal describing the ordinary avocations of the legionary officer of his own day —somewhere about 120 A.D.—mentions among them " diruere castella Brigantum "—to destroy the *castles* of Yorkshire Brigantes—tough enemies of the legion that lay garrisoned at the newly founded Eboracum.

Yet if Dorsetshire had not persisted in calling Maiden Castle by that name through long ages, which of us now would call it anything but an earthwork or a tribal camp of refuge? The name castle would not occur to us. There are other similar cases scattered all over the realm from Cornwall to Northumberland, where the enquirer, expecting to find mediæval stonework, discovers nought but prehistoric spade-work.

But at the other end of the scale this same deceptive word "castle" is applied to certain very large mansions of Georgian, Victorian, or even

"Maiden Castle," Dorchester

I

twentieth century date, which have a sufficiently pretentious and semi-military aspect to deter the auctioneer or the compiler of local guide-books from calling them Halls or Manors. Some of them stand on the sites of genuine castles of the Middle Ages, of which every external feature has disappeared, and have inherited the name from their vanished predecessors. Others are mere usurpers of the name of castle, solely in virtue of their battlements and towers—anything big and Gothic in style may get the designation, if its owner is hardened enough to bestow it on a building of yesterday or the day before. The only exception that I can see is that a dwelling of pure classical architecture will not earn the name, however large and pretentious it may be. Colonnades, pediments and statuary may make a " palace," perhaps—but not a " castle." For that public opinion requires loop-holes, machicolations, the semblance of a portcullised gate-house, and (above all) battlements that fret the sky line. I refrain from quoting examples of modern castellated architecture, lest certain owners should accuse me of malevolence. But a terrible example may be seen in the second illustration of this book.

The French of to-day are even worse than ourselves in the misuse of the name " castle "—they apply it to any large residential dwelling in the country-side, even when it has no signs of defensive decoration, and is of pure seventeenth or eighteenth century domestic architecture. Most of our " halls " and " manors " would be called *Chateaux* by our neighbours across the Channel.

But to get to the heart of the question, as to what is a Castle in the proper sense of the term, we must commence by ruling out prehistoric tribal camps at one end, and Victorian mock-antiques at the other. The Society of Antiquarians has a much-valued " Earthworks Committee," to which I relinquish the examination of the former class. The latter may be studied in the photographs of the auctioneer or the land-agent, which adorn the outside pages of the *Times* or the *Morning Post*.

We shall be getting near a definition if we rule that a castle is a " fortified dwelling intended for purposes of residence and defence." A British hill-camp is not a fortified dwelling—though it may once have contained many huts or wigwams,—and a Victorian castle is not intended for purposes of defence, however apparently formidable its aspect.

I do not think that we can properly include

Victorian Castellated Architecture—A Sad Example

among castles such military buildings as were not intended for purposes of residence. They may be called forts, blockhouses, towers, redoubts, or what you please. It is difficult to draw the line: for example the modern antiquary has determined to call the small garrison-towers, which lie along the Roman Wall in Northumbria at regular intervals, "mile castles." But I doubt the applicability of the term. On a parallel line of argument we should have to call each of the mural towers that line the *enceinte* of the Tower of London a "castle." In each case these structures are, in fact, only parts of a greater whole, not independent units. Nor could one properly describe Mr. Pitt's line of Martello Towers, along the coast of Kent and Sussex, as castles. They are small and non-residential, mere emplacements for a few guns to command a stretch of foreshore in a time of threatened invasion. And modern usage has also denied the name of castle to military structures of recent date, placed for purely tactical reasons to block a pass, or to deny access to the entrance of a harbour. To these the title "fort" or "battery" is applied, even though they may be so far residential as to afford shelter to a certain limited garrison.

On the other hand we must carefully exclude also, from our definition of castles, all fortified towns. These are residential, it is true, and essentially places of defence. But they are much too large to be considered in the light of a single fortified dwelling. They must be called fortresses, even though in some cases their whole circuit may be no greater than that of certain exceptionally large and complicated castles. It is quite common both in Britain and on the Continent to find a castle on a height, with a town which has grown up below it, and has ended by protecting itself by a line of walls joining on to those of the castle above—as did, for example, Edinburgh in the sixteenth century. And it is still more common to find an ancient walled town, in some corner of which a royal or baronial master has built himself a separate stronghold, long after the town was originally fortified—as happened at Lincoln or Exeter. But in all these cases the castle is a distinct unit from the town, though it may be either enclosed within it or built against one of its sides. Invariably the castle was cut off from the town, and was built so as to be capable of further defence, even after the town had fallen into the hands of an enemy. It was not a mere part of the town.

I have seen the castle defined in one excellent book as "the private stronghold of a single owner," and in another as "the product of the feudal system, and the home of the feudal lord." While acknowledging that there is much plausibility in each of these two definitions, I must point out, with regard to the first, that a castle need not be the property of a single owner, unless the body of citizens composing a republican state can be said to be a single person, and to have private property—which seems to be an over great stretching of terms. For example the "Castello" at the south-eastern extremity of the main island of Venice is certainly a castle, but as certainly it did not belong to the Doge or any other individual, but to the State of Venice. And equally so the Swiss Cantons sometimes built, and more often maintained, castles which held down the regions which they had won from their Austrian, Burgundian,

3

and Milanese enemies. We can not, therefore, insist on a castle being necessarily private property. While with regard to the other definition which makes it " the home of the feudal lord," we can not call an Italian or a Swiss Commonwealth a feudal lord, and moreover many castles were not baronial but royal, built and maintained by the king, as the suzerain of all barons and the representative of the State. The King of England did not hold the Tower of London or Dover Castle as a private individual, but as king. I hold, therefore, that the question of proprietorship does not affect the definition of the word " castle," and that the only conditions which govern the proper use of the term are size, character, and purpose. That is to say, a castle is a military structure larger than a mere tower, peel, or blockhouse, but not amounting to a fortified town. It must be residential, but the name would not cover military buildings intended for residence but not for defence—*e.g.*, modern barracks. For the same reason the name ought not to be applied (but often is applied) to modern residences quite unsuited for defensive purposes, but having some delusive show of fortification. Lastly, a castle must, however complicated in its internal arrangements, be a unit in itself, and not a mere part of a town or some other agglomeration of buildings. But a castle may exist inside a town, or adhering to it, provided that it is essentially separate, and can be cut off from it—*e.g.*, by the closing of gates and the lifting of drawbridges.

We have arrived at this definition guided by commonsense and logic only. But it may be well to make a note on the curious history of the word " castle," since much confusion has been caused both to mediæval monastic chroniclers and to modern historians by mistranslation of the words castrum, castellum, castel, castello, chateau. *Castrum* in classical Latin was a very vague word, meaning a closed place such as a fort, a walled enclosure, or a stronghold of any sort. Its plural *castra*, as every schoolboy knows, means a military camp, of the type of the great legionary square, girt by ditch and palisade, such as the Romans built in their prime. *Castellum* was a diminutive of *castrum*, and should have meant a closed place of a smaller sort—as Wycliffe thought when translating the Latin Bible into English, for by *castella* " he understondeth litil touns." But he was not quite correct—at the time when the Vulgate translation was made, in the earliest years of the fifth century, *castellum* was being used in a very vague sense, as was also *castrum*. Both seem to have applied to populated places, small and great, whether they were regularly fortified or not. And when St. Jerome was translating the Septuagint or the New Testament into Latin, he regularly rendered κώμη into *castellum*, though the Greek word meant a mere village of any sort. This turned out to be a trap for unskilled Latinists in the later Middle Ages, when the feudal castle had become a familiar phenomenon. And so we find the author of the *Cursor Mundi*, about 1300 A.D., stating that Bethany was the " Castle " of Lazarus, Martha, and Mary, in which they entertained Our Lord. No doubt he conceived them as a feudal family, with a portcullis and a coat of arms.

Now both in Carolingian France and Anglo-Saxon England *castellum* was used in the eighth and ninth centuries, as St. Jerome had used it in the fifth,

4

to mean merely an inhabited place, not always a small one. Egbert of Kent and Offa of Mercia in charters call Rochester a *castellum*, and the considerable towns of Mâcon and Vitry were *castella* to a Frankish chronicler. Hence much confusion has arisen, and subsequent historians, both mediæval and modern, failed to understand that *castellum* merely meant a town in the days of Egbert or Charlemagne, and not a fortified residential building. It was only in the tenth century that the word began to be used for what was then a new thing— the stronghold that the feudal lord, who had risen on the ruins of the Carolingian Empire, was beginning to build all over Continental Europe. It is a misfortune that no new word was coined to express what was actually a new phenomenon. But both chroniclers and clerks drawing up charters preferred to use old terms, not only *castellum* but *arx, munitio, turris*, all words old and familiar and with no necessary connection with the feudal castle, and so all equally delusive to readers in later ages. There is a transitional period in the tenth and eleventh centuries during which it is impossible to discover, except from the context, whether a writer is speaking of a *castellum* of the sort that St. Jerome or Charlemagne knew, or of one of the new royal or baronial strongholds. But finally the old sense was forgotten, and the new use of the word passed from the Latin into the spoken tongues of most of the nations of Europe, and castle, chateau, kastel, castello, castillo, in the sense of a baronial stronghold, appears on the map all over Christendom, even as far as the Ægean, where kastros and kastris are in many cases legacies from the Frankish barons, who built their castles to hold down the scraps which they had torn away from the Byzantine Empire.

The First of the English Castles

THE name of "castle" first occurs in English records under the date 1048, eighteen years before the battle of Hastings and the coming of William the Conqueror. The Anglo-Saxon chronicle there mentions, obviously as a thing new and notable, that certain foreign *protégés* of King Edward the Confessor erected a "castle" in Herefordshire, and treated the king's subjects dwelling around with roughness and contumely. Their local patron was, no doubt, the Confessor's Norman nephew, Ralph of Mantes, who had been made Earl in those parts in 1046. But within a year or two there must have been more than one such a building, for when Earl Godwin returned from exile and scattered his master's alien favourites in 1052, we are told that " some fled west to Pentecost's Castle, and some north to Robert's Castle." Now "Pentecost's Castle " must have been a stronghold of Osbern Pentecost, a well-known Norman settler, and may have been either Ewyas or Richard's Castle, both in Herefordshire and both connected with Osbern's family in later Post-Conquest days. Where " Robert's Castle " may have been is a puzzle : the owner was possibly that Robert Fitz-Wymara whom the Confessor had made Sheriff of Essex ; and Canham and Clavering in that county have been suggested as the site. These are the first mentions of " castles " in England—the things were new to the chronicler, and he utilized a foreign word because there was no English term that would serve.

This does not mean that fortification was unknown in early England, but that fortified residences of moderate size, intended to house a military retinue, were a novelty. The kings and magnates of the late Anglo-Saxon centuries were well acquainted with walled towns, which had played a great part in the history of the Viking wars, but they had not been accustomed to build strongholds for themselves in the countryside, nor even (it would appear) to shut off any corner of a walled town, as a special house of defence if the outer *enceinte* should be pierced. The system of covering the whole face of England with walled towns, " burhs," started by Alfred and continued by his successors, had proved effective. It was purely urban, and each earl or thegn was expected to trust the security of his family and goods in time of war to the stone or wooden walls of a " burh," not to any private fortress of his own. In days of peace they dwelt in halls, such as we see represented in the Bayeux Tapestry, where Harold Godwineson is seen feasting his friends at Bosham, on the eve of his unlucky voyage to Normandy. The picture shows a two-storied building, with pillared vaults below and living rooms above. There is no indication of any external defences—probably a hedged or palisaded enclosure sufficed to keep off robbers or wolves. That the English had not begun before 1066 to copy the example of Osbern Pentecost, or Robert Fitz-Wymara, and build themselves private strongholds, is well illustrated by the remark of Orderic Vitalis, who says that the easy subjection of England by William the Conqueror was in no small degree due to the fact " that there were practically no fortresses such as the French call *castella* in the land, wherefore the English, though warlike and courageous, proved too feeble to withstand their enemies."

The Normans of 1066 on the other hand were essentially castle-builders, though their castles were at this time structures of the simplest sort. They had learnt the practice from the French neighbours among whom they had intruded themselves in the tenth century. The outburst of castle building which began in the Carolingian Empire late in the ninth century, and became universal in the tenth, had partly been produced by the necessity for coping with the heathen invader from without—Viking, Hungarian, or Saracen—but it continued to develop long after they had ceased to be dangerous, and is explained by the chronic condition of feudal civil war all over the disrupted Empire. In the days of Charlemagne a magnate might live in his country manor, under the security of the " king's peace." But in the tenth century it was a case of " eat or be eaten," with every man. When life had become a practical exposition of the doctrine of the " survival of the fittest," the animal with the hardest shell had the best chance of winning through.

The shell was often of a sufficiently simple sort—a rocky hill strengthened with cuttings or palisades, in regions where nature had been lavish of stones and precipices—but in flat lands often nothing more than a mighty artificial mound of earth, girt by one (or even two) ditches, and well stockaded. The mound which was the foundation of so many castles, in England no less than abroad, was generally called a *motte* (mota): on top of it surrounded by the innermost palisade was the tower or dwelling of the lord [*arx, turris, domus, munitio* indifferently].

What these mound-castles were like we can see from the sections of the Bayeux Tapestry whereon Duke William's invasion of Brittany is portrayed. The pictures of Dol, Dinan, and Rennes each show us a pointed hill with a ring of palisades at its top encircling a large building. Exigencies of space have prevented a proper rendering of the ditch at the foot of the mound, but its existence is vouched for. There is careful representation of a bridge leading up to the mound. That the bridge is available even for horsemen is shown by the fact that in the pictures of Dol and Rennes one of the Norman attacking force is shown mounting up it on his steed. That the upper palisade is only wood and not masonry, is clearly indicated by an incident in the picture of Dinan, where two of the besiegers have crept close under it, and are endeavouring to set it on fire by means of torches or cressets.

It is quite possible that, even from very early days, a castle was occasionally built, in whole or in part, of stone. But this was very exceptional : there were two hindering causes—the first was the excessive cost of stone as compared with earth and timber, and the length of time which building in stone took up. The second was that heaped up earth takes years rather than months to settle down and become solid : if, therefore, a very heavy weight of masonry were superimposed, immediately after the throwing up of the mound, the soil would undoubtedly slip or crack in irregular patches, and parts of the tower

7

would sink or break away from the rest. There are occasional notices of such disasters, caused by "settlement" following the imposition of too great a weight on new earth. But of course where, by way of exception, the keep was built on actual rock, there would be no danger. And there are plenty of cases where a stone keep has been placed on an artificial *motte* when long years have permitted the complete settling down of the soil—as *e.g.*, the polygonal keep of Oxford Castle (now vanished) which superseded the original building of Robert D'Oilly.

But, as we shall see, the use of stone in the earliest English castles was so uncommon that it would be possible to count on the fingers of the hands those in which it was certainly employed during the reigns of the first two Williams. Over ninety per cent. of the original Norman castles were built with ditch and palisade and not with masonry.

Below the *motte* or mound which constituted the essential part of an eleventh century fortification, there was usually an outer enclosure, called in those days a Bailey (ballium). It was surrounded by an earthen bank topped with a palisade, and by a ditch. It would be capable of defence for some time, but might have to be evacuated in case of a serious attack with regular siege machines. The Bailey had room enough to pen the cattle of the garrison, and to contain the wooden hall for their common meals, for the workshops of the artisans employed about the place, and no doubt in many cases for their flimsy dwellings. In time of war it was the space in which the outlying retainers of the lord of the castle would take refuge with their goods and their beasts. Baileys differed in size according to the opportunities given by the lie of the ground; they might range from an acre up to six or eight, where nature had been exceptionally favourable in indicating a very defensible outer line to the castle-builder. In later ages nothing was more common than to find the Bailey turned into a serious outer *enceinte*, an integral part of the fortress—becoming its "outer ward" —while the *motte* or mound, also much improved, became the "inner ward."

From the very moment of his landing on the English shore William the Conqueror started castle-building on the widest scale. Even before the decisive battle on the slopes of Senlac had given him the crown, he had thrown up a castle of the usual type at Hastings, to cover his port of disembarcation. The Bayeux Tapestry shows us a mound rising under the busy spades of his soldiers, and a palisade is already beginning to appear on its top. And this start was logically continued: every town and shire that he occupied was to be held down by systematic fortification. For he was well aware of the precarious nature of his tenure during the early years of his reign, when any English district that got the chance might flare up in sudden insurrection.

The vast majority of William's castles were originally structures thrown up hastily on the "*motte* and bailey" scheme. They were almost invariably constructed in timber and not in stone—as is shown by the fact that many are recorded to have been finished in a few months or even weeks. The Castle of York, for example, was ordered to be built in the summer of 1068: it was finished and garrisoned by five hundred men before the winter. In March,

8

Bayeux Tapestry. *Dinan* besieged by Duke William and its palisades fired

Bayeux Tapestry. The Building of Hastings Castle

Bayeux Tapestry. Duke William captures Dol and Rennes

THE BAYEUX TAPESTRY

1069, the Northumbrians rose and besieged it. William returned in haste to relieve it, and supplemented it by the erection of a second castle on the other side of the river Ouse. This structure was completed in *eight days*. But in the following September the Yorkshiremen rose again, encouraged by the arrival of a Danish fleet. They besieged both castles, and in ten days had taken and destroyed them. Obviously such hastily constructed works cannot possibly have been composed of masonry, and must have been ditched and palisaded structures, not stone keeps in the later Norman style.

Domesday Book mentions forty-nine castles as existing in 1086, but this is certainly not a full list, as the great inquest is not a complete record of all England. Modern research can count up to at least 85 castles built before the year 1100, and showing definite indications of their early date. And there undoubtedly were others, which have now vanished so completely that no statement can be made about them, and a few more which have been so overlaid with later buildings that it can be suspected, but not proved, that they were in existence under the first two Williams. Of the 85 castles undoubtedly belonging to the eleventh century only six or seven would appear to have been wholly or partly built of stone. The great square stone keeps which are generally regarded as the typical Norman buildings were, with few exceptions, erected in the reigns of Henry I., Stephen, or Henry II. There are only a handful of keeps which may be attributed to the Conqueror's period—such as the Tower of London, Colchester, Pevensey, and Richmond (Yorks). We know that Rochester was rebuilt by Bishop Gundulf about the year 1088, but the enormous keep, which now forms the prominent feature of that imposing structure, was undoubtedly reared in the time of Henry I. At Exeter (see page 91), where there never was any keep, the very early gatehouse still visible may go back to the Conqueror, but the rest of his castle appears to have been banked and palisaded, not built of masonry. Where, as at the Tower of London, and at Colchester, the earliest Norman architect did embark on construction in stone, he worked on no small scale—both of these keeps vie in size and strength with anything that was built in later days—but they were wholly exceptional.

The castles, therefore, which the kings and barons of the eleventh century reared all over the face of England, to hold down a discontented nation, were in a large majority " mound and bailey " structures. How the palisade and the timbered house of defence within it was gradually replaced by masonry arranged in various schemes must be explained later on. Meanwhile before going into the question of architectural development, it is necessary to classify the English castles from the historical point of view, showing the various ends which they were intended to serve, and the divergence of character which was caused by the difference in the builder's purpose.

The Two Classes of Castles—Royal and Baronial

WHEN men set themselves to build places of defence, it is because they know that they are in danger either from a foreign enemy, or from civil wars within the state, or from the uprising of a discontented subject population. This is equally true whether the building be that of city-walls, or of castles, or of modern forts and batteries. When a region enjoys a long period of internal quiet, as did the greater part of the Roman Empire in the first and second centuries after Christ, or Great Britain in the eighteenth and nineteenth centuries, there is no building of new strongholds in the interior : the only fortifications erected or maintained are those on frontiers or seaboards, where the state is in touch with a possible foreign enemy.

When, therefore, we find a country set thick with fortresses over its whole extent, as were most of the states of mediæval Europe, we know that one, two, or even all of the three dangers mentioned above must have been impending. Foreign invasions, such as no mere frontier defences could ward off, were seen from time to time. Such were the raids of the Vikings in the ninth century and the Hungarians in the tenth, such also in later times were the great Mongol raid into Eastern Christendom in the thirteenth century, and the westward advance of the Ottoman Turks in the fifteenth and sixteenth. To deal with such cataclysmic invasions even internal provinces needed their strongholds.

Systematic fortification of a whole countryside to hold down conquered and discontented populations may be seen in cases such as that of the Anglo-Norman adventurers who subdued first Wales and then Ireland, and of the German adventurers who won from the Slavs the "marks" beyond the Elbe, such as Brandenburg and Misnia, and in later days conquered from the wild Prussians and Lithuanians the broad dominions of the Teutonic Order.

But undoubtedly the most common and regular cause of fortification was the danger of civil strife within the realm, either between a king and his nobles, or between two great factions which divided the governing classes, or simply between individual magnates or families, venting personal or hereditary spite against their nearest neighbours. There are examples of all these three sorts of civil war to be found in English history. Of wars between the king and part or all of his baronage, we may quote such cases as the strife between Henry I. and the rebels headed by the house of Belesme, and again the war between John and the barons of the Great Charter, and in the same century that between Henry III. and the league headed by Simon de Montfort. Of faction-strife the Wars of the Roses are the most obvious but not the only example. Purely private wars between barons were much less frequent in England than on the Continent, but instances occur, such as the bickerings of Bohun and de Clare in South Wales in 1290, the Courtenay-Bonville fight in front of Exeter in 1455, and last, but not least, the Berkeley-Lisle feud in 1470, which ended in the considerable private battle of Nibley Green. In all these cases neither side was making any pretence of fighting for the king, or for a constitutional cause, or even for a party inside the state : the grounds of quarrel were purely personal.

The original outburst of castle-building in England during the reign of William the Conqueror must be ascribed in the main to the need for holding down a newly-subdued and resentful subject population. The king could not have felt himself safe from general rebellion, nor his newly-enfranchised tenants in chief have escaped assassination in detail, unless they had possessed strongholds secure against any sudden explosion of popular violence. Hence it was that, although kings disliked as a rule castle-building on the part of their vassals, and sometimes claimed to be the only lawful holders of castles, yet William permitted and encouraged the erection of private fortresses by his more prominent followers. He knew that they could not have preserved their existence without them.

From the first, therefore, we find the castles of England divided into two classes, the royal and the baronial. This division goes very deep, affecting the position, character and object of each stronghold. The king required castles either to overawe large towns, which might have become centres of revolt, or else to guard strategical points both on the circumference and in the interior of his realm. There was a political meaning in each of his castles. The baron, on the other hand, was, in most cases, merely seeking either for the strongest site that could be found in his fief, or else for the spot from which he could most easily dominate and administer it. At the most his purpose would be tactical, rather than strategic like that of the king, since normally each fief was a unit in itself. It is only on the Welsh and, to a lesser degree, on the Scottish marches, that baronial castles are found supporting each other, and built on a common scheme, though belonging to different masters.

The king, as we have already said, required castles to overawe the larger centres of population, most of which were already towns walled in the old Saxon style, with ditch and palisade. Of some thirty royal castles which can be reckoned up as built before 1100 the majority are inside, or alongside of, the walls of some considerable town. Such were the castles of London [the Tower], Cambridge, Chester, Colchester, Exeter, Gloucester, Hereford, Lincoln, Old Sarum, Winchester, Worcester, and York. It is curious and interesting to find that in many cases the king built his castle not *inside* the town, but against its outer wall. This was a mark of suspicion—he did not wish to have it hemmed in with houses or too easily accessible. In cases where the chosen site was intra-mural, the dwellings of the citizens were torn down in ruthless fashion. Domesday Book records many instances of tenements " waste " because a castle had been recently built. The Tower of London, Colchester, Exeter, Rochester [Gundulf's stone castle] and Lincoln were intra-mural castles Hereford, Norwich, Winchester, Chester and York were extra-mural.

But the king also required, outside great centres of population, another class of castle, which we must call strategical, since they were placed at points where defence was vital to the whole realm. Some were reared to block obvious landing places for an enemy coming from over-seas. Such were

Dover, Hastings, Pevensey, to which in successive generations were added many more, such as Portchester, Southampton, Scarborough, and Orford. Much later Henry VIII. constructed a whole line of such castles from Kent to Cornwall, including many famous haven-guarding fortresses, like Walmer, Camber, Portsea, Hurst, Calshot, Portland, Dartmouth, Pendennis and St. Mawes.

There was a different but hardly less important class of strategic castles—those in the interior, which were designed to command those critical fords, passes and defiles, through which the main routes, commercial and military, then ran. In many cases these arteries of communication were already guarded by the walled towns dotted along them. Where this was not the case, a royal castle was often reared to watch the critical point. Obvious instances are Newcastle-on-Tyne, placed to block the lowest ford on the Tyne, and Wallingford, commanding the most important ford on the Thames. When a private castle had arisen on a spot which turned out to be of high strategic importance, the king generally endeavoured to get hold of it—as was the case with Newark, taken from the Bishop of Lincoln by Stephen in 1139, and Corfe, forfeited from William of Mortain as early as 1105 by Henry I.

Baronial castles on the other hand were, as a rule, simply the spots which the new Norman landholders chose as the most eligible sites in their fiefs. Eligibility might mean one of two things—either great natural strength, or convenience of situation for the purpose of dominating the lands of their fiefs. It is generally known that King William served out the forfeited lands of the English thegnhood to his followers in a complicated fashion. It was seldom that a whole region was bestowed on a single grantee, usually his lands were scattered in several counties, in non-contiguous patches. It was only in certain great frontier earldoms, such as Shrewsbury, Hereford, and the palatine bishopric of Durham, that the earl was the main landowner, and might, if he chose, build several strongholds, placed in military relation to each other. But, as a rule, if a Norman magnate had more castles than one, they were remote from each other, each the centre of a separate holding.

The sites of some of the earliest baronial castles were apparently selected for mere inaccessibility—such were the cliff-guarded strongholds of William de Mohun at Dunster, of William Peveril in the Derbyshire Peak, and—if he was the first builder—of Reginald, Earl of Cornwall, or the black rock of Tintagel. But a baron whose estate lay in Kent or Essex could find no such precipices. He took what advantage he could, and often discovered that water or marsh gave good protection. In some of the early feudal fortresses morasses or muddy watercourses covered most or all of the front—as at Castle Acre, Kenilworth, or Tonbridge. In later ages streams were dammed up so as to make artificial lakes, as at Leeds (Kent), Shirburn and the lovely Broughton [both in Oxfordshire], or Caerphilly in Glamorgan. There was a special advantage in water-girt fortresses: the use of mines—one of the most formidable methods of siege-craft in the Middle Ages—was impossible against them. But neither cliffs nor water defences were available for most of the baronial castles, which usually started with simple mound and bailey. If a baron could find a rising ground

13

with fairly steep sides, or could cut off the end of the spur of a hill by a deep ditch—as at Chepstow, Okehampton, or Morpeth—he was generally satisfied.

Apart from the castles of the Welsh March the great castle-building age in this realm was the twelfth century. There had been, as we have already said, about a hundred castles, small and great, erected between the battle of Hastings and the death of William Rufus. But the next century more than trebled the total, despite the endeavours of strong kings like Henry I. and Henry II. to restrict the multiplication of private fortresses, and the heroic effort of the younger of these two to destroy all the unlicensed castles which had sprung up in the anarchic reign of Stephen. He had much success—" adulterine " castles, built without the royal leave, perished by the score, and have often left no trace behind but a green mound and the relics of a ditch. For in a great proportion they were still earth and timber strongholds of the earliest Norman type, easily built, and ready to crumble easily when dismantled and deserted. Probably the actual number of English castles in occupation was higher at the end of the reign of Stephen than at any other moment before or after. But even Henry II. was not able to do away with all the castles which had sprung up, though he thinned them out. And occasional additions continued to be made after his death. Both new royal castles, called into existence by some strategical necessity, and new baronial castles, still kept appearing, though in diminishing numbers.

The distribution of castles in the various regions of the realm is irregular, and sometimes difficult to understand. Two tracts are set very thick with them. The first is the Welsh March, and South Wales ; the other the Scottish March—and more especially Northumberland. In both war was endemic—in Wales till 1410 and the crushing of the last great insurrection under Owen Glendower: on the Scottish Border almost till the union of the two realms under " James I. and VI." But there are notable divergencies of distribution in shires which were not near to habitually turbulent neighbours.

The first cause that we discover is that where church lands were very widely spread, castles are few. For though most bishops owned a castle (and some of them two, or even three) the abbeys, whose lands were much broader than those of the bishops, were not castle-building institutions. The bishop was a tenant-in-chief with military obligations, as well as an ecclesiastical potentate, and generally got permission to fortify a stronghold—e.g., the bishop of London had the strong castle of Bishop's Stortford, the bishop of Winchester Farnham and Wolvesey, the bishop of Hereford Bishop's Castle, the bishop of Sarum Sherborne, the bishop of Worcester Hartlebury, the bishop of Wells his crenellated and moated stronghold opposite his cathedral. But bishops were personalities—abbots did not need castles, because they were but chairmen of corporations, often kept in check by a jealous body of brethren. At the most an abbey sometimes got leave to embattle its monastic buildings. Hence wherever we get a great stretch of abbey lands, we get a dearth of castles—e.g., on Cotswold, where the Abbots of Evesham, Tewkesbury, Cirencester, Hailes, and St. Peter's, Gloucester, dominated the whole region. A similar scarcity of castles may be discovered round St. Edmundsbury, Glastonbury, and the great group of South Lincolnshire Abbeys.

The next point to note is that a very large and compact holding, whether belonging to an earl or a baron, would show one first-rate fortress commanding the whole region, rather than a number of small ones. When a great tenant-in-chief had many castles, it was because his estates were scattered all over England, and he wanted a castle in each fief. The holdings of the richer barons were dispersed in the most eccentric fashion, partly owing to the way in which William the Conqueror distributed the confiscated Saxon lands among his first followers, but quite as much owing to marriages by which an heiress brought to her spouse an estate far remote from his original sphere of influence, e.g., the Cliffords, originally marcher lords on the Wye, got half Westmoreland as the dowry of a Vipont. The Bigods, earls of Norfolk, obtained Chepstow with the hand of a lady of the house of Marshall. The Fitz-Alans of Clun in Shropshire, became the greatest magnates in Sussex when their head married the heiress of Arundel. As to the accumulation made by the house of Lancaster, the descendants of Henry III.'s son Edmund Crouchback, they were portentous after successive earls and dukes had married the heiresses of the earldoms of Lincoln, Salisbury and Hereford, and of the Marches of Kidwelly and Brecknock. Edmund, their progenitor, had been already gifted by his father with the confiscated lands of the Montforts of Leicester, and the Ferrers of Derby. Hence the Duchy of Lancaster under John of Gaunt bestrode all the realm from Northumberland to Wiltshire, and from Essex to Kidwelly. He owned about twenty of the greatest castles in England, but when we look at their positions on the map we see that they are strategically without any correlation to each other. The Duke of Lancaster was a person of enormous territorial influence, but he had no solid and connected block of lands anywhere. It is only the king's castles which have any common purpose and bearing, whether as part of a system of coast defence, or as covering internal points of strategical value.

A much-castled district, putting aside the Welsh and Scottish Marches, was usually a region where proprietorship was much divided, either where a cluster of second-class barons lived near each other, or where fragments of the holdings of several greater barons, whose main interests were in another county, were each sufficient to require a separate military centre.

Where population was very thin, because of woods, fens, moors, and bare downs, we do not expect to find many castles. The only object of a builder in going off into the desert was to secure inaccessibility. And such builders were not very common, though they included those of the castles in the Peak, Dunster and Tintagel. As a rule unpopulated regions are bare of castles—note the long stretch in the wooded weald of Kent and Sussex between the line of castles north of it—Tonbridge, Reigate, Guildford, Farnham, and those near the sea—Amberley, Lewes, Hurstmonceaux, Bodiham, Hastings. North Devon, similarly, has nothing but Barnstaple and Torrington. The woodland of Dorset is very bare, so is Chiltern, and so are the Cornish Moors.

Castles of the Twelfth, Thirteenth
and Fourteenth Centuries

AT the accession of Henry I. the immense majority of the castles of England were simple " *motte* and bailey " structures, with their wooden tower or house of defence perched on a mound, whose summit was surrounded with palisading. The base was girt with a ditch, beyond which lay the bailey or outer court, with another palisade and ditch of its own. Only a few castles had, like the Tower of London, been provided already with a stone keep.

In a general way the architectural progress of the twelfth century consisted in the substitution of stone for wood in castle-building. It was very gradual; not merely did many earth-and-palisade castles survive all through the century, but more were being continually built, up to about 1154, though the proportion of them was always growing less. In the anarchy of Stephen's reign the advantages of cheapness and rapid construction caused many landowners to run up hasty " *motte* and bailey " castles for the purpose of self defence, rather than to start on stone building, which would certainly be costly, and perhaps not completed when the hour of trial came. Henry II., when he suppressed the " adulterine " or unlicensed castles, destroyed scores of these buildings, but others survived, and were not turned into stone till the thirteenth century had set in.

There were several types of development by which the original " *motte* and bailey " castle was turned into something more capable of long and obstinate defence. The first and most obvious was the following of the example which William I. had set in the Tower of London, the building of a large stone keep, to replace the original wooden tower on the *motte*. The twelfth century was the golden age of the great keep, which grew more and more common as it advanced, but was seldom built after the day of Henry II.—under the later Plantagenets it became very abnormal. Keeps might take several forms, and be fitted into different parts of the castle. Sometimes they stood, like the Tower of London, isolated in their own passive strength within the inmost ward of the castle. Good examples of this may be found among the castles which we are studying at Goodrich, where the keep is square, and at Pembroke and the little Tretower (Brecknock), where it is round—a much more exceptional shape. But the keep might also be inserted in the wall of one of the wards, often in the strongest corner of the *enceinte*, so as to give as good a final refuge as if it stood isolated in the court. Such were the positions of the round towers of Penrice and Cilgerran (Pembrokeshire), and of the rectangular keep of Chepstow, which occupied the whole breadth of the cliff-top from end to end, with an outer ward on each side of it : at Abergavenny, so far as the relics give guidance, it would seem to have been in the same way inserted in the wall. A more exceptional place for the keep was the fore-front of the castle, the most exposed point, where it covered the gateway, as would seem to have been the case at

16

Kidwelly, where the original Norman keep has been built up into the great thirteenth century gatehouse, and at Ludlow where it blocked the entrance of the inner ward.

But the solid keep, square or round, was not the only form of final stronghold which replaced the early house of defence on top of *mottes*. Sometimes the castle-owner found that the plateau was too large to cover with a solid keep, or that he could not afford to undertake such an ambitious piece of building. In such a case he often replaced the palisade on the *motte* by a curtain wall of stone, forming a ring or shell around the edge of the plateau, without a tower either inside it or built into its circuit. This type of mound-defence is called a shell-keep. It may be of any size : some are quite small, others very large, encircling a broad central area in which there was room for small subsidiary buildings. It lay with the twelfth century builder to determine whether he would accept the contour of the *motte*-top as it stood, or scarp its sides down to smaller dimensions, or throw up more earth to broaden it. But this last operation would need care, since newly-heaped soil might slip down, if subjected to the weight of a heavy wall.

Some of the most famous castles of England and Wales start with a shell-keep replacing the palisade of a pre-existing *motte*. Such are Berkeley, Totnes, Launceston, Cardiff, and Usk.

Meanwhile, when the *motte* was developing into a keep of some sort, the outer *enceinte* of the bailey was seeing its palisades replaced by stone masonry of more or less height and solidity. First came simple curtain walls—without bastions or mural towers, which were not developed on any scientific scale till the thirteenth century—their shape was not worked out on any mathematical principle, but was simply settled by the contour of the original bailey's earthwork and ditch.

Stone was, of course, far preferable to earth and palisading. Palisades can be battered down with rams, or pulled apart with hooks and picks, or—easiest of all—set on fire by heaping masses of straw or brushwood against them. The keep could defy such simple assaults, when its walls were twelve, fourteen, or even twenty feet thick, and it could also defy any bombardment with the primitive siege artillery of the early Middle Ages, the mangonels and catapults which threw stones by the force of tension or torsion. Such missiles would do no more than chip its solid bulk, or at the best bring down battlements. More dangerous, but very slow of operation, were the bore (*terebrus*, or *teretrus*) and the battering ram. If the enemy had got through the enceinte-wall of the bailey, he would run trenches up to the foot of the keep, covering the head of his sap with pent-houses or mantlets, in the old Roman style, and having reached the foot of the inner ward would attack a chosen spot either with the battering ram, or by setting his engineers to work with bore and pick against the lower courses of the structure, in the hope that he might pull out or shake down enough stones to cause a general collapse, and open a breach.

Now the weak point in Norman castle-building was that both keep and curtain were ill-provided with means for molesting an enemy who had worked his way up to their foot.   Apertures for discharging missiles were few and small, and vertical shooting down from them almost impossible.   Presently, however, before the twelfth century was very far advanced, the idea was introduced of throwing out projecting galleries of wood, from the upper courses of the wall or the keep, with holes in their flooring, from which bolts might be shot, or unpleasant things such as stones, boiling water or pitch, or even molten metal, dropped on the heads of besiegers who had actually reached the wall-foot. These wooden galleries were called *hourdes* ("hoardings") or later *bretèches* (brattices).   It was not till the end of the thirteenth century that we find them replaced by the much more satisfactory device of "machicolation," *i.e.*, of building the projecting gallery, with the holes in its bottom, in stone instead of in timber, so as to be an actual part of the castle, not a rickety adjunct.

But the assailant had a more effective device than either the bore, or the ram, or battering with mangonels. This was the mine.   The besieger worked down from a shaft-head in his trenches till he had got below the foundations of the wall.   He then began to remove foundation stones, replacing them with props of timber, till he had excavated a chamber of considerable size : this he would stuff with brushwood and other combustibles, which, when fired, would bring down the supporting woodwork.   If the plan had been properly carried out, the superincumbent wall would then fall into the excavation, and open a broad breach.   The classical instances of success in this fashion were King John's capture of Rochester Castle in 1215, and Hubert de Burgh's dealings with Bedford Castle in 1224.   The great Justiciar first mined the outer *enceinte*, then the keep.   When the latter began to crack and crumble the garrison surrendered—and were promptly hanged to the number of eighty, including several knights.

But obviously mining was useless against either a rock-castle or an island castle.   With the former it would be an endless task to hew through many yards of solid stone : with the latter a mine would be flooded out when it got below water-level.   Neither Rochester nor Bedford were of either of these classes.

The first series of improvements in defence had to do with the idea of securing flanking fire against an enemy working up to the wall-foot.   The problem of how to keep him off was solved, by the device of furnishing the hitherto straight walls of the curtains with projecting mural towers, which afterwards developed into bastions.   Such towers, built well forward out of the line of the *enceinte*, were furnished in their sides with loopholes which looked right along the foot of the wall.   A small square castle would require no more than four, one at each corner, the distance between any two of them being easily within bow-shot.   A large castle would require not only corner-towers, but several intermediate ones.   In the vast Portchester (Hants) the sides had four projecting circular towers : in the much smaller Whitecastle (Mon.) there was only one on each side over and above the corner towers.   A small place like Chirk (Denbighshire) would depend on the four corner towers alone.

In the end of the reign of Henry II., when the square keep began to go out of fashion, the development of a strong gate-house became a main feature of castle-building. The idea that the entrance might be made the strongest point of the fortress was not altogether new. At Ludlow and Exeter some such notion had already been seen. But about the end of the twelfth century, and all through the thirteenth, it grew usual to heap such heavy defences on the gate-house that it became the most imposing part of the castle, unless there were still an early Norman keep in existence, to dwarf all other building. But from 1200 onward most new castles developed gate-houses of great strength, often with extra and supplemental detached works in front of them. These were called barbicans (the word is of uncertain derivation): they served to narrow down the approach to the gate-arch, before the besieger could get anywhere near it.

The typical gate-house of the early thirteenth century was that formed by two projecting circular towers, guarding on each side the actual gate, which lay somewhat recessed between them. The towers, and the chambers above the archway between them, made a single solid building, always cut off from the rampart-walls, which ran along the curtain on each side of the gate. The chamber on the first floor above the arch was devoted to the management of the portcullis, which was let down or lifted up by windlasses. Often there were one or two stories of good rooms above the portcullis chamber. Fine examples of the typical gate-house with two drum-towers may be seen at Chepstow, Whitecastle, Criccieth, Upton (Pem.), Kidwelly, Rockingham; in later castles the towers are sometimes polygonal and not round—as at Wells and Raglan.

Barbicans, when they were added in front of the gate-house, might be of almost any size and character. At Kidwelly and Pembroke they are elaborate, but not very large, and placed close in to the gate-house. At Warwick the barbican is big and lofty, very thoroughly dominating the main entry, narrowing the space, and compelling an enemy to advance on a very small front. At Broughton (Oxon.) we can hardly deny the name of barbican to the very solid tower blocking the bridge across the moat, at some distance in front of the main works. And it would seem that at Kenilworth the two separate stone works across the causeway over the now-vanished lake, a very long way from the *enceinte* of the castle, must also be called barbicans. The term is indeed a very vague and deceptive one, which may cover anything from a strong and elaborate outer gate to a mere pair of converging external walls.

By the later years of Henry III. any new castle that was being built, or any old castle that had been brought properly up-to-date, would be equipped with mural towers or bastions, and have very strong protection for its entry—though this might not necessarily be a towering gate-house, and might or might not have a barbican in its front. It was also now the rule to have living apartments other than those that might be contained in the limited space of the keep. Indeed the keepless castle built since 1180 would certainly have hall, chapel, kitchen, and other chambers built into the walls of its inner, or less frequently its outer, ward. The idea of the fortress was still dominant, but that of the palatial residence of a feudal magnate had already come in. The living apartments of many thirteenth century castles are well lighted, spacious, comfortable and often highly decorated.

It was not till the very latest years of Henry III. that a single definite scheme of fortification begins to be visible in most parts of the realm, and shows the rise of a new school of military architects of a rather mathematical turn of mind. This scheme is often called the " Edwardian " style, because it was most prominently displayed in the great group of castles which Edward I. built, for the holding down of the newly conquered principality of North Wales. But there is definite proof that it was already in existence before the accession of that great king, and was in no sense his invention. The style is also called the " Concentric " system, though the literal meaning of that adjective must not be pressed too hard. If we were to insist that a concentric castle must be one in which each ward is completely enclosed in that next without it, like circles of different sizes drawn round a single centre, we should get a wrong idea. The term really means that each line of defence protected that immediately within it, which could not be assailed till the outer line had fallen—*e.g.*, Conway is a concentric fortress, though, being built on a headland projecting on to the sea, its innermost ward has water on two sides, and the middle ward only on the third.

Undoubtedly the earliest castle which answers the test by which we can declare it to be a concentric castle of perfected style, is Caerphilly in Glamorganshire, which was started in 1267 by Gilbert de Clare Earl of Gloucester, five years before Edward I. came to the throne. A full account of this massive and scientifically planned fortress will be found in the chapter dealing with the county in which it stands. And in another place the details of Harlech, the most picturesquely placed of all King Edward's castles, may be found. In each case the striking feature is the complete surrounding of the innermost ward by that which lies around it, and the accurate mathematical regularity of both.

With the reign of Edward I. the great castle-building age came to an end, though real castles, and many more great residences that called themselves castles, continued to be reared for another two hundred years. It was not till Tudor times that all magnates set on providing themselves with new abodes, finally abandoned the pretence of making them defensible, planned them for ends of convenience and splendour alone, and relied for protection upon the " King's Peace " rather than on moats and barbicans. We do not mean to say that many fine houses unsuited for military purposes were not reared before Tudor times ; nor, on the other hand, that some semblance of defensive strength was not given to halls and mansions built in Elizabethan, or even Jacobean, days. But large residences of a frankly non-military type were rare in the fourteenth century. and only beginning to come into vogue in the fifteenth.

The End of the Castles

CASTLES which were purely military in purpose continued to be built for some time after the fourteenth century had commenced, and even after artillery had begun to show signs of its ability to sweep away stone walls, however strong. But that the old feudal period was drawing to an end is shown by the extreme paucity of first-class castles built on new sites after the death of Edward I.—Dunstanburgh (1313) is about the only instance that can be quoted. Such new fortresses as were planned were nearly all on a small scale, and intended to serve local ends—e.g., to give protection against French raids by sea or Scottish raids by land. Or else they were built to minister to the pride of a rising family, which thought itself sufficiently important to require a baronial hold instead of a mere manor-house. Farleigh Hungerford is a good example, and Donnington another. But this latter class of castles developed very soon on the non-military side, and came to be planned for mere convenience rather than for efficiency in war.

When a magnate wished to set to work on his chief seat, either because it was only a manor-house, or because as a castle it was out-of-date, he had to ask for a " licence to crenellate " from the king. The tendency of the times can be shown from the fact that Edward III., in his long reign, issued 181 such documents, Richard II. 60, Henry IV. no more than eight, Henry V. only one, Henry VI. five, and Edward IV. three. Many of these licences relate to repairs to old castles, others to trifling additions to mere manor-houses which never became real castles. Out of the whole 260 only a few dozen relate to the building of serious military structures on new sites. By the fifteenth century there was much construction in progress, but either that of castles which were not primarily fortresses but rather splendid residences —like Raglan—or that of great manor-houses like Minster Lovel or Wingfield, which were obviously civil in character.

What was the underlying cause of the progressive decadence of the system of castle life, and of the triumph of the residential mansion ? Not, assuredly, that the times had grown less turbulent, nor till a late date in the fifteenth century that

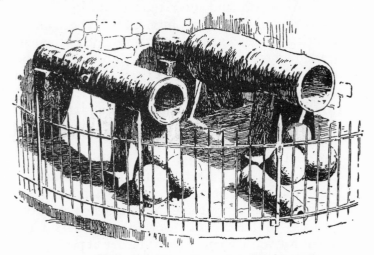

Captured English Siege Guns (bombards) temp. Henry VI. at Mont St. Michel

artillery had grown all-powerful. It is only necessary to remember the portentous length of Henry V.'s sieges of Rouen or Meaux, while reflecting that he possessed what passed in his day for a first-rate royal siege train. Yet instead of sieges we get in the fifteenth century history of England battles in the open, on such a scale as had never been seen in earlier centuries. The fate of the realm was settled at Shrewsbury, Bramham Moor, St. Albans, Northampton, Mortimer's Cross, Towton, Barnet, Tewkesbury, Bosworth, Stoke Field and Blackheath. In the twelfth century Henry II. spent twenty years on war without fighting one general action : in the thirteenth the victory of Lewes was followed by the interminable siege of Pevensey, and the victory of Evesham by the almost equally protracted siege of Kenilworth. What had happened in the meantime to change the face of war ?

The only convincing answer would seem to be a military one—*viz.*, that it had at last been discovered that a system of passive defence behind stone walls may protract a war, but does not decide it. Though sieges may be as long as those of Pevensey or Kenilworth in the Barons' War, or those of Aberystwyth and Harlech during the rebellion of Owen Glendower, there comes a time when the last barrel of salt beef has been emptied and the last cask of beer drained. And then the game is up for the besieged party. Protracted local defences have no practical effect on the general fortune of a war, if one combatant has got possession of the open country, the capital, and the machinery of government. The chance of final success lay with the party that mobilized the strongest force, struck first, and compelled the enemy to accept a battle in the open field. If he were there beaten, and then shut himself up in castles, his doom was certain, though it might be long in coming. As a rule the defeated side did not do so, in the War of the Roses : there were still hundreds of castles in England susceptible of defence, but we can not count a dozen sieges in thirty years of strife. The leaders of a faction beaten in the field either fled to France, Scotland, or Flanders, or else made an insincere submission to the victor, hoping to stab him in the back on some better opportunity. For political discontent and treachery not infrequently intervened ; the army of a leader who had made himself unpopular might refuse to fight, like Richard of York's host at Ludlow in 1459, that of Edward IV. in 1470 during Warwick's rebellion, or the unwilling levies of Richard III. at Bosworth Field.

This simple fact enables us to understand why a baron of the fifteenth century began to spend little money on bastions and gate-houses, and much on comfortable residential quarters. All would depend on the battles if war broke out : the man who shut himself up in a castle would probably end with his head on the block, even if he held out for many months before surrendering. And the siege might not be so very long—cannon were improving, as Sir Ralph Grey found out at Bamborough in 1464, when the stones of the most formidable rock-fortress of the North "flew like flinders into the sea." So if money was spent for warlike ends, it was rather in paying large bands of "household men," or in spreading the detestable practice of "livery and maintenance," by which a great baron could raise hundreds of adherents for the battle-day, than on mortar and masonry.

The end of many, perhaps of most, castles, was that their owners abandoned them as places of habitual residence ; some modernized the cramped, dark, and uncomfortable dwellings, and continued to dwell in them. But more abandoned them as hopelessly inconvenient and let them go to ruin, building less military and more splendid manors or halls, in some less inaccessible spot. Berkeley and Kenilworth, Cardiff and Warwick were modernized, and many others, but when Leland went on his antiquarian tour round England and Wales in 1540-42, he reported everywhere castles " nearly down," or " far gone to decay," or " once a great thing, but now a pound for cattle." And this was not the result of a series of destructive sieges during the wars of the Roses, but of deliberate desertion and neglect. Liskeard and Tintagel, Dinas Bran and Clun, Torrington and Caer Cynan were wrecks long before the artillery of Fairfax's " New Model Army " blew down so many royalist castles in 1645-46.

The king's castles had a particularly humiliating end. Since they were so many that he never by any chance visited the majority of them, since constables were negligent and often non-resident, and sheriffs parsimonious, they dwindled down into jails for the most part. For as the castle of the county-town always contained the *gaolia regis*, the part of the building that served as a prison was kept up, but all else was allowed to slide into permanent disrepair. One of the odd results of this is that the word donjon, originally used for the keep or dominating tower of a castle, passed into common parlance as the modern " dungeon." " The lowest dungeon below the castle moat," to which the tyrant of mediæval melodrama consigns his victim, is a contradiction in terms, for the donjon was always the highest point of a fortress. To the regret of every archæologist the jail-aspect of the shire-capital castles so much prevailed over all others, that many of the venerable relics of the earlier Middle Ages, being inconvenient and insanitary from the point of view of the practical eighteenth century, were gutted or pulled down entirely, in order that buildings more suitable for the modern prisoner should replace them. Oxford Castle is a prominent example—there remains nought of the old fortress save St. George's Tower and the *motte*. Lancaster has kept its mighty gate-house intact, but its hinder parts are smothered by the modern prison. Carmarthen shows scraps of thirteenth century work peering through an eighteenth century classical façade. The bulk of Chester Castle was pulled down as late as 1797 to make way for a new county jail and barracks. The famous " Rougemont " of Exeter was gutted to make way for an assize hall, though not for an actual jail. At Launceston by 1740 there was nothing left save the castle keep and the common jail : in 1830 even the latter disappeared, and only greensward was left. Of Gloucester, Bristol and Hereford Castles, all mighty works, only the eye of faith can discover the sites, for not even a modern prison survives to show where they once stood.

By 1500 we have got to the point where even a show of defensive strength was abandoned, and those of the English magnates who wished to build sacrificed all other ends to beauty and convenience. If a gate-house or a tower was still in the design, they were made the mere vehicles for armorial display or artistic carving. And battlements were retained for mere picturesque effect—as they were in so many sixteenth century Oxford and Cambridge Colleges, which had no military end whatever.

By this time it may fairly be said that artillery had come into its own, and that no sensible man would build a keep eighty feet high, or curtain walls of forty feet, merely to give a good mark for cannon balls. The fall of the great triple wall of Constantinople, under the siege train of Mahomet II. in 1453, marks the point at which really formidable and first-class fortifications began to succumb to the cannon ball. But many a year more was to go by, before it was generally recognized that to defend a mediæval castle against modern guns was a hopeless business. Castles and even manor-houses were repeatedly held against artillery during the great Civil War of King and Parliament in the seventeenth century. Indeed they were often so held by desperate partisans, in the scrambling and amateur warfare which marked the first two years of the clash between Cavalier and Roundhead—but seldom (as we shall see) to good effect, if the besieger had even a moderate provision of great guns.

In the sixteenth century military building did not cease, but it was no longer employed on castles of the old sort. Modern fortification was invented to cope with the modern siege train. The Tudor military architect built his fortress low, and intended it mainly as an emplacement for artillery. The last "castles," such as Portland or Pendennis, St. Mawes or Walmer, were really forts rather than castles. They are not to be found in the interior of the realm, but only along the south coast, where Henry VIII. threw up some dozens of them when, in his later wars with France, he had lost, or almost lost, the command of the sea, and saw the coast of the Channel raided again and again by French landing forces. The chain runs from Walmer, Camber, and Sandgate on the Dover Straits, past Portsea, Hurst and Calshot, as far as Falmouth in the extreme peninsula of Cornwall, where Pendennis marks the end of the series.

Their typical aspect was a circle of broad but stunted semi-circular bastions surrounding a low central keep. The bastions were casemated, with bomb-proof roofs, and splayed-out embrasures through which the concealed and protected guns could play.* Details differed : sometimes there was provision for two tiers of guns, one in the keep : but often the latter was only pierced for musketry, and furnished on top with swivels and wall-pieces. The castles were built low, so as to give as little mark as possible to the guns of a hostile fleet, and the only thing which they had in common with mediæval fortresses was the great thickness of their walls. Oddly enough, I do not think that any of King Henry's haven-protecting castles were ever actually subjected to the test for which they were built—action against a French fleet—any more than were Mr. Pitt's " Martello Towers " of the Kent and Sussex coast exposed to the cannonade of Napoleon's squadrons. Both were curious examples of a precaution quite justifiable, but—as it turned out—unnecessary, since England never really lost the command of the sea.

* For a typical embrasure, see the illustration to St. Mawes in the Cornish Chapter.

There were practically no sieges on this side of the channel in the sixteenth century—it is hardly worth while to mention King James IV.'s successful bombardment of Norham, Wark, and Ford in 1513, or the half-hearted defence of Barnard Castle in 1569, against the rebel Earls in the Rising in the North. And meanwhile the nobility and gentry of England built not castles but the splendid Elizabethan and Jacobean manor-houses which are the glory of the land. Nothing seemed more unlikely than that there would be one more short period of turbulence, in which dozens of famous mediæval castles were again to play a part in war.

The " Great Rebellion " has peculiar interest, as a unique specimen of a military experiment worked out by the English people undisturbed by any interference from outside. Neither side had any trained army, and hardly a single English town or fortress had seen a new stone laid since Henry VIII. had built his chain of harbour-guarding forts a hundred years before. The first year of the war was really a struggle between weak forces, hastily embodied, for the control of the separate regions in which each unit was interested. When the Royalist and Roundhead squires of a county divided in spirit, such as Cheshire, Warwickshire, or Wiltshire, set to work to molest each other, the weaker party was thrown on the defensive, and seized some strong point on which to rally. As often as not this strong point was a castle or a big manor belonging to some leading landowner, though sometimes it was a town. The local forces bickering in a remote county had often no guns, or at best only two or three small pieces. So a really solid castle could be held for some time against an enemy, gunless or only provided with a few old-fashioned sakers or falconets, retrieved from some forgotten store, or brought up from a seaport.

Hence came all manner of interesting amateur sieges, of which we sometimes have personal narratives from those who took part in them, like the Roundheads' defence of Wardour, or the Royalists' defence of Corfe. Mines were sometimes used for want of cannon, and the primitive device of trying to burn down a gate by heaped-up brushwood set on fire was not despised. It was worth while to defend an out-of-date castle, or even a strongly-built house which had not been erected for any military need—like Basing or Bletchinton— if the enemy had no adequate siege train. And the same was seen with towns no less than with castles, as witness Blake's defences of the improvised works of Lyme and Taunton.

For nearly three years of the war both sides used the principle of trying to hold every point of vantage, partly because a castle or a town dominated the countryside, but much more from the simple fact that a castle-owning squire or the burgher of a little town wanted to keep their own homes safe. Hence on both sides an intolerable number of combatants were locked up in petty garrisons, and took no part in the decisive fighting of the pitched battles. Yet when a decisive battle had been lost, all the small strongholds of the neighbouring region were doomed to fall, sooner or later, into the hands of the party which dominated the countryside.

It was not till 1644-5 that the Parliamentarians saw the folly of this policy, and adopted the principle of " slighting," *i.e.*, putting out of action, all captured castles, by blowing them up rather than garrisoning them.   And a few months later the king, who was even in greater straits for men than the Parliament, had to take up the same system, and suppress minor garrisons.   But it was very difficult to induce the local leaders to fall in with this " self-denying ordinance." When we read the surrender-rolls of the king's Welsh fortresses in 1645-6, we find statistics of far more than enough men to replace the infantry lost at Naseby. Though the commanders had persistently asserted that no troops whatever were available there to reconstruct a field army, places like Carnarvon, Berkeley, Denbigh, Raglan were found full of men.   Localism all through the war was even more ruinous to the king than to his enemies.

Meanwhile Fairfax and Cromwell with the battering train of the " New Model Army " moved slowly round the West Country and Wales blowing in the defences of time-honoured castles, and then blowing up their gate-houses, keeps and curtains.   On the whole it is surprising to find how much survived even after a thorough " slighting."   Mediæval walls were thick and mediæval mortar was tenacious, and the putting of a castle out of action did not really mean that it was razed to the ground.   But the large majority of the castles that were defended in 1645-6 were never inhabited again.   For one that was restored after the Civil War, like Arundel or Powys (Castel Coch) or St. Donats, there were a dozen that were abandoned.   A few came safely through because their owners had been stalwart Parliamentarians, who secured that their homes should escape "slighting"—such were Warwick, Cardiff, Chirk and Broughton (Oxon).   But when we look round England as a whole we must formulate the conclusion that survival as an inhabited abode was exceptional after 1646.   The large majority of such old castles as had not been already deserted in Tudor times were deserted after the Great Rebellion—like Nunney and Donnington, Carew and Montgomery, Wallingford and Winchester, Pembroke and the vast courts of Raglan.   Wind and rain, the deadly embrace of the treacherous ivy, and stone-filching neighbours have brought them to their present state of desolation.

WINDSOR CASTLE : VIEW FROM RIVER

WINDSOR CASTLE: EXTERIOR OF ST. GEORGE'S CHAPEL

THE THAMES VALLEY

UNDER this heading we have to consider the block of country formed by Oxfordshire, Berkshire, and the southern third of Buckinghamshire. The last-named most anomalous county— a very artificial creation of the early tenth century—was divided across its centre by the wilderness and woods of the Chiltern Hills; and all its northern part drains into the Ouse, and belongs to the Midlands, not to the Thames Valley. Hence the shire-capital, Buckingham itself, with its ancient but almost vanished castle, does not fall into the sphere of our enquiry, nor do the scanty remnants of the old baronial fortresses of Bolebec and Hanslape. The comparatively narrow point of South Buckinghamshire, which reaches down to the Thames, is singularly deficient in castles, though it contained one or two well-known monasteries. Probably the explanation is partly that much of the land belonged to St. Albans and other religious houses, partly that much more was the king's, Chiltern being royal forest, while royal Windsor lay just across the river. At any rate there are in South Bucks no more than the remains of small manorial strongholds, like the tower of Little Missenden, and one or two crumbling mounds, traces of Norman "*motte* and bailey" castles which vanished early, such as those at High Wycombe and Kimble. None of these are worth a visit from the archæologist, and the only place of which some notice will be taken in this chapter is the late, but picturesque, Boarstall—which is, after all, almost on Oxfordshire ground.

The Thames has been from the earliest days an important waterway—it used to be navigable as far as Oxford—and also a well-marked boundary, which had separated early British tribes and Anglo-Saxon Kingdoms. It was in the Middle Ages a bigger stream than it is now, and a more formidable obstacle for other reasons—its frequent double channels, backwaters, and sodden water-meadows made it unapproachable for long reaches, and there was no road which followed its banks. Hence the places at which it was easily passable were limited in number, and most of them were notable strategical points. To these William the Conqueror turned his attention in the earliest days of his castle-building, and chose as sites for first-class castles Windsor, Wallingford and Oxford. The latter two were old Anglo-Saxon "burhs" of considerable importance, each covering a favourite point of passage. Windsor was a new site, occupied not because it covered any notable road from north to south, but because it occupied an exceptionally commanding position, on a steep chalk hill, rising directly above the river. Before the Conquest there had been a royal residence at "Old Windsor," but this was two miles from the present castle, and not on strong ground.

Quite early, but more probably in the time of Henry I., than in that of his father, there was a castle built at Reading also, not down by the river at Caversham Bridge (where was a ford or ferry, no bridge, in those days), but beside the old Saxon town, which was already a place of some importance, though not walled.   But Reading Castle has vanished even more completely than Reading Abbey :   it was gone by the time of Leland's travels.   That indefatigable wanderer could only say " the name of Castle Street yet remaineth, but I could not perceive or clearly learn where it stood.   But by all likelihood it may have been at the west end of Castle Street."

There was only one other castle on the Thames, that far towards its source at Castle Eaton near Lechlade, where Leland saw " great ruines of a building *in ulteriori ripa*, which was the Lord Zouche's Castle."   Since all is gone, its date is not to be fixed, but it evidently covered the passage across the stripling Thames from Fairford to Cricklade.   There was not a castle, but what Leland calls a " pile," or peel-tower, covering Radcot Bridge, apparently built by the Lovells in the fifteenth century.

The Oxfordshire lands north of Thames had a larger number of baronial castles than those of Berkshire on the south of the river.   The explanation probably was that in Berkshire an enormous proportion of the county was dependent on the two great royal strongholds of Wallingford and Windsor— the Honour of Wallingford alone contained over 100 knights' fees, mostly in Berks, and the Abbot of Abingdon, also a very great territorial magnate, had 30. But in Oxfordshire the king's lands were not very broad—mainly Woodstock Chase, an uninhabited region—and the titular Earl of Oxford had no hold whatever over the shire save his " third penny " and his title.   The De Veres ought to have been Earls of Essex, in which the bulk of their lands lay—but that appellation had already been granted to the Mandevilles, and Henry II. put off Aubrey de Vere with another and a very empty comital name.   Oxfordshire was really in the hands of a number of minor families all through the Middle Ages, and this is why it was rather well provided with castles, though many of them are of late construction.   Arsics, D'Oillys, Iverys, Chesneys and Bassetts had estates scattered all through the county: the first-named had the head of their barony at Cogges, the second were for three generations constables of Oxford Castle, till the king took it out of their hands, as well as great landowners in the surrounding region.   The Chesneys would seem to have been the builders of the castle of Deddington—at least they had it by the time of Henry II.   Later the Broughtons built their lovely lake-castle in the north end of the shire, and the Lisles Shirburn, by Watlington—also water-girt—while the Greys of Rotherfield " crenellated " their manor into a real fortress—all three in the reign of Edward III.   Bampton Castle was the head of a large outlying patch of Valence land, Banbury was the southernmost stronghold of the great bishopric of Lincoln.   The Harcourts and Lovells, whom one would have expected to show castles of some pretentions, never built anything more than large manor-houses—the ruins both at Stanton Harcourt and Minster Lovell are those of splendid fifteenth century residential houses, not of earlier buildings of the military sort.   There were in addition several early Norman *motte* and bailey castles which did not survive the twelfth century, and had vanished—all but their mounds—by the thirteenth, such as those at Chipping Norton and Middleton Stoney.

By Leland's time only the royal castle of Oxford, and the baronial castles of Broughton, Shirburn, and Rotherfield, were standing and inhabited. And with these only we shall deal in detail. At Deddington and Chipping Norton the curious may discover traces of earthworks, at Bampton a window and the vault of a gate-house may be seen built into a modern farm-house. At Banbury the townsfolk have succeeded in making as complete a clearance of their castle as they have of their splendid church—now replaced by a Georgian abomination.

In Berkshire, with the exception of the glorious pile of Windsor, on whose history and architecture whole books have been written, there is comparatively little to visit. At the date of Domesday Book only one important baronial holding, that of Ferrers, is notable. The east end of the county was wooded and little inhabited, covered mainly by the royal chace of Windsor: in the central parts the great Honour of Wallingford occupied most of the land, and had but its single enormous castle—one of the lost marvels of England, for it is now but a grassy mound. Reading Castle, not so important as Wallingford as a military post, but still a strong royal fortress, has vanished completely. So have an ephemeral " adulterine " castle at Newbury, and another at Faringdon, built by Earl Robert of Gloucester, which stood a famous siege in 1144. " I asked there," says Leland, " for the castle that the favourers of Matilda the Empress held, and that King Stephen after pulled down, but they could tell me nought of it." Of Beaumyss, the Castle of the De la Beches of Aldworth, only the dry moat remains. Indeed, in all Berkshire, west of Reading, there is nothing worth a visit save the splendid gate-tower of Donnington, built in 1386, which came through a Chaucer heiress to be an important item in the much-scattered holding of the De la Poles, Earls and Dukes of Suffolk. Uffington and Letcombe " castles " are prehistoric earthworks—in that sort of military architecture, which does not concern us, the shire is very rich.

Windsor

The Saxon kings, as has already been mentioned, had a residence or hunting lodge at Old Windsor, two miles from the present castle, whose scanty foundations have recently been discovered and investigated—with no great profit to archæology. But William the Norman, set on occupying a point of military value, fixed on a hill in the parish of Clewer, which seems to have had no special name of its own hitherto, and ordered a "*motte* and bailey" fortress to be constructed there. It appears to have been by some mere chance that it came to be called after the old royal hunting lodge in the neighbouring parish, and not after the village to which its land belonged. The site was excellent for a primitive Norman castle, a steep chalk cliff rising abruptly to a height of 100 feet above the bank of the Thames, which flows under its northern front, with well-marked slopes to east and south, and only accessible by an easy gradient on the west side. Here William threw up a very large circular *motte*, represented to-day by the dominating " Round Tower," but then no more than a mound crowned by a wooden house of defence. It had two baileys, or outer wards, not one, as was the case with many other Norman castles. The Lower Bailey was to the west, on the gentle slope; the Upper Bailey on the higher ground, to the east of the *motte*: they were almost entirely separated from each other by that elevation, only a narrow passage being left between the mound and the cliff, and this was protected in front by an inner ditch, cutting off the Lower Ward from the mound and the passage round its foot.

If, as in other Norman castles, the later stone buildings of the twelfth century replaced in position the earlier wooden buildings of the eleventh, the Lower Ward may have contained the stables, storehouses, kitchen, chapel and great hall for the garrison, while the Upper would have held the king's private lodgings and offices, and the tower on top of the *motte* would have been intended for a final place of refuge, if either of the outer wards should have been breached by an enemy. The weak side was the west, where lay the Lower Ward, much less well protected by nature than the rest of the castle, and relying for defence on its ditch and palisade more than on the slope of the ground, which is less steep here than on the eastern and southern fronts, while the northern front, that looking toward the Thames, was absolutely precipitous.

The area of the castle was so large—13 acres or thereabouts—that there was no need for it to grow beyond the limits of its original site. For centuries all that was done was to strengthen its *enceinte*, and to line its two baileys with many successive buildings, which grew progressively more solid and more picturesque, first as stone replaced timber, and then as " Decorated " and " Perpendicular " architecture superseded the heavy Norman style of the earliest masonry.

It is probable that Henry I. started the conversion of the castle from wood to stone, as Henry of Huntingdon, a respectable chronicler, notes that in 1110 he, for the first time, held his Whitsun Court at New Windsor, " which he himself had built," and in 1121 he married, in its chapel, his second wife, Adeliza of Louvain. Probably Henry's " building " was that of a stone royal residence and chapel in the Upper Ward. That the mound was still the main fortification, and not the stone outer *enceinte*, is probably indicated by the fact that in 1153, at the Pact of Wallingford, King Stephen and his rival, Henry of Anjou, mention that the *Tower* of London and the *Motte* of Windsor shall both be in the custody of the justiciar, Richard de Lucy.

Henry II., a great builder in stone, as we have already shown in an earlier chapter, would seem to have been responsible for the replacing of the circular tower on top of the *motte* by a solid structure of masonry, much of which is visible to-day, and for surrounding the whole of the Upper Ward with a stone *enceinte*, apparently furnished with slightly projecting square mural towers at irregular intervals. He would also seem to have started, but not to have completed, a similar *enceinte* for the Lower Ward, of which two towers at its north-eastern corner, and two in the south-eastern, are in their substructure apparently of his date. But except on the east front of the Upper Ward, and in the *Motte*, all his work has been so much pulled about and overlaid by later builders that it is not easy to distinguish. The troublous times of Richard I. and John brought little change to the fortifications, but saw the only two sieges to which the castle was ever subjected. The first was a spiritless affair in 1193, when the justiciar Walter, Archbishop of Rouen, beset the castle, which was occupied by the partisans of the rebellious Prince John. The leaguer was in the months of March-April, and was ended by the general submission of John and his adherents. The Archbishop is accused of criminal slackness, for not pressing the attack and waiting for the result of political negotiations. But the second siege in 1216 was a serious business—the only military event of importance which ever took place around the walls of Windsor.

The insurgent barons, who had taken arms after John repudiated Magna Carta, and had called in Louis of France to be their counter-king, beset Windsor for three months. The castle was held for John by Engelhard of Cigogné, one of those foreign captains who are specially denounced, and delated for expulsion, in the Great Charter. He would seem to have been a good soldier, and his garrison comprised the pick of the king's mercenaries, including 70 men of knightly rank. The siege began in July, 1216, and was conducted by a mixed Anglo-French force, the Count of Nevers being in command. They set up *trébuchets* before the castle—presumably attacking the Lower Ward as the easiest point of approach, and the least completely fortified, and reduced it to an evil condition, so that an assault was impending. King John appeared at Reading with a considerable army of succour, but refused to attack the rebels in their siege-lines, and suddenly wheeled off and disappeared (Sept. 14). This looked like an abandonment of the garrison, but the king had another scheme. He went off by forced marches eastward, and began to ravage Norfolk and Suffolk with such ferocity, that the besiegers of Windsor suddenly burnt their siege machines and huts, and hurried off to defend the eastern counties (Sept. 20).

Thus Windsor was saved, and Engelhard of Cigogné held it for the Crown all through the remaining year of the civil war, being of course continued in command by the council of Henry III. after John died in October, 1216. It was the southernmost post in the hands of the royal party, save Dover, and was so completely isolated that we wonder that the siege was not resumed. But the rebels, though they beleaguered and took Hertford and Berkhamstead, and afterwards laid siege to Lincoln, seem to have left Windsor alone, after their first attack in 1216. In September of the following year they submitted, and by the Treaty of Lambeth, the young Henry III. became sole king in England. He showed his appreciation of Englehard's defence of Windsor by continuing him as constable till his death in 1241, though he had been one of his father's most unpopular adherents, and had been displaced for a few years by Hubert de Burgh.

Henry III. was one of the great building kings—an enormous proportion of the taxes with which he irritated his subjects was spent on stone and mortar, and Windsor was one of the spots on which he lavished most money. All through his long reign he was intermittently making additions and improvements to

31

the castle. Not only did he finish the fortification in stone of the Lower Ward, which his grandfather had only begun, but he reconstructed and ornamented the royal residence in the interior of the castle. We find in the Close Rolls accounts for rebuilding the king's and queen's private apartments, for erecting chapels, halls and cloisters, and for much spent on frescoes, panelling, and carved work, as well as for lead roofs, in all directions. Yet there is comparatively little of the work of Henry III. visible to-day, little more, in fact, than two fine towers to the south of the *motte* on either side, one in the Upper and one in the Lower Ward, known at present as King Henry's and (wrongly) King Edward's Towers, and three more (" Garter," " Belfry " and " Chancellor's ") Towers, in the west front. Most of his energies were devoted to the royal residential apartments, and these were repeatedly and completely transformed by his successors—especially by Edward III., Charles II. and George IV.

The next great innovator at Windsor was Edward III., who has left behind him far more visible traces than did his great-grandfather. This chivalrous, if somewhat flamboyant, monarch, made the castle his favourite residence, and held in it the most famous of his ceremonial festivities, the setting up of the " Round Table " for his fellowship of knights, after the manner of the legendary Arthur (1344), and the more permanent establishment and endowment of the Order of the Garter in 1348. The tournaments and feasts at the inauguration of the Round Table involved the construction of a great circular building, 200 feet in diameter, in the Upper Ward, which was intended to be finished in stone. But the growing expense of the Hundred Years' War stopped its progress : it was removed, and in 1348, after Cressy, Edward changed his scheme. After establishing the Order of the Garter, he erected for the knights his great St. George's Hall in the north-east corner of the castle, and his chapel of St. George, which incorporated the old garrison chapel of St. Edward, in the Lower Ward. He filled the northern half of that ward with dwellings for a dean and twenty-four canons, who were to serve the chapel, and along its southern side erected lodgings for twenty-four knights, who were destined to become the " poor knights of Windsor " in later generations Edward also rebuilt the royal lodgings—the structure on which Henry III. had spent so much money having been wrecked by a fire. And he lined the eastern and southern sides of the Upper Ward—where the apartments of the courtiers and officials had hitherto been timber structures reared against the walls of Henry II.—with stone buildings of comely aspect. The inside of the tower on the mound was also refitted and improved, and a fine covered way was made to it.

It has been said that Edward III. turned Windsor from a fortress into a palace, and this is true in the main. Many of the buildings which he put up would have incommoded the defence from a purely military point of view, and splendour rather than strength was always in his eye. His architects served him well—the best known of them was William of Wykeham, who has left his name to one of the new towers, and who was destined in later years to rear

WINDSOR CASTLE : AERIAL VIEW

WINDSOR CASTLE : INTERIOR OF ST. GEORGE'S CHAPEL

WINDSOR CASTLE : KING HENRY'S GATEWAY

WINDSOR CASTLE : EAST TERRACE [WYATVILLE'S RECONSTRUCTION]

the stately quadrangles of Winchester College and New College, Oxford. But posterity has not dealt kindly with Edward's work at Windsor—his chapel of St. George's, which was a reconstruction of the original chapel of Henry III., was superseded by the far more magnificent St. George's of to-day, built by Edward IV., and was pulled to pieces by Henry VII., who cut it down in size and made it into a Lady Chapel, intended for the tomb-house of his dynasty. And St. George's Hall suffered in a different but almost as unfortunate

St. George's Hall, Windsor.

a fashion at the hands of Wyatville, the egregious architect of George IV., who destroyed all its proportions by throwing other chambers into it, and spoiling its symmetry.

Between the death of Edward III. in 1377, and the twelfth year of Edward IV. (1473), the buildings of Windsor suffered comparatively little change, but into this period falls the one occasion on which it was captured by enemies. In 1399, after the deposition of Richard II., his partisans, headed by the Earls of Kent, Huntingdon and Salisbury, hatched a plot for seizing and slaying his supplanter, Henry of Lancaster, who was celebrating the festival of Christmas in the castle, with no military force about him. They collected 400 lances at Kingston, and pounced on Windsor before dawn on January 5, 1400. One of the posterns was opened to them by confederates within, and they thought for a moment that they had captured the new king and all his family. But

Henry had been warned by a traitor a few hours before, had got to horse with his sons, and had ridden off to London through the darkness of a winter's night. The insurgents made no attempt to hold the castle, but swerved off and retreated westward, to meet their unhappy end a few days later.

The House of Lancaster made few changes in Windsor, but the House of York altered its silhouette against the sky for ever. In 1472, Edward IV., fresh from his victories of Barnet and Tewkesbury, gave orders for the construction of a new St. George's Chapel, which should dwarf and supersede the earlier work of his Plantagenet ancestors. In the middle of the Outer Ward he laid out the lofty broad-windowed structure, all glorious within with the banners and insignia of the Knights of the Garter, which dominates the whole west end of the castle, and towers above its walls. And here he himself was buried, to the north side of the high altar, before the chapel was quite completed. Before he had been dead a year, the bones of Henry VI. were brought from Chertsey Abbey and interred on the south side of the altar, as a sort of pendant to those of his murderer. This was probably an ingenious if futile freak of Richard III., who was supposed to have been Edward's willing instrument in the assassination of the last Lancastrian king. Did he wish, by showing honour to the corpse of Henry, to advertise that he had no part in his death? Or was he desirous of stopping a crop of recent miracles at Chertsey?

Henry VII. completed the new St. George's Chapel which his father-in-law had left unfinished, and built in the Upper Ward a small addition to the royal residence, which still goes by his name. But the main impression which he left on Windsor was the practical destruction of Edward III.'s old chapel of St. George, which he pulled to pieces and cut down in size, intending to make it a mausoleum for future kings of his dynasty. This reconstruction of his is the building, much decorated outside with his badges of the Portcullis and the Tudor Rose, which is now known as the Albert Memorial Chapel, since its last change of fortunes. Henry himself altered his mind late in life, and left his body, and the magnificent bronze tomb which the Florentine artist Torregiano made for him, to Westminster Abbey. But many of his descendants lie in the Royal Vaults below the two chapels, Henry VIII., and Queen Jane Seymour, as also Charles I., and George III., with all his numerous family, and finally Edward VII. Queen Victoria's original intention, when she redecorated the chapel and changed its name to the Albert Memorial, was that her husband the Prince Consort, and she herself, should lie there. But his tomb, in the midst of the nave, is but a cenotaph, as he and his long-surviving spouse now rest together in the separate mausoleum at Frogmore.

The story of one tomb in the Royal Vault, that of Henry VIII., is an odd one. Cardinal Wolsey, in the day of his power, had expended much money on preparing for himself an elaborate monument in bronze and marble. After his fall, his ungrateful master laid hands upon it, and determined to utilize it for himself, after having filed off many cardinal's hats and archiepiscopal crosses from the decoration, and replaced them by royal crowns and Tudor Roses. But he never found time or money to complete those parts of the

34

canopy and roof of the tomb which Wolsey had not finished. Hence when he was placed in the vault below, the usurped monument above was like a torso, and most unsatisfactory in appearance. Of Henry's three children, Edward VI. died young, and Mary and Elizabeth had no reason to love their father—he had divorced the mother of one, and beheaded the mother of the other. James I. and Charles I. were too distant relatives to feel much interest in the tomb, and it was in a state of considerable disrepair when in 1646 the Long Parliament, declaring that it was covered with "scandalous images of saints and angels," ordered it to be demolished. The brass-work was sold for £400 : the empty sarcophagus, after being long stored at Windsor, had a surprising end : it was utilized in 1806 for Lord Nelson's tomb in St. Paul's Cathedral—where it may still be seen.

Beside leaving his body to Windsor, Henry VIII. laid up one other memorial for himself, rebuilding the great arched gate-house on the south side of the Lower Ward, which remains to-day the main entrance of the castle. Though its surface has several times been refaced, the outline and decoration repeat the original Tudor details. The only other alterations of importance made under his dynasty were the work of Elizabeth, who added to the amenities of the place by constructing the long gallery leading from the royal apartments to the descent into the Park, which now forms part of the Great Library. Below this gallery and the whole north front of the Upper Ward she made a long terrace, with a pleasant view towards the river and the Chiltern Hills, and a solid summer-house, apt for *al fresco* meals, at one end. This was one more sign that Windsor was no longer regarded as a fortress—the terrace seriously impaired the military strength of the north front.

Between Elizabeth's modest additions to the castle, and the coming of the next innovator there was a century during which little change took place—save that all manner of small and unsystematic residences, for hangers-on of the court, kept springing up in vacant spaces, especially in the Lower Ward. The storm of the great Civil War of 1642-46, which ruined so many castles, passed lightly over Windsor, which was held for the Parliament all through the combat. The canons were evicted, the rich plate of St. George's Chapel sold, and some "idolatrous" images removed, but no structural damage was done. The vandal at Windsor in the seventeenth century was not the Puritan but the Merry Monarch, who found the rooms of his palace (as did his contemporary, Mr. John Evelyn) "melancholy and of a decayed magnificence." Hence came a craving for modernization, a crusade against narrow mullioned windows, useless battlements and pinnacles, dark corners and small rooms. Charles, as he put it in one of his warrants, "thought fit to pull down and alter in several places the outer walls and other buildings in our royal Castle of Windsor, for making our apartments and lodgings more convenient." This meant the demolition of the outer walls of most of the buildings of Edward III., in the royal residence in the Upper Ward, and the cutting of round-headed modern windows, without tracery or mullions, as substitutes for mediæval forms of lighting, all round the castle. The worst work was done in the north-west corner of the Upper Ward, where a square four-storied building all of one piece, without relief or exterior decoration, appeared instead of the towers and bays of King Edward's old front. It would have done for a barracks or a county jail. Instead of battlements fretting the sky, there appeared a stone coping, and a symmetrical row of chimney pots.

But Charles and his architects understood interior decoration, and his new rooms were well lighted, well panelled and frescoed, and flamboyant with the carvings of Grinling Gibbons. But his crimes against the exterior of Windsor were flagrant—he even cut out Edward III.'s windows in St. George's Hall, destroyed their tracery and rounded their tops. It is melancholy to compare Hoefnagel's silhouette of the north front of Windsor in 1570, or Hollar's of 1667, with the dreary picture of 1700—fit setting for Miss Burney's intolerable existence at the court of George III.

The remedy was almost as bad as the disease—but not quite. The next rebuilders of Windsor set themselves to undo all that Charles II. had done, and to make the castle mediæval at all costs—much more mediæval than it had ever been in the Middle Ages. In fact there was an "archaistic revival" conducted with more zeal than historical knowledge. The Gothic style was the reaction against the seventeenth century vandals. Two generations of patrons, employing two generations of architects, remodelled Windsor once more. The beginning was made by George III. in his old age, with James Wyatt (the wrecker of Salisbury and Hereford Cathedrals) as his guide. It was finished by George IV. and Sir Jeffrey Wyatville—as he absurdly called himself—the nephew of the Elder Wyatt. George III. started in a modest way with some restoration in St. George's Chapel and the Lady Chapel, but in 1800 authorized Wyatt to begin the undoing of the evil work of Charles II. on a large scale. In that year the word "Gothic" appears in Wyatt's approved plans, and begins to pervade every estimate—there are to be "Gothic" windows and "Gothic" turrets everywhere. And much was done between 1800 and 1812, when there came a pause in the reconstruction, owing no doubt to the insanity of George III. But when his son became king instead of Prince Regent, he launched out, with Jeffrey Wyatville as his adviser, into a complete refacing of the whole castle, with the avowed intention of "removing the many tasteless additions and alterations which had been made to the exterior of the building," and restoring its original character. Both George IV. and his architect were lovers of the grandiose and great spenders of money.

To them, Windsor Castle owes, in the main, its present appearance, and it cannot be denied that they created a palace much more magnificent and less offensive to the eye than that which Charles II. had left behind him. Unfortunately it is possible to be too mediæval : and if the seventeenth century erred in the direction of sweeping away picturesque detail, the nineteenth century overloaded the castle with unnecessary wealth of decoration. Wyatt, and Wyatville still more, crammed in "Gothic" detail everywhere, often where it was entirely unnecessary. "Machicolation" was a practical military expedient in the reign of Edward III., but wholly inappropriate in 1825, when applied to buildings which were not intended for defence. And immense projecting bow-windows, full of elaborate tracery, can be set too frequently to the face of a building. Moreover the two Wyatts did not content themselves with undoing the work of Charles II., they sometimes fell upon and altered good mediæval walls, which the Merry Monarch had respected. For example the end of St. George's Hall was knocked out, and the ancient king's private chapel thrown into it—altogether destroying its proportions. A less unhappy liberty taken was the addition of 30 feet of masonry to the great Round Tower on the *motte*; this has really improved its silhouette, which was rather squat compared with its diameter in the earlier days. We owe to the Wyatts most of the state apartments in the north-west angle of the Upper Ward, and the staircases and vestibules leading to them—the Throne Room, Waterloo Room, and the rest. Where some of Charles II.'s rooms survived, they got new Gothic windows. The result was certainly sumptuous and impressive, though examination of the architectural and æsthetic value of details is sometimes disappointing. On the whole we must conclude that, considering the time at which they were built, they might have been much worse. And they certainly replaced seventeenth century arrangements which could well be spared: a comparison of the castle as it stood in 1750 with its state in 1850 is all to the credit of the Wyatts. We also owe to them the removal of many mean buildings which had been intruded into odd corners of the castle, for the private convenience of favoured courtiers and dependents of the Stuart and early Hanoverian kings.

Windsor in recent centuries has seen more of the pageantry of the English monarchy than any other spot outside London, and it would be a hopeless task to recapitulate all the royal feasts, marriages, and funerals, which it has witnessed. Perhaps the picture which lingers longest before the mind is that of the white burial of Charles I., whom his slayers permitted to be laid with his ancestors in the desecrated sanctuary. The coffin and pall, deeply covered with the snow that had overwhelmed the whole region that day, were laid in a hasty grave, over against the eleventh stall on the right side of the Lady Chapel. Around the handful of melancholy royalist mourners stood the serried ranks of Parliamentary musketeers, watching to see that no demonstration should be made and no unruly words uttered. Bishop Juxon was not even permitted to read the burial service of the Church of England over his master, who held (not without some justification) that he had died as a martyr for that church as well as for his ideal of royalty.

Wallingford

Of the first-class castles of England this is one of those which have most completely disappeared—not because its site has been built over like those of the great castles of Gloucester and Bristol, but because it was deliberately destroyed and nothing left of it but a green mound. It was one of the marvels of England, founded by the Conqueror as a great strategic fortress, the head of an "honour" to which belonged over a hundred knights, a worthy endowment for several

37

successive royal princes. Leland visited it in 1540, and describes it : " The castel joineth to the north gate of the towne, and hath three ditches, large and deep, and well watered. About each of the two first ditches, on the crest of the ground, thrown up out of them, runneth an embattled wall, now for the most part defaced. All the goodly buildings, with the towers and the donjon, be within the third ditch. There is a collegiate chapel among these buildings within the third ditch ; the last dean before him that now is built a fair steeple of stone at the west end of the chapel." Of donjon, towers, steeple and chapel there is nothing now left, barely two or three fragments of masonry sticking up from a wooded rising ground above the River Thames. The internal arrangements of the castle before its destruction can only be guessed at, despite of an alleged plan, temp. Edward VI., showing it as an irregular polygonal block of about 480 feet by 400, which does not seem to fit into the site as at present visible. But evidently the mound to the north must represent the site of the Norman *motte*. Wallingford Castle was prominent in English history; it saw three sieges in the reign of Stephen, when Brian Fitz-Count held it obstinately for the Empress Matilda, and two more during the Civil Wars of Charles I., when it was perpetually keeping in check the Parliamentary garrison at Abingdon. Colonel Blagge held it for the king to the end—it was the last place in Berkshire to surrender (July, 1646) and only yielded when the news came that Charles had handed himself over to the Scots at Newark.

The victorious Parliamentarians were, no doubt, irritated by the long resistance of Wallingford, and marked it out for destruction immediately after its surrender. But the castle received a reprieve, owing to its excellent qualifications for a prison—there were suggestions that it would easily hold not only royalists, but prisoners of all sorts. And this suggestion was destined to be fulfilled, though not to the pleasure of the ruling party in the Parliament in 1646. For after Pride's "Purge" in 1648, the army clapped into it a great number of the hitherto predominant Presbyterian party in the Commons, and some of them were still imprisoned in Wallingford as late 1650-51, when they were accused of secret correspondence with the royalists. Cromwell finally decreed the doom of the castle, which was to be entirely pulled down and the materials sold, according to a warrant of 1652. It is interesting to know that the demolition cost £450, while the lead and timber was sold for £516, so that the Government had a handsome balance left after the clearance. This must have been a much more complete " slighting " than most of the condemned fortresses endured, for there is less left of Wallingford than of any other great castle in the countryside which received a similar condemnation.

Donnington

It would not be quite correct to say that in the whole county of Berkshire Windsor and Donnington are the only two places in which there is the least remnant of the masonry of a mediæval castle standing above ground. For though this would be true enough concerning the castles of Reading and

DONNINGTON CASTLE: THE GATE-HOUSE

OXFORD CASTLE : ST. GEORGE'S TOWER

Faringdon and Newbury, and Beaumyss (as we have seen) some fragmentary blocks survive from the inner stonework of Wallingford. But they are a negligible quantity, while at Donnington, though the castle is mutilated, one very large and imposing section of it remains almost intact, and is well worthy of a visit.

The manor of Donnington, one mile to the north of Newbury town, belonged in the fourteenth century to the family of the Abberburys; and in the year 1385, Sir Richard—last male of that house—got his "licence to crenellate" from Richard II. He built a castle on a well-marked eminence above the stream of the Lambourne, choosing a knoll on the highest part of the hill as his site, and adapting the shape of the building to the contour of the knoll; it was, therefore, not square, like the almost contemporary castles of Oxfordshire—Broughton and Shirburn—but roughly pentagonal. Its main distinctive feature was that its lofty and disproportionately large gate-house formed the strong point of the whole—there was no other keep, and the circular corner-towers were small. This great gate-house has in front two very tall drum-towers, slightly tapering toward their summits, and ringed round for decoration with five well-marked string-courses, the third and fourth of which show at intervals curious grotesque heads. Between the drum-towers is a portcullis-chamber with a handsome window above it. This forms the front of a square battlemented building, much lower than the two drum-towers which rise above. The whole gate-house projects greatly from the bulk of the pentagonal castle, its back only being in line with the rest of the walls. It is so complete that its lower stories are used for a dwelling house, a modern cottage front having been built on to the back of it. Of the rest of the castle there is nothing but a ground plan on the hill-top discoverable; at no point is the masonry more than two or three feet high. But we can trace small corner towers at four of the angles, and small square mural towers set in the curtain between these corner towers, and the ditch outside is still well marked.

Sir Richard Abberbury, being old and childless, sold Donnington, in 1415, to Thomas Chaucer, sometime Speaker of the House of Commons, the pushing and capable son of Geoffrey the Poet. Thomas made it over to Sir John Phellip, as the dowry of his daughter Alice, having probably purchased it for that special purpose. But Phellip died childless, only one year later, and his widow—still quite a young woman—married in succession two great peers, Thomas Montague, Earl of Salisbury (*circ.* 1425) and William de la Pole, Earl of Suffolk (*circ.* 1430). Alice Phellip was an heiress of considerable wealth, as she owned not only Donnington, but the manors of Ewelme and Hook Norton, and other lands, which came to her at her father's death. She was most unlucky in her husbands—Phellip died young: Salisbury was slain by a cannon ball at the siege of Orleans (Nov. 3, 1428) just in time to escape a contest with Joan of Arc. By neither of them did Alice have issue. Suffolk was the unlucky minister of Henry VI., who incurred much ignominy and hatred as the advocate of a "peace at any price" with France. His master gave him a dukedom, but could not save him in the day of his adversity—banished from

39

the realm in 1450, he was murdered on the high seas by his political enemies. By this unfortunate and much maligned statesman Alice Chaucer had a family—a son and several daughters. The boy was only eight at his father's death, and was for many years under the tutelage of the duchess, dwelling at Donnington and at Ewelme. Oddly enough—considering his father's history—he became a resolute Yorkist when he grew up, and married Elizabeth Plantagenet, the sister of King Edward IV.

This was a grand marriage—a wonderful rise for the great-grandson of Geoffrey Chaucer, whose father had been but a vintner. But it brought in the end death and destruction to the house of de la Pole. For the children of Elizabeth Plantagenet were in the direct succession to the crown, when Richard III. had lost his only son, and had declared his two brothers' issue illegitimate. In his last year Richard saluted Elizabeth's eldest son John de la Pole as his destined heir—a fatal heritage when the House of Tudor came to the throne after Bosworth Field. The unlucky heir-presumptive died in arms against Henry VII., at the Battle of Stoke (1487), his brother Edmund, attainted on very doubtful evidence, was nineteen years a prisoner in the Tower, and finally was beheaded. The only surviving male of the house, Richard de la Pole, whom obstinate Yorkists called the "last flower of the White Rose," lived long years in exile, and died at the Battle of Pavia in 1525, fighting for a foreign cause on Italian soil. Donnington had, of course, been confiscated to the crown on the attainder of Edmund de la Pole, and was given by Henry VIII. to his favourite and brother-in-law, Charles Brandon, on whom he also conferred the forfeited dukedom of Suffolk. The new duke, however, twenty years later (1535) exchanged Donnington with the crown for other lands, and the castle was a royal possession from 1535 to 1600, when Queen Elizabeth made a gift of it to the Earl of Northampton. The heirs of this nobleman alienated it not many years later, and by 1640 it was in the hands of a Mr. John Packer, a member of Parliament of Puritan tendencies.

This Mr. Packer must be reckoned a most unlucky man, for while he was a strong Parliamentarian, the Royalists seized his castle, which was in good order, and well furnished, and turned it into one of their strategical forts covering Oxford. Hence it was twice besieged by the owner's friends, who ended by knocking it to pieces. The second battle of Newbury was fought all around and about it. Donnington was being besieged by a Parliamentary detachment, who had breached it and broken down three of its towers, when the king came out of Oxford with some 11,000 men and relieved it. An organized attempt was then made to crush him, by a general concentration of all the Parliamentary corps, consisting of the Eastern Association Army under the Earl of Manchester and Cromwell, and the wrecks of Waller's and Essex's recently defeated forces, with a brigade of London train-bands added. They numbered 19,000 men, but Charles (who was unaware of their great strength) offered battle (Oct. 27, 1644), holding Newbury town with his right, while his centre lay between the Lambourne and Kennet rivers, with the fortified mansion of Shaw House covering his left centre, and Donnington behind his left rear. The

Parliamentarians, relying on their superior numbers, detached a large flanking column to turn the king's left, consisting of the infantry of Essex's army, and of Cromwell's and Waller's horse, while Manchester lay in front of the Royalist line, having promised to deliver the main attack when the flanking column should have come into action. But the combination miscarried—the turning force made too long a wheel, and appeared actually in the rear of Charles's centre, instead of on his left wing. It got fiercely engaged with the king's reserves, instead of attacking his flank, seized Speen Hill and then was gradually fought to a standstill. To the great disgust of Cromwell and Waller, Lord Manchester let the critical moment pass by, and only attacked the king's centre a little before dusk, to be repulsed with loss while trying to storm Shaw House. Meanwhile parts of the Royalist reserve or rear line had sought shelter under the castle, and the guns of Donnington were firing into the flank of the Parliamentary detached force, and helping to bring it to a standstill. At nightfall the king, who had held out while the light lasted, in a most uncomfortable position between two hostile forces, slipped away toward Oxford, having first thrown his artillery and heavy baggage into Donnington. The battle was, in a sense, a defeat for both parties, rather than a victory for either.

While the Parliamentary generals were wrangling, Charles made an unexpected sortie from Oxford ten days later, and carried off the guns and baggage from Donnington, before the enemy could collect from their cantonments in and about Newbury, and bring him to action. Colonel John Boys, who had defended his castle during the first siege, was knighted for his services, and justified his promotion by holding Donnington right down to the end of the war. It was again besieged in the spring of 1646, but held out till the news of the king's surrender to the Scots came round. Sir John Boys then hauled down his flag, and handed over a castle so much battered that it took small trouble to complete its " slighting." In 1647 it was an absolute ruin, save the gate-house, and so it remains to-day. Mr. Packer wisely resigned himself to living in a town-house in Westminster, for the short remainder of his days : he died in 1649.

Oxford

Oxford, like Wallingford, was an old English *burh*, fortified early in the tenth century, to guard an important point of passage on the Upper Thames, and also to serve as a military centre for the newly formed (and rather artificially shaped) territorial unit of Oxfordshire. The town, though less than 200 years old in 1066, had grown into a place of considerable size, had witnessed meetings of the Witan, the coronation of one king and the death of another. It was the obvious place for King William to select as the third of his great fortresses for the guarding of the line of the Thames : even if it had not been so notable as a strategical point, it would have demanded a castle on account of its political importance. The Saxon *burh* was an oblong town built on the slightly rising ground between the many-channelled Thames on the one side, and its tributary, the Cherwell, on the other. It was surrounded by marshy meadows on the east, west and south, only the roads from the north reaching it on high and dry ground. On what was then the navigable channel of the Thames, outside its west wall, was its "Hythe" or wharf, to which merchandise came in barges from Reading and London. They could not go to any higher point.

William's castle at Oxford was built adjoining the west side of the town, and commanding the river and the wharf. It was not (as in many other places) on the highest available ground, but slightly sloping downwards from the town-wall. But to give it a certain dominating power, William ordered the construction of a very lofty and prominent *motte* on its north side; the house of defence on top of this mound overlooked the whole neighbourhood. The shape of the castle was rather circular than polygonal—there were slight angles in its circumference, but not such marked ones that one could speak of its having definite sides. The defences were the normal ones for a primitive post-conquest fortress—a *motte*, a bailey below, marked by ditch and palisade, and probably a second outer palisade beyond the ditch—for traces of such a structure appear in our earliest maps of the locality—those of Agas (1578) and Loggan (1675). The low-lying position of the bailey made it possible to fill the ditch with water for all (or nearly all) its circuit.

The building and custody of Oxford Castle was consigned by the Conqueror to Robert D'Oilly, a trusted follower, to whom he had given many manors in Oxfordshire, and who got more by his marriage to Ealdgyth, daughter of Wigod of Wallingford, one of the few English magnates who had earned the king's favour, by early submission and loyal service. Wigod's son, Tokig, having fallen in battle in the Conqueror's service, his sister inherited all their father's lands, and Robert had become, when Domesday Book was compiled, the greatest man in Oxfordshire. The chronicles of Osney and Abingdon Abbeys, both places which owed much to the D'Oillys, fix the completion of Oxford castle in 1071.

Only two years after that date D'Oilly built a church, dedicated to St. George, within the castle precincts, on its lowest or westward front, close to the river and the castle mill. The crypt and walls of this church still survive, and adjacent to them there rises a Norman tower of immense strength, a typical square stone keep. This was undoubtedly the tower of St. George's Church, but as undoubtedly a military work of importance, destined to guard the lowest and weakest side of the castle. Was this D'Oilly's work, and did he build a stone keep here, because the earth of the newly raised *motte* would have been unable to bear such a weight? Stone keeps of King William's time were so rare that one must hesitate to attribute such work to Robert, and suppose that it was reared under Henry I., forty years later: some would even put it a hundred years later than 1073. And it is a notable fact that in the Pact of Wallingford between Stephen and Henry of Anjou, in 1053, Oxford is spoken of (like Windsor) as a *mota*, not as a castle. At that date, then, the mound was still its most prominent feature.

I am driven to conclude, therefore, that St. George's Tower is much later than St. George's Church, whether we ascribe it to Henry I. or to Henry II.,

BROUGHTON CASTLE: THE BARBICAN OR OUTER GATE

BROUGHTON CASTLE

whose rolls of accounts show that he was spending much money on Oxford Castle between 1165 and 1173. Possibly the "keep" mentioned in them may be St. George's Tower, and not (as might have seemed more probable for some reasons) the stone building on top of the mound, which certainly existed in the thirteenth century. For of this last we have a good drawing in Agas's map of Oxford in 1578, showing a decagonal building with string-courses, elaborate battlements, and rather large windows, which seems to demonstrate thirteenth century date, and to point to Henry III. as the builder.

It would seem probable, then, that Oxford had a "*motte* and bailey" castle only in the eleventh century, that the palisades of the bailey were replaced by stone outer walls somewhere in the early twelfth century: inserted in them was the Tower of St. George's by way of a keep, while the very fine ornamental donjon on the mound, and the five large mural towers in the *enceinte* were thirteenth century constructions. This is hypothetical, but thanks to Agas's map, we can be certain what Oxford Castle looked like at the end of the Middle Ages. It was nearly circular, its strong point was the great tower on the mound, which Agas calls "the Castle Prison." The tower of St. George's at the mill covered the weakest part of the front, and is shown with three stories. There were five smaller mural towers, all residential, as their windows indicate. The main entrance was on the south-east side, by a high-level wooden bridge crossing the ditch, and ending in the south-east tower, which no doubt had a portcullis and drawbridge. This entry must have been at the end of the present Castle Street—as the name of that thoroughfare suggests. The existence of a small footbridge over the stream at the south-west side of the castle, not far from St. George's Tower, shows that there must have been a postern, opening towards the river, on the south-west side of the place. At this side took place the escape of the Empress Matilda in 1142, when she and the three knights who escorted her, were let down by ropes from the castle at night, in a time of snow and frost, muffled in white cloaks, and walked on the ice of the frozen Thames till they got to Abingdon, and from thence rode to the friendly walls of Wallingford.

The map of Agas shows no detached residential buildings in the middle of the bailey—nothing indeed save a small two-windowed structure with a tower, which looks like a well house or a very small chapel, and a little to the left of it the county gallows, in permanent evidence. It is certain that in Robert D'Oilly's time,

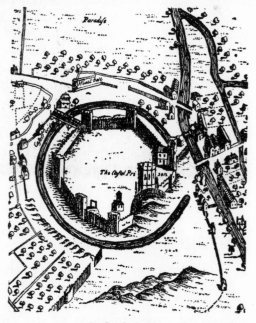

Oxford Castle. Agas's Map

and long after, there must have been a wooden hall for the garrison, kitchens, and the other usual buildings of a Norman castle, somewhere within the bailey. But these were all cleared away by the fourteenth century, chambers and offices being, no doubt, found in the various large towers of the rebuilt stone *enceinte*, and the splendid tower on the *motte* providing a residence for the governor. St. George's Church, certainly, was from the first used as the garrison chapel. In the fifteenth and sixteenth centuries the castle became more and more the king's jail, like so many other strongholds in county towns, and less of a fortress. But, as Agas's map shows, it was standing complete in the late sixteenth century, and was utilized again during the Civil Wars of 1642-46 for military purposes. The Parliamentary general, Edmund Ludlow, mentions in his memoirs that when taken prisoner in 1644, he was confined in Oxford Castle, and found there very many other officers of mark in like case.

At the end of the Civil War Oxford Castle was " slighted," and most effectually, as can be seen by comparing Loggan's map of 1675 with Agas's of 1578. Everything in stone was cast down, save St. George's Tower and Church, the castle mill, and the small building (whatever it was) that stood isolated in the middle of the bailey. The outline of the walls survives in the map of Loggan as a mere earthen bank above the ditch, and the great decagonal tower on the *motte* has been removed, leaving only Robert D'Oilly's conical mound in evidence.

Of all the old buildings there survive to-day only St. George's Tower, and the ruined lower string-courses and crypt of St. George's Church. Those who ascend the *motte*, however, will find the castle well still in existence there, going right down to the bottom level of the mound. The entrance of the sunken chamber is decorated with Tudor-style coats of arms of the bishoprics of Durham, Winchester and Exeter, which must have come from some other defaced building in the castle or city.

But the terrible thing about the fate of Oxford Castle is not its almost complete destruction by the Long Parliament, but the insult that has been inflicted on its remains by the imposition on them of quite the most abominable pseudo-Gothic assize-court in all England, a compound of mock-Norman arches, pepper-box turrets, meaningless machicolation, arrow-slits in inaccessible places, and large round-topped windows. This triumph of early Victorian architecture must be seen to be believed ! It has been placed in our first chapter as the illustration of the lowest modern conception of what a " castle " should look like. That a large nineteenth century prison hides behind this atrocity is a comparatively trifling addition to the woes of the visitor of antiquarian tastes.

Broughton Castle

This is, in my private opinion, about the most beautiful castle in all England, not from majesty and splendid situation like Harlech, Caer Cynan, or St. Michael's Mount, but for sheer loveliness of the combination of water, woods, and picturesque buildings of the later and more decorative age of military architecture.   There are many lake-castles in England, such as Leeds, Bodiham, Maxstoke, and Shirburn (Oxon), but of none is the effect so charming to the eye as that of Broughton.   Seen on a sunny summer's day, when the sheets of water-lilies in the lake are in flower, it is almost theatrically lovely—the visitor half believes that a beautiful panorama has been produced by some landscape-artist for his special benefit.   The explanation can be found in the fact that the site chosen for defence by a fourteenth century builder, who was honestly seeking for military strength, happened to be picturesque, but that the effect of the present scene is mainly produced not by the remnants of the original castle, but by the many-pinnacled and many-windowed Elizabethan and Jacobean buildings which have incorporated the old walls in their broader and loftier mass.

Broughton is quite late as castles go.   The first builder would seem to have been Sir Thomas Broughton, nearly the last of a race which had held the manor for two centuries.   Somewhere about the year 1300 he took advantage of the obliging Sor brook, which could readily be dammed up to produce a lake, and created a broad sheet of water with a rectangular island in its centre.   The only approach was by a narrow causeway across the lake, which was defended by a very solid barbican or gate-tower.   Seventy or eighty years later Sir Thomas Wykeham got a " licence to crenellate " and turned what may have originally been no more than a moated manor into a castle.   To him belong the battlements along the eastern and part of the northern front, whose shape shows that he left Broughton as a rectangular castle with square corner-towers. It may also have been Wykeham who erected a low stone *enceinte* all round the island, so turning it into a " bailey," of which the castle proper formed the inner house of defence.   This outer stone wall was still visible as late as 1700, but was taken down before 1800, so that what was once a bailey is now only a broad lawn.

After the Broughtons died out, their castle went rapidly through the hands of several successive owners—Mauduits and Hungerfords.   Bishop William of Wykeham, bought it from a Hungerford and gave it to his nephew, Sir Thomas Wykeham : but this family only endured for two generations, and the lands devolved on an heiress, Margaret Wykeham, who married William Fiennes, Lord Saye and Sele, the son of that Lord Treasurer Saye who was murdered by Jack Cade's mob in 1451.   Since his day, however, Broughton has descended in regular succession to the owners of the title of Saye, with only one break in the male line, when, in 1781, Richard Fiennes, last of the original stock, died, leaving as his heir, by a female descent, his cousin, Thomas Twisleton, from whom came the Twisleton-Wykeham-Fiennes, owners of Broughton down to this day.

The Lords Saye of the times of Elizabeth and James I., like so many of their contemporaries, were discontented with the residential amenities of their castle, but did not destroy it, merely adding a very great mansion in the best style of their day to the north and west sides of the building, and inserting in some places larger Tudor windows in the parts of the old front which were allowed to stand.   In our illustration of Broughton the battlemented walls of the old castle can be seen joining on to the gabled bays of the new, with their immense projecting windows, which form such a large proportion of the whole house. The interior is even more effective than the exterior would lead one to guess— long galleries and fine rooms, with plaster ceilings in the most elaborate and intricate patterns, sometimes showing pendants, armorial stained glass, and excellent panelling and carved work on and over doors. This is in all respects a model Jacobean mansion of the best sort.

The great man of the House of Fiennes was the eighth baron, William, who held the title from 1613 to 1662, and was one of the main contributors to the new building. He was the eldest and most wily of the knot of peers who took the side of the Parliament, and from his skilful guidance of their policy got the nickname of "Old Subtlety." Local tradition points out an upper room in the third story in which he is said to have gathered together Hampden, Pym, St. John, Essex, and the younger Vane for a consultation at which they made up their minds to press matters even to the point of civil war. Lord Saye was the first peer who refused to pay ship-money in 1636, and his name was prominent in every subsequent political move till 1648, when he refused to side with Cromwell and the military party, and retired from public life. He strenuously declined to sit as a member of the Protector's new House of Lords, and in 1660—though now 78 years of age—emerged from his retirement to declare in favour of the Restoration of the Monarchy. He accepted honorary office under Charles II., and was one of the very few leading Parliamentarians of 1642 who came unharmed through the whole eighteen years of turmoil, and died in prosperity, aged four score years and over.

After visiting the castle it is worth while to inspect the church, where there is a fine group of recumbent effigies of Broughtons and Sayes, ranging from the time of Edward I. downward. It lies hard by the bridge-tower, so that the Lord of Broughton had not far to go, when he wished to gaze on the tombs of his ancestors or to hear mass.

Shirburn

Oxfordshire is fortunate enough to boast of two lake-castles, both of great beauty, though Broughton by the diversity of its architecture and the pleasant undulating country above it, and the breadth of its water-protection, has some-what the advantage of Shirburn in general effect. The latter, nevertheless, is a most comely and interesting building, and has preserved all its original shape, while Broughton lost in architectural symmetry, though it gained much in picturesqueness, by the additions made in Tudor and Stuart times. The dates of their building were much the same, Sir Thomas Wykeham's " licence to crenellate " for Broughton being only a few years later than Sir Warren de Lisle's similar warrant for Shirburn (1378). And both were originally square castles with corner-towers, on an island in an artificial lake. But there are considerable differences—Shirburn is built on a much smaller island, and all

SHIRBURN CASTLE

ROTHERFIELD GREYS : S.W. TOWER

its walls rise straight from the water—there is no external space not covered by buildings in the isle. Secondly, we note that the corner-towers of Shirburn are round, and not square like those of Broughton. Thirdly, it has no outlying barbican or gate-tower like the more northern castle, but simply a drawbridge, made of a scale sufficient to allow it to span the narrowest point of the lake. And fourthly (though the eye does not at first detect the fact) Shirburn is a brick castle, like some of those of Kent and Sussex, with the red carefully dissembled under a thick coating of grey rough-cast. It is only in the few places where the surface has flaked away that the inner material is visible.

Of course, Shirburn, though never added to in the course of the ages, could not escape internal and external changes in the comfort-loving sixteenth and seventeenth centuries. Very nearly every one of the external windows has been cut out and replaced by much broader seventeenth century windows of the round-topped Charles II. type. This has made a good light from the outside for rooms which were previously furnished with windows on the inside only, looking into the court, and had nothing much better than arrow-slits on the front that looked outward. The sixteenth or seventeenth century improver of amenity has also been at work in constructing large and imposing long galleries in the second story, where previously there were only many small chambers opening into each other. He has also blocked up the lower story of the small quadrangular court of the castle with modern offices, not leaving any open space within. But the internal alterations make little difference to the general aspect of the place, which is just as Warren de Lisle left it, save that his small and narrow external windows have everywhere been replaced by much larger openings, which give it a false air of seventeenth century rather than fourteenth century construction. The surroundings are flat, a well-wooded park lies all round the lake, and there are no natural features of any prominence to distract the eye from the trim and symmetrical castle.

The existing Shirburn dates, as we have already said, entirely from Warren de Lisle's activities in 1378. There was an earlier building, some parts of which were said to go back even to Robert D'Oilly—but no single stone of it is visible. The history of the castle since its building consists of three centuries of constant change from owner to owner—no house held it long. Warren de Lisle left no son, and the castle was, soon after his death, in the hands of the Quartermaynes—an Oxfordshire family of some note in the fifteenth century. In the time of Henry VI., Richard—the last male Quartermayne—left Shirburn to the son of his favourite clerk, Thomas Fowler, who afterwards became Chancellor of the Duchy of Lancaster. But Richard Fowler was " a very unthrift," and sold all his lands in the reign of Henry VII., " leaving his own children full small living." The buyer was one John Chamberlain, whose descendants held the manor till late Stuart days—they were lucky enough not to see it destroyed at the general " slighting " of castles in 1645-6, because the Chamberlain of that day was a loyal supporter of the Parliament, and " begged off " his house. After other transferences of proprietorship Shirburn was purchased by the Whig Lord Chancellor, Thomas Parker, in the reign of

Rotherfield Greys. N.E. Tower

George I., and has remained with his descendants, the Earls of Macclesfield, ever since. The archæologist owes them thanks for having preserved the outward aspect of the castle almost unchanged till this day.

Rotherfield Greys

This, like Broughton and Shirburn, is a fourteenth century castle, but unlike them, is not water-girt, but situated on a knoll overlooking the narrow and picturesque valley of the Rother brook, an outlying corner of the highlands of Chiltern. The castle, and the branch of the prolific family of Grey which built it, and held it for the first years of its existence, start from a churchman, Walter de Grey, Archbishop of York (*obiit* 1255), who bought the manor and left it to his nephew, Sir John de Grey (*obiit* 1312). The castle, however, is the work of the second John de Grey, a favourite of Edward III., and one of his original Knights of the Garter, whose banner—*barry azure and argent a bend gules*—may still be seen hanging in St. George's hall at Windsor. He got his " licence to crenellate " in 1348, and built a rectangular castle with octagonal or square corner towers*, of which three survive to-day, but the fourth has disappeared, as has most of the connecting curtain wall between them. The space inside is much cut up with modern garden enclosures, and the general aspect of the ruins is rather puzzling, from their want of coherence. Only the wall between the north-east and south-east towers is continuous. The material of the towers is flint and brick mixed—a curious blend in the way of colour : the bricks are very thin, even for fourteenth century work, and sometimes laid in herringbone fashion as in the earliest Norman style. The north-east tower is larger than the other two survivors : against the south-west one a small modern [seventeenth century?] residence has been built, little better than a cottage.

The last de Grey died in 1387: his daughter and sole heiress, Joanna, married John Lord D'Eyncourt, but had no male issue by him. Her child, another heiress, Alice D'Eyncourt, took Rotherfield and many other possessions to her husband, William Lord Lovell, already a great magnate in Oxfordshire. Alice's grandson, Francis Lord Lovell, was that resolute and unscrupulous supporter of Richard III., who has achieved immortality, along with Catesby and Ratcliffe, in the famous lines about " the cat, the rat, and Lovell the dog," who " ruled all England under the hog." He was attainted after Bosworth Field, and all his wide lands distributed among Lancastrians ; Rotherfield Castle fell to Henry Tudor's aged uncle, Jasper Earl of Pembroke. It went back to the crown on his death, childless, and after several other changes was granted to Francis Knowles, a relative of Queen Elizabeth. He was her Treasurer for many years, and his son William Knollys was created Baron Knollys of Rotherfield Greys, and afterwards Earl of Banbury. Their heavy Jacobean monument is conspicuous in the village church. Earl William is remembered for two unhappy reasons. He was made, by James I., the gaoler of the wicked Earl and Countess of

* See plates : The S.W. Tower octagonal ; the N.E. Tower square.

49

Somerset, the murderers of Sir Thomas Overbury. After their release from the Tower, he had unwillingly to lodge them for two years at Rotherfield.† He probably owed this invidious duty to the fact that his young second wife was the elder sister of the infamous countess. That this lady herself was not an estimable character, may be sufficiently gathered from the fact that when Knollys died, at the age of 86, the House of Lords refused to recognize as his heirs the two sons who had been borne by Lady Banbury a few years before, when her husband had sunk into his dotage. The lawsuits resulting from this decision lasted intermittently for a hundred and fifty years, only came to an end in the reign of George III., and form the longest record in all " Peerage Cases."

Rotherfield Castle was completely gutted at the end of the Civil Wars of 1642-46—having been held as a royalist garrison much incommoding the Parliamentarians at Henley and Reading. No attempt was made to restore any portion of it, but a new house was built just outside the old precincts in the time of Charles II., and was occupied by Stapletons down to quite recent days. It has been much modernized and only part of it has a seventeenth century appearance. It looks out, across a lawn, on to the picturesque ruins of two of the ancient towers of John de Grey.

Boarstall

This interesting fragment of a castle is, as has already been observed, the only building in Buckinghamshire which demands a mention in this book—we may add that it is surrounded on three sides by Oxfordshire land, and is only

Boarstall Castle.   View from within, South Side

eight miles from Oxford City. Its position is odd, just at the foot of the lofty hill on which stands the large village of Brill—a less commanding site in that neighbourhood it would be hard to find. But being in the flat, it was capable of being provided with a wet-ditch, which, perhaps, was the attraction that led Sir John de Handlo to use his " licence to crenellate," obtained from Edward II. in 1312, for this particular spot.

†Somerset and his wife are said to have conceived such a distaste for each other's company that they refused to speak to each other, and were confined at their own request in two separate towers of Rotherfield. When they were allowed in 1623 to choose separate places of internment they parted for ever.

BOARSTALL

WINCHESTER CASTLE : EXTERIOR OF GREAT HALL

Handlo's castle was quadrangular, surrounded by a deep moat, sixty feet across, and with a large gate-house as its strong point. As at Donnington little more than the gate-house survives to-day. The other buildings (probably already in very bad order) were pulled down late in the eighteenth century. Apparently Boarstall Castle had (like Shirburn) a simple square outline with small corner towers, and the water defence formed a great part of its efficiency.

The surviving gate-house has suffered badly from sixteenth century and seventeenth century alterations, which have given it a much less military appearance than it must originally have possessed. When it is looked at from outside, the very large window over the gate-arch, and the balustrades, which have replaced battlements on the central front, destroy the general effect of the building—whose real aspect in its early days can be much better realized by going through the gate and looking at the comparatively undamaged interior face, which looked toward the courtyard. It consisted of a three-storied central block with four hexagonal corner towers, furnished with battlements and arrow-slits. The central building had, no doubt, very small window-space on the outside, but competent lighting from the side that looked into the court. There was a drawbridge across the moat, but water and bridge have alike disappeared, though three of the four sides of the ditch can still be traced. In 1716 Boarstall could still be described as " an old house moated round, in its north side a tower much like a small castle." It is probable, therefore, that its other three fronts had no very strong military features by this date. It is quite likely that after it was " slighted " by the Parliamentarians in 1646, there was a rebuilding of the quadrangle on non-military lines, to replace the parts where large breaches or similar demolitions had been made. But alas! Sir John Aubrey, whose family had been owning the place for two centuries, thought fit about 1780 to cast down everything save the gate-house front.

Boarstall had its place in history in 1642-6, when it was one of the outlying garrisons which protected the royalist capital at Oxford. Brill, above on the hill, was often held by the Parliamentarians, as a good observation point overlooking Otmoor and the whole plain of central Oxfordshire. Boarstall was once evacuated in 1644, and the enemy at once threw a garrison into it, who proved such a nuisance to communication that the king had to recover it, after a little battering. The walls were, of course, wholly unfitted to resist cannon-shot, and the Parliamentarians surrendered. But Boarstall was lost again in 1645, after the general breakdown of the royalist strength that resulted from the defeat of Naseby. And like most other castles it was then " slighted " by the victors. But the destruction was obviously far less complete than that of most strongholds of the region—e.g., Donnington or Rotherfield Greys. After some patching it was still habitable, and the strange seventeenth century balustrades above the main gate are probably post-civil-war adornments—the vast window below them looks somewhat earlier—of Jacobean rather than Charles II. style. But speculation as to how far reconstruction went after 1660 for the rest of the buildings is futile, since Sir John Aubrey's unhappy resolve swept everything away.

WESSEX

THE boundaries of our sphere of investigation permit us to deal with only a few of the castles of the South Country; but some of these are among the most important centres of English history, and others have points of high architectural interest. Bristol would have been the most notable of all, if only it were still standing—but the keenest investigation can only discover one minute fragment of what must have been a most imposing fortress. The local antiquary can point out this relic, a small chamber behind a confectioner's shop, and this none but he could discover, for no passer-by would suspect its existence. But we can deal with fine remnants of the almost equally historical castles of Winchester and Taunton: Dunster gives us an example of a first-class baronial stronghold on a most picturesque site. Wells is the best specimen of a moated palace-fortress that survives; the fourteenth century strongholds of Nunney and Farleigh Hungerford have both many interesting features, and the two Dorsetshire harbour-protecting castles reared by Henry VIII. at Portland and Sandsfoot give us a logical end to the annals of English mediæval military architecture. But of the Tudor scheme of coast-fortification we shall have more to say when we get to the most perfect examples of it—the twin castles of St. Mawes and Pendennis on Falmouth Harbour.

Winchester

The ancient capital of Wessex can boast—like York, the ancient capital of Northumbria—of two castles, as a sign of its exceptional importance. But there is this difference between the cases, that the two strongholds of the northern city were both royal, while Winchester had the king entrenched at the top of its sloping site, on the highest ground, and the bishop almost as strongly lodged at its very bottom, among the ramifications of the streams of Itchen. Both the Conqueror's castle on the hill, and the fortress which the contentious bishop Henry de Blois built for himself among the waters, have been treated hardly by the hand of time—or rather by the hand of man—for deliberate destruction by human agency, not the wind and the weather, wrecked each of them. Of the episcopal Castle of Wolvesey only rather shapeless fragments of masonry survive. The royal castle above has vanished, all save one splendid fragment, but that—the great hall—is one of the most famous buildings in England, for its historical associations as well as for its intrinsic beauty.

The old Saxon kings had dwelt in the flat ground around the cathedral, where the traces of their palace can only be discerned by the eye of faith. William the Norman transferred his residence to the top of the hill, and built his castle just outside the West Gate, adjacent to the city, but not within it. It was very large, and had two wards. Probably it was one of the first castles in England to see stone substituted for earthwork and palisading. But William's building has absolutely vanished : in the one surviving fragment of the castle—the Great Hall—there are a few Norman stones in an inner doorway, and others, probably, in the dais at the head of the great and lofty structure. The site remains the same, but the walls have been twice and thrice recast. It was on this spot, but not in these surroundings, that Rufus wrangled with Anselm, and the envoys of King Stephen with the arrogant Henry of Blois, who wished to exploit his position as Papal Legate to give him jurisdiction over the whole realm.

It was that unwearied builder, Henry III., who transformed the Norman hall, and gave it an appearance not much differing from that of to-day. Very probably he rebuilt the whole interior of the castle, but as not only *enceinte* and outer walls, but all chambers save the hall, are completely gone, we cannot say. What he did to the hall is clear ; he took out the small round-headed Norman windows, and substituted large " Early English " dormer-topped ones, making the lighting of the place three times as effective. And he replaced the heavy and low original arches inside by very lofty and slightly built pointed arches, borne on clustered pillars, making the whole into a broad central nave, with two much narrower aisles—if we may use words more usually applied to ecclesiastical architecture. An entry in a roll of expenses shows that the windows were all glazed with good glass, not merely furnished with shutters, or frames of inferior semi-translucent stuff. The only appreciable changes made in the structure of the hall since 1240 are that Richard II. somewhat altered its external appearance, by taking down the dormers above the windows, and making them flush with the outer wall, while Edward IV. inserted the wooden braces which strengthen the tie-beams of the roof. But it is certain that the dais at the west end, where the king's seat and table stood, was a more lofty affair all through the Middle Ages than it is now, and that there was a good wooden minstrels' gallery at the east end : the corbels or brackets on which it rested can be detected on the easternmost pair of pillars. The eighteenth and nineteenth centuries, usually so fatal to Gothic buildings, seem to have done no more than remove the gallery, and make the two easternmost windows, which were originally somewhat shorter than the rest, of an equal size to them. This change was made in 1845, and cannot be said to have done any harm, fatal though Victorian reconstruction generally was.

The hall has seen much of the pageantry of English history : in it Henry III. repudiated the " Provisions of Oxford," and made the Barons' War inevitable : here Edward I. held his first court after returning from the Crusades (1274), and presided over the Parliament which passed the celebrated Statute of Winchester (1285). There were several other Parliaments held here in Plantagenet days. It was in this hall that Henry V. in 1415 declared war on France, by the truculent speech to the ambassadors of Charles VI., of which Shakespeare has given us a hypothetical reconstruction. Here Henry VIII. entertained the Emperor Charles V., and Mary held her state reception after her unlucky marriage with Philip of Spain in the Cathedral below. Notable trials all through English history have been held here—from that of Edmund of Kent, the brother of Edward II., judicially murdered by the tools of Mortimer and his paramour, the "she-wolf of France," down to the equally atrocious condemnation of Alice Lady Lisle by Judge Jeffries. The longest set of state trials which took place in the hall were those of 1603, when the investigation of the dark business of Raleigh's plot (or Lord Cobham's plot) for the

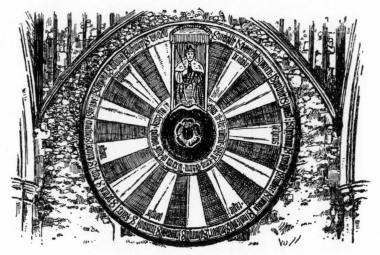

King Arthur's Round Table, Winchester

deposition of James I., went through its tortuous course, and ended in a series of convictions and reprieves.

The most striking object in the present hall, which fixes the eye of the visitor as he enters, is the immense circular board of "King Arthur's Round Table," fixed above the dais in the western wall. The actual painting on this great round is of the reign of Henry VIII., as the Tudor rose in its centre, and the royal robes of King Arthur himself, make evident. From the rose there branch out, like the spokes of a wheel, alternate stripes of white and green, broadening gradually as they approach the outer rim, on which are painted, one for each stripe, the names of the twenty-four knights—Modred and Galahad on each side of the king, with Lancelot on Galahad's left, and Tristram three places further off. The queerest name is "Sir Côte mal taillé," which the painter would seem to have taken straight from Mallory's *Morte Arthur*. Who made the original Round Table, over which the sergeant painter of Henry VIII. executed the present designs, it is hard to say. It was there, and reckoned very ancient, when Hardyng and Caxton wrote of it in the fifteenth century. Some would take it back to Henry III.: the tyrant Mortimer is recorded to have set up a "Round Table" in the day of his ostentatious triumph and practical regency over the realm, and Edward III. had Arthurian legends in his head before he finally created the Order of the Garter. All three were sometimes at Winchester, and are possible devisers of this vast council-board, eighteen feet in diameter, which was certainly once fitted with legs, though for centuries it has been braced up against the west wall of the Great Hall.

As to the castle of which that splendid remnant alone survives, we can only know of its two wards and many towers, by old engravings, such as Speed's Jacobean map. After the capture of Winchester by the Parliamentarians in 1645, it was most scientifically destroyed, three years being occupied in the task. The site with the Hall, alone left intact, was granted to Sir William Waller, who

WINCHESTER CASTLE : INTERIOR OF GREAT HALL

TAUNTON CASTLE

sold it for the modest sum of £100 to the County of Hants, to be used for assizes and other public functions. Charles II. took possession of the ground in 1660, and proposed to build himself a palace, for which the plans were drawn out by Christopher Wren. But though its central block was begun—a long red brick pile with classical decorations—it was never completed, and the unfinished palace was converted into barracks, which served for many years as headquarters and depôt both for the Hampshire Regiment and the Rifle Brigade. It was burned down by accident in December, 1894—no great loss so far as beauty went, though Wren had been the architect—and perfectly modern barrack-buildings have replaced it.

Ruins of Wolvesey Castle, Winchester

The Bishop's Castle at Wolvesey—originally, as its name shows, an eyot between two branches of the Itchen—was built (in simple Norman style two wards with wet ditches)—by Henry de Blois, the brother of King Stephen: it is said that he finished it in 1136, the year after his brother's accession. Its main feature was, evidently, the square keep set in the eastern wall of the inner ward, of which two stories still survive. A certain amount of the curtain—flint and mortar, with no mural towers—remains, but very nearly all the inner arrangements are gone, though it is possible to make out the hall, in which there are a good round arch and one surviving Norman window. Within five years of its building, Wolvesey stood its first and only siege, when it was held for Stephen by the retainers of his brother, Bishop Henry, against the besieging forces of the Empress Matilda. There was lively fighting, during which the garrison burnt with fire-balls all the houses of the city which came too near their *enceinte*, and gave cover to the enemy. Finally the siege was raised, after three weeks [Aug.-Sept., 1141] by the arrival of the king with a relieving army. Henry II. is said to have dismantled Wolvesey after the death of his cousin the Bishop, in 1171, but this does not mean that he destroyed its residential quarters, as we find many later occupants of the see of Winchester dwelling there in high state. Possibly the gate and portcullis were removed, or some breaches made in the curtain. But Wolvesey was, perhaps, less frequently inhabited by its owners than might have been expected, since Farnham—a stronger castle—was available, and Winchester House in London was a tempting abode for bishops who were often great political personages, like William of Wykeham, Cardinal Beaufort, and Bishop Fox—who never took up his abode in Winchester till he was an old and broken man. Both he and Cardinal Beaufort died within the walls of Wolvesey, though they may not have lived much within them. It was " slighted " by the Parliamentarians at the same time that they destroyed the royal castle in the hill above. But Bishop Morley, after the Restoration, built a modern palace, designed by Christopher Wren, on part of the old site—some of the lower stories of his chapel are Norman work still *in situ*. The new palace was voted damp and unhealthy by eighteenth century bishops, who preferred to make Farnham their chief abode. And Bishop Brownlow-North—the brother of George III.'s prime minister—pulled down nearly half of it—a vandalic act, for it is a pleasant and comely building. The surviving wing and the chapel are now used as the Diocesan Church House. The ruined Norman walls make a somewhat chaotic background.

SOMERSETSHIRE

The greater part, but not quite all, of Somersetshire, comes within the boundaries of our sphere of operations. This was a county never particularly rich in castles : there was much ecclesiastical land in it—notably the enormous estates of the Abbey of Glastonbury : the king was also a large landholder, and overlooked all his manors from the single great castle of Taunton. There was no great and early family of earls—the Beauforts only got the title in 1397—to rear a first-class castle in the centre of the shire. Once, during the anarchy of Stephen, the Mohuns aspired to the dignity, and got a grant of it from the Empress Matilda : but it was disallowed, and they had to content themselves with their baronial status, and their castle of Dunster, of which we shall have much to say, as it is by far the most important item in our county survey. One large Norman castle—Montacute—existed in the first epoch after the Conquest, but nothing but its " sharp mount " survives—its stones having (no doubt) gone to help in the building of the Cluniac priory and the beautiful Elizabethan manor-house below. There are only scraps left of Stoke-Courcy [Stogursey], destroyed during the Wars of the Roses, Richmont [Harptree], an " adulterine " castle dismantled by Henry II., and Nether Stowey, which was —if Leland speaks correctly—more of a " goodly manor place " than a castle. Castle Carey has left its name to a village, but its site—long unknown—had to be discovered by deep digging, and is now covered in again with earth. Neroche was apparently a prehistoric earthwork, converted for a short time into a Norman bailey, but soon allowed to go to decay. Cadbury, with its Arthurian legends of Camelot, is a " castle " only in the same sense as " Maiden Castle," near Dorchester—*i.e.*, is a primitive Celtic stronghold of uncertain date. These excisions leave us only five names on our list of places that should be seen, three of them of primary importance—Taunton, Dunster and Wells—the other two secondary, but well repaying a visit, Farleigh Hungerford and Nunney.

Taunton

The history of Taunton as a fortified place starts early, for here King Ine of Wessex, in or about the year 710, " timbered him a *burh*," which his consort, Ethelburga, as an odd entry in the Anglo-Saxon Chronicle relates, destroyed twelve years later. This was not, apparently, a gratuitous " breaking up of a happy home," but a recapture by the royal lady, who was on the best terms with her husband, of a stronghold which had fallen into the hands of rebels, for the Etheling Ealdberht was, at the moment, vexing Ine with insurrections. But Saxon burhs were not castles, and we need not trouble ourselves with the chronicles of Taunton till it received the regular mark of Norman occupation. The town is found in Domesday Book as a moderate-sized borough with 64 burgesses, belonging not (as might have been expected) to the king, nor to the Bishop of Bath and Wells, but to the Bishop of Winchester. The castle owed its origin either to Bishop William Gifford, the Chancellor of Henry I. (1100-27), or to his successor, Henry de Blois (1129-1171) the builder of Wolvesey Castle at Winchester. For certainly we have here a typical Norman keep of the first half of the twelfth century, not one of the lofty sort, but squarely built, 50 feet long by 40 wide, in three stories, with walls some 13 feet thick. No doubt this was let into the walls of an inner ward with a stone *enceinte*, and no doubt, also, there was an outer bailey, represented by the modern " Castle Green," with wet ditches round it, supplied from the Potwater stream—they were only filled up in the end of the eighteenth century. But the present aspect of the castle is Edwardian rather than Norman, and shows trace everywhere of the work of Bishop Langton, a great builder in the time of Henry VII.

The outer ward is mostly spoilt—it has been invaded by two hotels, which have crenellated themselves, in order to be in keeping with the genuine battlements of the inner ward. But the great gate, opening into the enclosure, where they stand, is in part a genuine antique, having the arches of an "Early Decorated " gate-house of about the time of Edward I., though the superstructure is a restoration of 1816. The almost triangular inner ward is complete, and would be a very fine example of its type, if so many of its windows were not still eighteenth century insertions in the original masonry. The Somersetshire Archæological Society, who purchased the place in 1874, have replaced many of these eyesores with more appropriate openings, but some still survive.

The apex of the triangle, if we may use the word of a rather blunted figure, is formed by the Norman keep, and a round tower separated from the keep by a narrow entry only. The north side of the triangle is formed by the immense Great Hall, the south side contains the gate-house, with chambers

57

in two stories on each side of it, the base (with a round tower at its south-east corner) was occupied by the minor offices. If there was another tower at the north-east angle of the base, it has vanished.

The gate-house of the inner ward was probably of Edward's date, but it was pulled about by Bishop Langton in 1496, when he inserted a large two-lighted Tudor window, and placed a tablet bearing his own arms, supported by angels, above it, and the royal coat of Henry VII. below. The Great Hall, which stands just opposite the gateway, is 120 feet by 31 feet, with walls apparently in part Norman, but much pulled about by later generations. Bishop Langton inserted Tudor windows, but all of them, save two in the north front, have been replaced by less satisfactory seventeenth or eighteenth century substitutes.

It was in this hall that Judge Jeffries in 1685 held the "Bloody Assize," and condemned more than 200 of the misguided rebels who had followed "King Monmouth" to the gallows, and many more to servitude in the plantations, or whipping at the stocks. A later generation cut up the great chamber by a partition across the middle into two courts. By 1780 it, and many other portions of the castle, had got into bad condition, and were handed over to the tender mercies of an energetic Georgian repairer, Sir Benjamin Hammet, who put on a new roof, inserted many windows, and recast many other details all round the castle. It is presumably to him that we owe the large inappropriate windows which disfigure the round towers at the angles of the ward. But apparently he must not be over-censured, for the castle was getting quite out of hand—its south-east corner had been turned into a private school-house, and the encroachments in the outer ward seemed likely to invade the inner.

Taunton Castle changed hands several times during the great Civil War of 1642-45, but only along with the town: it had no separate history,

Taunton.
Gateway of Inner Ward

WELLS : INTERIOR OF THE BISHOP'S FORTIFIED PALACE

WELLS : THE GATE-HOUSE AND MOAT

and the famous defence by Blake from July, 1644, to July, 1645, was that of the whole place, not merely that of the castle. It was a most creditable achievement, considering that many of the fortifications were only extemporized earthworks.

Wells

Not the least beautiful corner in the little cathedral city of Wells—where everything is beautiful—is the palace-castle of the Bishop, set in the middle of its broad moat of running water. Its fortification came late, in an age when already some idea of splendour and comfort had replaced that of mere military strength in the building of a castle. And Wells lay in a reasonably quiet corner of the land, not—like the castles of the Bishops of Hereford or St. Davids—in one where strife, with the unruly Welsh, was endemic. We shall have to deal with Bishop Robert Burnell in another place, when we tell of his building of the castle of Acton Burnell in Shropshire, in the vain hope that it would be for many a year the home of a baronial house springing from his cherished nephew. But he worked not only for his family but also for his successors in the see of Bath and Wells, leaving them a fortress, where he had taken over only a fine manor house. The core of the present residential part of the palace was a spacious building erected by Bishop Joceline, early in the reign of Henry III., to which belong the two lower stories, now visible—the upper story and roof are comparatively modern. Robert Burnell, having got his " licence to crenellate " in 1285, turned the palace and its precincts into a very effective fortress. He fashioned the abundant waters of St. Andrew's spring, which wells up from the ground beside the palace, into a broad quadrangular moat, and inside the moat, on each side, threw up a rampart wall of earth faced outwardly with stone, and on the rampart put a stout battlemented wall, with towers at its four corners, and a bastion or half-tower here and there projecting from its curtains. The extremely broad water defence was the most effective protection. There was entrance only at one point, in the face which looks toward the cathedral, and here the curtain is broken by a very large and strong gate-house, two octagonal towers with battlements and arrow-slits, and between them a portcullis chamber, in which were also the chains by which a drawbridge could be lowered or raised. This is a very pleasing building, and its effect has not been spoiled by a queer little Tudor bow-window thrown out from the left-hand tower.

These were Burnell's really military buildings, under his " licence to crenellate," but he gave a certain military effect to his domestic buildings, a very large hall and a chapel and other chambers, which he threw out at right angles to the old palace, into the middle of the green space now forming a sort of " outer ward." For they are battlemented from end to end, and have several towers set in them—also battlemented ; but everywhere their large and beautiful " Early Decorated " windows show that they are really civil structures, not intended for defence.

All these buildings of Burnell's in the palace enclosure, except the chapel, are in ruins and roofless. The abominable Bishop Barlow (1548-53), of whom we shall have more to say when discussing his earlier vandalisms in the diocese of St. Davids, by some sort of a corrupt bargain with Protector Somerset, disposed of them to him. And Protector Northumberland's creature, Sir John Gates, who got this fragment of Somerset's plunder, sold the lead of the roofs and the carved beams and panelling. Barlow's Marian and Elizabethan successors got back the palace, but had not the heart or the means to repair all Burnell's ruined buildings, which now stand in picturesque fragments in the middle of the lovely garden, enclosed by the outer *enceinte* and its swan-haunted moat. The chapel above, adhering to the old palace, survives intact.

Dunster

In the long western projection of Somersetshire, which runs along the Bristol Channel and slopes up into Exmoor Forest, there has always been one predominant family—the Mohuns, from the Conquest down to 1376, and the Luttrells, their successors, from 1376 down to this day. It is an almost unparalleled thing (but compare Berkeley) to find a castle like Dunster, which has only changed hands once, otherwise than by inheritance, since its first erection. We may add that it would be equally hard to find another castle fitting in so well with a scene of sylvan beauty as this—others, like Harlech or Caer Cynan, may stand on sites higher, more precipitous, and more majestic, but Dunster, rising from its curtain of woods above its little river, presents a silhouette of towers and gables against the northern sky which cannot be excelled for grace. And it is equally effective when seen not from the river and meadow below, but from the high street of the quaint little town which straggles up the slope towards its lowest entry, and makes a perfect foreground, from which stand out the wooded ascent to its gatehouse, and the cluster of towers far above the tree tops.

William the Conqueror gave to William de Moion, a baron from the Côtentin, a great cluster of manors in West Somerset, as well as many others in Devon and Dorset. But his chief seat was on the Tor where Dunster Castle stands: "William of Mohun holds Torre, and there is his castle," says Domesday Book. The Tor was the isolated circular final spur of a ridge (Grabbist Hill), which runs west towards Exmoor. Its slope drops suddenly towards the town below and the end of the shore-plain of Somersetshire. It is cut off by a broad depression from the main length of the ridge to which it belongs, so as to form by its natural situation a most eligible site for a Norman castle of the early type. The point of the Tor made a perfect *motte*, without any need for artificial piling of earth: it is a small flat, 35 feet by 70, round whose edge a palisade of timber from the woods below could easily be drawn. The outer bailey was formed on a broad ledge half-way down the slope of the Tor, about 125 yards long by 33 broad; below this ledge the hillside gets very steep again, so that there is a sharp fall towards the town at its foot. All that was needed to make the Tor-fortress practically impregnable was to scarp the already precipitous slopes of its summit on all sides, leaving space for a descent to the lower ward by means of a path, or perhaps steps, on the only section which was not cut into sheer impracticability. The same could be done with almost equal ease for the lower ward, both of whose flanks were very steep, the only comparatively easy section of the slope being blocked by a palisade with the entrance gate in its centre. This was somewhere above the spot where the present gate-house stands.

Dunster. Inner Gate-house

Nothing could be more formidable, but of course the later Mohuns, like all their contemporaries, replaced palisading with stone, which was easily procurable on all sides. The ring on top of the tor became a shell-keep. The ledge on which the lower ward stood was walled, or rather its edge was cut into a low cliff, with retaining walls and a parapet above, from which (no doubt later) projecting towers to give flanking fire were thrown out. It seems likely that all the residential chambers and offices of the castle were in the lower ward—chapel, hall, kitchen, etc., as there is absolutely no trace of inner buildings within the shell-keep on top of the Tor.

The most prominent man in the annals of this family, whose castle dominated all Western Somerset, and whose lands were scattered so broadly over it, was the third William de Mohun, a contemporary of Henry I. and Stephen. He was a furious supporter of the Empress Matilda in the Civil Wars, and made

61

himself odious by his reckless plundering and burning, so that he was known as the " Scourge of the West." His mistress would appear to have conferred on him the title of Earl of Somerset in 1141, and he employed it in a Charter which he issued to the priory of Bruton; but it was never recognized by Stephen or Henry II., as were some other of Matilda's creations, and the later Mohuns did not employ it. Some would attribute to this William the building in stone of the shell-keep of Dunster, and the earliest stone walls of the lower ward, but their date, since they have almost entirely disappeared, is very problematical. It is safe, however, to place the credit of the projecting towers in the curtain of the lower ward to a much later generation, the Mohuns of the time of Henry III.

Their house died out in direct male line in 1376, and the widow and daughters of the last baron sold Dunster to the Lady Elizabeth Luttrell, widow

Dunster. Outer Gate-house

of Sir Andrew Luttrell of Chilton, and daughter of the Earl of Devon. From her descend the second dynasty of owners of the castle, who have now held it for five centuries and a half continuously. It was an early Luttrell, probably just before or soon after 1400, who built the imposing gate-house, which stands well outside the lower ward, as an additional defence to it, joined up to it by walls. This is a very large quadrangular structure, 63 feet broad by 23 deep, in three stories. Over its front arch is an interesting carved panel with nine heraldic shields, showing the arms of Luttrell impaled with those of Courtenay and other famous baronial houses. It contains two stories of rather handsome rooms, instead of the usual portcullis chamber, for it

62

DUNSTER CASTLE : FROM THE RIVER

DUNSTER CASTLE : THE MAIN FRONT

does not seem to have possessed that usual fitting of castle gates. The inner gateway of the ward, a smaller but more elaborately ornamented structure, is a square between four turrets of polygonal shape, much pierced with arrow slits, and much crenellated. It is quite a century older than the outer and larger gate-house below, and may go back to Edward I.

Luttrell Monument in Dunster Church

The main front of the residential buildings in the lower ward is largely Elizabethan, built by George Luttrell in 1589—his shield is above the central door. He must have pulled down much mediæval work when erecting his own: for while scraps of inner and outer walls belonging to older buildings are incorporated in his masonry, there are traces of foundations of vanished blocks outside the circuit of the existing residence. By this time the upper ward or shell-keep on the top of the Tor must have been completely deserted, for already half a century earlier, Leland (a great admirer of Dunster) had remarked that the donjon above "hath been full of goodly buildings, but now there is only a chapel in good case, which of late days Sir Hugh Luttrell [temp. Henry VII.] did repair."

There is now not a trace of this chapel, or of any other old building, or indeed of the ring-wall, on top of the Tor, which is levelled into a grass plot, with a summer house or gazebo of small dimensions on one edge of it. The

63

clearing away of such mediæval stones as may have survived is attributed to an eighteenth century Luttrell, who disliked scraps of ruins, and wanted a bowling green and a fine view over hill and dale.

Dunster, like most other West Country and Welsh castles, had its times of trouble in the great Civil War, but came through them more easily than most of its equals. The Luttrells of the day were not Royalists, but their castle was seized, and held by a royalist garrison throughout the war, down to the great collapse in 1646, after Hopton's defeat at Torrington. It was then besieged by Blake, who lay before it for some time, battering it with guns placed in the town below. The attack against such a precipitous place was not easy or effective, but the governor, Colonel Wyndham, surrendered in April, when all the neighbouring royalist strongholds were also hauling down their flags in despair at the general collapse of their party, after the western field-army had laid down its arms in March. Though Dunster did not belong to a "Malignant" it was put into the general list of fortresses to be "slighted," but the order was carried out without little zeal, no doubt in consideration for the owner. Probably some holes were blown in the curtain wall of the lower ward—conceivably the decayed walls on the Tor may have been cast down, but neither the inner nor the outer gate-houses, the real strength of the castle, appear to have suffered much.

The later Luttrells, as was natural, devoted themselves to making their castle more comely and comfortable rather than to restoring its military strength. They made a circular carriage drive, by which the front door of the main building could be reached without passing under the great gate-house, which no coach could have got through. They levelled a broad stretch of ground in front of the house, where their carriage drive ended, burying under the new gravel many traces of mediæval foundations. They also levelled the top of the Tor, and they cut many windows on ill-lighted parts of the older buildings. The last changes were made in Victorian days by the architect Salvin, who added to the Elizabethan buildings, built a new tower, and reconstructed the exterior of much of the east front in the modern Gothic style. On the whole the eighteenth and nineteenth century alterations have not destroyed the general effect of the mass of buildings, and they have certainly rendered them more habitable. The castle remains the greatest baronial survival of the West Country, and the most romantic and picturesque of all the old strongholds of Wessex.

Nunney

This small, little-visited and much neglected castle lies in a well-watered valley five or six miles to the west of Frome. It is quite late—going back only to the reign of Edward III.—the founder, Sir John Delamere, is said to have built it with ransom-money got in the great wars of France. It is quite small and consists only of one ward surrounded by a good moat formed by a running stream. Its plan is curious : it is formed by four large drum-towers, of which the southern and northern pairs are close together, with no space between them, but the east and west fronts, between the two pairs of towers, are long stretches of curtain. It was built of beautiful ashlar masonry, and shows surviving windows with cusped tops and mullions of Early Perpendicular style. It had no outer buildings whatever, the water of the moat coming up to the foot of the *enceinte* all round, as at Shirburn (Oxon) or Bodiham.

Its interior arrangements consisted of three stories and a basement, access to all being by a large newel stair in the north-western tower. There are visible

Nunney Castle from the Village

a hall with a large fireplace on the first story, and an oratory or small chapel, indicated by a large mullioned window, on the top story. The whole interior is at present blocked with fallen masonry, a great section of the west curtain having fallen inwards through mere decay in 1910. This was the side on which the gate lay—its character and size cannot be guessed at, as the whole stonework lies in a crumpled mass.

Seventeenth century drawings, which chance to have survived, show that the four corner towers were once surmounted with high conical roofs, and that there was a rampart walk below them, going round the whole top story of the castle. The projecting corbels on which it rested are still very visible, and seem to hint that the walk was partly or wholly of timber, standing out from the face of the castle.

The site is very low, and despite the water defence of the narrow moat, seems a weak one for a castle of the later fourteenth century, when cannon was coming in. For there is rising ground quite comparatively close, from which even Edwardian siege guns could have made havoc with the walls. Moreover the houses of the village are only a stone's throw from the moat—the castle was actually in the middle of it. On the rising ground on the other side of the street is the church, containing the monument of the founder, Delamere, and others of the families of Pawlett, and Prater, who succeeded the Delameres. A

65

Prater held his own house against Fairfax in the great Civil War, and saw it breached by the guns of the " New Model."   A traitor is said to have warned the besiegers that the west curtain was the weakest section of the walls, and so it proved to be.   It was probably ineffective repairs after 1660 which caused this same front to fall down in our own day.   More will crumble soon, if the owners do not take steps to cut out the ivy, which is doing its usual treacherous work on many parts of the still imposing towers and east curtain.

Delamere Monument in Nunney Church

Farleigh Hungerford

This, like Nunney, is a castle of the late fourteenth century : but it was not, like the former, a completely new structure built on a hitherto unoccupied site, but resembles rather Stokesay in Shropshire (of which more elsewhere), in that it represents the already existing domestic buildings of a great manor house turned into a castle under a " licence to crenellate."   But the fates of the two have been different : at Stokesay the *enceinte* has disappeared, but most of the inner buildings survive : at Farleigh it is the inner buildings which have practically perished, only the chapel remaining in good order, while the gate-house and the outer walls make a good show.

NUNNEY CASTLE

FARLEIGH HUNGERFORD CASTLE

Farleigh was a manor of the knightly family of Montfort, from whom it was purchased in 1369 by Thomas Hungerford, " citizen and merchant of New Sarum." He was a greater man than this modest designation would suggest, as he was steward to John of Gaunt, and for a short time Speaker of the House of Commons. His father had been bailiff of Salisbury, and his uncle one of the king's Justices in Eyre. But clearly Thomas Hungerford was a " new man " like his contemporary, Michael de la Pole, the son of a citizen and merchant of Hull, who came to be Earl of Suffolk and the king's chief minister. Thomas got himself knighted by John of Gaunt's influence, and in 1383 obtained a licence to crenellate his mansion, which was henceforth known as Farleigh Hungerford instead of Farleigh Montfort : he also purchased other manors in the neighbourhood.

His son Walter, a great fighting man and a comrade of Henry V. at Agincourt and the siege of Rouen, was raised to the peerage in the fourth year of Henry VI. He became a Knight of the Garter, and rose to be Lord High Treasurer before his death at a good old age in 1449. This is a good parallel to the similar exaltation of the mercantile family of the De la Poles—and like that of Suffolk, the Hungerford peerage ended by the axe. The third baron, a Lancastrian, as befitted the descendant of a steward of John of Gaunt, was beheaded after Hexham Field, where he had been taken prisoner. The last Hungerford who bore the baronial title was a victim of one of the suspicious fits of Henry VIII., and lost his head in 1541. As his attainder was never reversed, the barony disappeared, but Hungerfords continued to hold Farleigh down to the time of Charles II., when they lost it by the persistent folly of the head of the house.

In its prime Farleigh was a square castle of two wards. Leland gave careful observation to it during his Somersetshire tour. He notes the situation " was strong, set on a steep hill, with a stream in a ravine covering its rear." It had a gate-house and " divers pretty towers " in the outer ward, also an ancient chapel, with a new chapel annexed unto it. The inner ward had also a fair gate-house with the arms of Hungerford richly carved in stone, and within a hall and three great chambers, all very stately. Unfortunately there remain to-day only the outer gate-house, part of the *enceinte* with the stumps of two towers, and the double chapel, the large chapel of St. Lawrence with the chantry of St. Anne built on to it. These are the only buildings of the whole castle which remain intact. They have been made into a sort of museum, containing not only the tombs of the founder and three or four of his successors, but a collection of armour, brought over when the old hall was destroyed in the eighteenth century, some Jacobean woodwork, and fragments of carved stone from the vanished buildings ; also some early books and letters in cases.

In Tudor times Farleigh saw some domestic tragedies, of which the legend still survives. Lady Agnes, second wife of the Hungerford of 1522, was accused of poisoning her husband, and hung, along with one of her servants, as Stow's chronicle records. Her step-son, the last Lord Hungerford—whom Henry VIII. beheaded, for keeping a chaplain who called his sovereign a heretic, and casting the royal horoscope—was apparently a domestic tyrant. He kept his wife immured for four years in the tower still known as the " Lady's Tower," allowing her to see no one but his chaplain, half starving her, and (if she is to be believed in her petition to Secretary Cromwell) twice or thrice attempting to poison her. Local legend has it that he was jealous of attentions paid to her by a well-known local reprobate, " Wild Darrell," of Littlecote— but the dates do not at all tally. When her husband's head fell on Tower Hill, Lady Hungerford emerged, married Sir Robert Throckmorton, and bore him four daughters and two sons. So her health would not appear to have suffered permanent injury from her imprisonment.

The Hungerford family was approaching its end when two seventeenth century knights, father and son, were its successive heads. Sir Edward Hungerford was a zealous Puritan, long commander of the Parliamentary levies of Wiltshire, " of eminent zeal for his country," as his tomb of 1648 in the chapel records. Revulsion against parental strictness may, perhaps, account for the lamentable career of his son, the last Sir Edward, best known as " Hungerford the Waster," who was one of the least worthy members of the court of Charles II. He gave £500 for a wig to which he had taken a particular affection, and gambled away in succession twenty-eight manors—he is said to have paid £30,000 across the green cloth. His last attempt to get money was to turn his house and garden in London into a public market—known ever after as Hungerford Market. After this he lived to a poverty-stricken old age, on the one manor— Black Bourton in Oxfordshire— which he had not succeeded in alienating. And with the death of his childless son in 1748 this unlucky house came to an end.

The "Waster" sold Farleigh to a Mr. Baynton in 1686, and since then it has passed through many hands. The main authors of its destruction would appear to have been a family named Houlton, who are recorded to have carried off its panelling and carved beams to their other house at Trowbridge. But the bulk of

Arms of the Hungerfords
From a tomb in Farleigh Hungerford Chapel

the stones went to build the handsome Farleigh House, in the park outside the castle. Earl Cairns saved the remnant of the buildings from complete destruction, by purchasing them and presenting them to the Board of Works— and now the Commission for Ancient Monuments takes care of the interesting chapel and gate-house.

Portland and Sandsfoot

These twin castles, whose origin is the same, but whose present aspect is so different, are far later in date and style than any of the others which we have been discussing. Indeed some might call them forts and not castles, and deny their right to a place in this book. But we have already determined that the lowest limit of our chronological survey goes down to the building of the great series of haven-protecting castles, destined for the use of artillery against hostile fleets, or landing forces, with which Henry VIII. covered the south coast during his last war with France. The English had lost the permanent command of the sea which they had hitherto enjoyed. It was not the time to say—

> " Britannia needs no bulwarks,
> No towers along the steep."

Several dangerous descents at exposed points of the coast—*e.g.*, the sack of Brighton—had set the king and his council on the policy of intense fortification, of which we shall speak in full when dealing with St. Mawes and Pendennis —the best sample pair of haven-guards. A section of the accessible coast needing strong protection was the long sweep of Portland Harbour, an admirable and well sheltered place for a possible disembarkation of the French. Hence came the creation of the twin castles of Portland and Sandsfoot at the two ends of the roadstead. They were, like most of the other castles of the series, low-built batteries with many embrasures placed close above the shore at commanding points, and with a solid battlemented tower, generally circular, in their centre, overlooking the battery below. From their roof platform, or from upper embrasures, musketry fire, or swivel-fire, could supplement the work of the big guns below.

Of this pair Portland, at the southern end of the haven, presents a trim and complete appearance: if it was much injured in the great Civil War it was thoroughly repaired in the time of Charles II. Sandsfoot, on the other

Sandsfoot Castle

69

hand, a great royalist stronghold in 1643-44, seems never to have been touched after its destruction by the Parliamentarians in 1645. It shows only the battered remains of its central building—a core of inner masonry and a row of four large windows above. Numismatists may, perhaps, find more interest in this melancholy ruin than other people, as it was the site of one of the ephemeral Civil War mints of Charles I., while the royalists were in possession of the neighbouring Weymouth. Some rather rudely designed half-crowns with the mint-mark SA for Sandsfoot, as well as more numerous pieces with $\overline{\text{W}}$ for Weymouth, were struck here in 1643-44, before the governor, Colonel Ashburnham, was battered out of the place in the June of the latter year. He retired with his garrison across the water to Portland, which held out till the end of the struggle, and only surrendered in April, 1646.

Portland Castle. Outer Gate

PORTLAND CASTLE : THE SEA FRONT

KENILWORTH CASTLE: THE KEEP AND LEICESTER'S BUILDINGS

THE WEST MIDLANDS

THE shires of the West Midlands, unlike those which lie beyond them in the Welsh Marches, were never very rich in castles. When Leland went on his famous archæological tours in 1540-42 he noted that he found in Warwickshire only six castles, of which three were utterly " desolated "; in Worcestershire five, of which one was in ruins, and another had but one tower left—" I saw the carts carrying stones thence to amend Pershore Bridge." In Gloucestershire he noted only four, and of these one is Cirencester, " which had a castle once belike "—in which speculation he seems to have been wrong : but (to compensate) he has by some odd lapse of memory left out the very important and interesting castle of Berkeley. Of the ten castles out of the whole fifteen which were existing in Leland's day five more have now passed into oblivion—the old royal castles of Worcester, Bristol and Gloucester—all three completely gone—Astley in Warwickshire, which has had a Tudor mansion built on top of it, and Abberley in Worcestershire. The bishop's castle of Hartlebury, sacked and " slighted " by Colonel Morgan in the great Civil War, was rebuilt in the time of Charles II. as a red-brick mansion in the style of the times. Sudeley, the old castle of the Botelers, was twice besieged and taken in 1643-5—once by Waller—and being already much battered was ordered to be " slighted " in 1649. It lay desolate for two centuries, and then was rebuilt very carefully by the Dent family in mid-Victorian times, so that it is now pleasing but not mediæval. Leland does not reckon in his list one or two castles which had gone to pieces long before his time, like Brimsfield, the old home of the Giffards, or the de Clare Castle of The Holm near Tewkesbury. They were scraps of mound and ditch then, and so they remain now ; wherefore we need not trouble ourselves with speculations as to their probable aspect in the fourteenth century. Beverston (Glos.) he mentions elsewhere, though not in his list, as " a pile one time very pretty," but now only a " castillet well moated." There remain for our consideration only three places—Kenilworth, Warwick and Berkeley, each one of which may be reckoned among the most notable castles of England.

Kenilworth

This, in its prime, was the most important of all the lake-fortresses in the realm, the great artificial sheet of water in which it stood exceeding in dimensions even those of Caerphilly and Leeds (Kent), much more those of Broughton, Shirburn or Bodiham, where the lake is hardly more than a very wide moat. Till this broad inundation, covering 111 acres in all, had been produced, Kenilworth was a stronghold of no especially favourable situation : after it had spread abroad to its destined limits, the place was almost impregnable.

The original castle stood in a gently rolling country, on the end of a low spur of gravel and sandstone between two brooks, the Inchford and Finham,

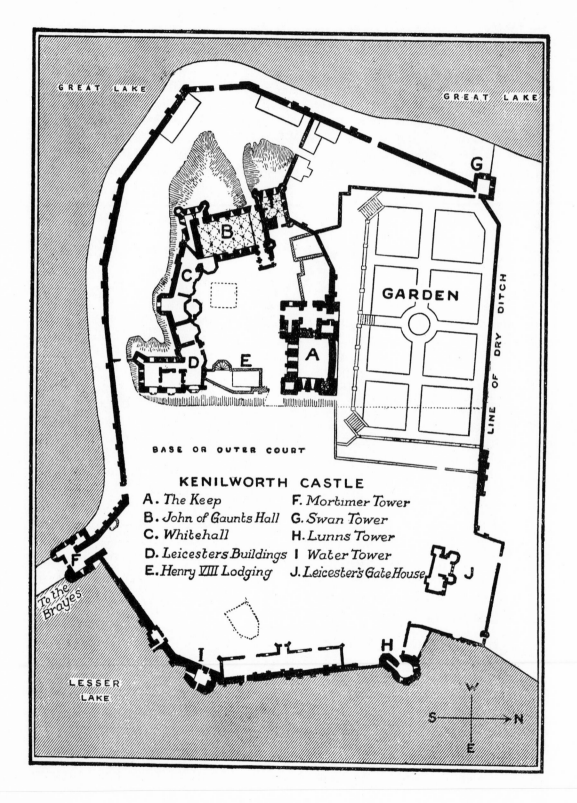

GREAT LAKE

GREAT LAKE

G

GARDEN

B

C

LINE OF DRY DITCH

D E A

BASE OR OUTER COURT

KENILWORTH CASTLE

A. The Keep   F. Mortimer Tower
B. John of Gaunts Hall   G. Swan Tower
C. Whitehall   H. Lunns Tower
D. Leicesters Buildings   I Water Tower
E. Henry VIII Lodging   J. Leicester's Gate House

F

J

To the
Brayes

I

H

LESSER
LAKE

W

S   N

E

which converge a little below it. On three sides the spur dips down rather steeply towards the brooks; on the fourth, which looks north and east, it was cut off from the rolling plateau of which it forms the end by a deep ditch, in front of the spot where the gate-house was afterwards to stand. At the time that Domesday was compiled the two holdings of which Kenilworth was composed, were only "members" of the great royal manor of Stoneleigh: they were held by different persons, Alberic the Clerk and Richard the Forester. Henry I. united the two holdings and gave both to Geoffrey de Clinton, his chamberlain and treasurer, in or about 1122. Before he died in 1129, Geoffrey is supposed to have built the first castle, possibly no more than a "*motte* and bailey" work, occupying the site of the present inner ward. There is certainly a trace of

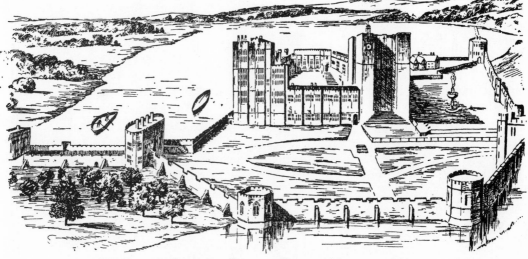

Kenilworth Castle in 1620. *From a contemporary picture*

thrown-up earth around the spot where the existing keep stands, and here the *motte* may have lain. Tradition links the keep itself with the name of the founder of the castle, as it is called Clinton's Tower to this day. But its architecture would date itself rather more plausibly from the time of his long-lived son, Geoffrey II., who lived all through the anarchical reign of Stephen and became chamberlain to Henry II., as his father had been to Henry I., surviving to at least 1265. The keep forms the north-east angle of the inner ward; it is rectangular, 58 feet by 87 in external measurement, and about 80 feet high, with slightly projecting turrets at its corners. Its present effect as a monument of Norman castle-building is very much spoiled by the fact that its windows, originally small apertures, much splayed inwards, were hewn square and made very large in the time of Elizabeth, when Robert Dudley's masons must have spent untold labour in hacking through the Clintons' masonry, in order to insert big mullioned glass-work letting in plenty of light. At a first glance the size of these Tudor windows deceives the eye into giving a much too modern date to the solid keep. Against its west side is a "forework," protecting its door

73

on the first story. No doubt there was, by the time of Henry II., a complete stone *enceinte* forming the inner ward, but of this only the keep survives, the rest of the buildings being of various dates, ranging from 1200 to 1580. The outer ward in the Clintons' day may still have been no more than a ditched bailey.

In the end of the reign of Henry II. the third Clinton owner was induced or compelled—one cannot think that he would do it willingly—to lease the castle to the king, and twenty years later the lease was made into a permanent cession to the crown. Since the Clintons were neither a specially rebellious nor a specially impoverished house, one can only suspect that the king wanted a royal stronghold in this region of the Midlands to balance the growing importance of Warwick, where the great Newburgh earls were making themselves very strong. Both Henry II., John, and Henry III. spent immense sums—according to the money-values of those days—in turning Kenilworth into a first-class fortress—a fact which the last named builder was to rue in his old age, when the castle became the impregnable rallying-place of his enemies. To one or other of these Plantagenets must be ascribed the perfecting of the water-defences, which made the place the strongest thing of its kind in the realm. In John's time there was already a " pool," and Henry III., in 1231, is found " repairing " the banks of the pool, and in 1237 ordering " a fair and beautiful pleasure boat " to be moored near the door of his private chambers. To him is probably to be ascribed the great dam that pent up the water of the brooks, and created the lake of 111 acres, which was in existence at the time of the great siege of 1266. Its effect was to flood the whole of the marshy meadow ground, and to make three of the four sides of the castle inaccessible. Except the main entrance on the north-east side, there was now left no access to the castle save along the crest of the dam, and this narrow approach was guarded, not only by a gate-house in the outer ward [Mortimer's Tower], but by a barbican tower at the south end of the dam (now called the Gallery Tower), and by a still more important work (called later the Brayes*) on the slightly higher ground where the causeway reached dry land. But the Brayes, of which only earth-work survives, and whose date is therefore hard to determine, may be much later than 1230. It may have been thrown up by the besieged barons of 1265, or even in still more recent days.

When Henry III. had completed his building and his inundation, Kenilworth Castle consisted of a high-lying inner ward, standing in the south-west corner of a much larger outer ward, and still dominated by the Clintons' great keep. The outer ward had a sharp fall to the water on its south and west sides, toward the greater lake, that west of the dam ; and though its east side is not on such high ground as its west, had very adequate protection there by the smaller and narrower " lower lake." There were five important mural towers in the outer ward, Mortimer's Tower which blocked the access to the dam, the Water Tower, and the Warder's Tower on the south-east front, and two more

---

* Cf. the term "Fausse-Braye" used by seventeenth and eighteenth century engineers for extra lower *enceinte* works placed round the foot of the main wall of a fortress. The word comes from the Latin *braccæ*.

KENILWORTH CASTLE : JOHN OF GAUNT'S BANQUETING HALL

WARWICK CASTLE: CÆSAR'S TOWER

(now known as the Swan Tower and Lunn's Tower, the latter from some forgotten worthy of much later date than the thirteenth century) at the north-eastern and north-western corners of the *enceinte*. The domestic buildings and chapel which Henry III. undoubtedly erected are now invisible. The later buildings of John of Gaunt and of Robert Dudley, Queen Elizabeth's Earl of Leicester, were imposed on their sites, after ruthless destruction of the earlier work, whose masonry nevertheless shows here and there in the core of the existing structures.

After perfecting a first-class fortress, Henry III. was unwise enough to present it to a some-time favourite, who was to become his greatest enemy. In 1248 he gave it as a residence for life to his sister Eleanor, the wife of Simon de Montfort, the great Earl of Leicester, and in 1254 he made a grant of it to Simon and Eleanor in common for their lives, little thinking what ten years more were to bring forth in the way of political changes. By 1264 the Earl was at the head of the baronial opposition, and the trusted head of a militant party, despite of his foreign birth and the unpopularity of his earlier years. He beat his brother-in-law in pitched battle at Lewes, took him and his son captive, and became the virtual ruler of England for one short year. The king's brother, Richard, Earl of Cornwall and titular emperor, was a prisoner in Kenilworth during the days of the Montfortian régime. In the campaign of 1265, which opened with the escape of Prince Edward from Simon's hands, Kenilworth and its neighbourhood saw the crisis of the action. While the earl and the prince were facing each other across the Severn, Simon the younger, the most vigorous of Montfort's sons, brought up the whole of the levies of his father's party from London and the south, to attack the royalists from the rear. They reached Kenilworth on July 31st, in such force that if they had been able to join the Earl they must have got the better of their enemies. But fatigued by a long march, and believing the prince to be at Worcester, thirty miles away, the younger Simon committed the gross error of camping outside the castle, without sending out scouts to look for the enemy, or planting pickets round his weary host. Edward, who had marched by night with all his force, on hearing of the approach of the enemy, fell upon them before dawn on August 1st, and took them completely by surprise. Many were captured in their tents, some few slain : many fled broadcast : only a remnant escaped into the castle : Simon the younger got there by swimming the lake in his night-shirt. Leaving the castle unmolested, now that the army of relief had been annihilated, Prince Edward swerved off westward without a moment's delay, and early on August 4th, overwhelmed the much smaller force of the elder Simon at the battle of Evesham, and slew the old earl and the best of his followers in that very bloody fight.

The events of the following year displayed the impregnability of a good castle against the siege-craft of the day, but also the uselessness of indefinite resistance against an enemy who has won complete control of the countryside. Simon the younger rallied at Kenilworth many of his father's scattered partisans, and refused to think of surrender, when he heard that general forfeiture of lands had been decreed against their party. Having stocked and garrisoned the castle, he made flying tours to keep up the resistance of the " disinherited " in Lincolnshire and those in the Cinque Ports. When these failed, Kenilworth was still intact, and it was not till the spring of 1266 was past that the royal army sat down to besiege it. They lay before its walls from June to December: all assaults proved futile; the king's men erected many military engines opposite the northeast side of the walls, the only part not protected by the lake: but their battering was futile, and they never got across the deep dry ditch which covered that section of the outer ward. An attempt was then made to escalade from the water side, by boats brought up by night and launched on the lake—it failed disastrously as was to be expected. Finally the besiegers grew weary, and as winter came on Prince Edward and the Earl of Gloucester agreed to offer somewhat better terms to the disinherited. By the *Dictum of Kenilworth* (Oct. 31) they were offered the chance of compounding for their treason by paying fines assessed at five years' value of the lands of each. So great was the confidence of the besieged in their walls, that they refused to accept the terms, and held out for two months more, almost till Christmas 1266. Then the approaching exhaustion of their stores, and epidemic disease which had broken out in the crowded castle, compelled them to treat. Instead of pressing his advantage, Prince Edward wisely gave them the terms of the *Dictum*. Many great families among the rebels were reduced to comparative poverty, but few were exterminated— The three younger Montforts, Simon, Guy and Amaury, betook themselves to Italy and vanished from English history, save for one discreditable episode— the murder of the king's nephew Henry of Cornwall at Viterbo (1272).

Thus Kenilworth once more became a royal castle. But the thriftless king at once made a present of it to his younger son Edmund " Crouchback," the founder of the Lancaster branch of the House of Plantagenet. From 1266 to 1399 Kenilworth remained the proudest abode of all that ambitious race, till by the accession of the heir of Lancaster to the throne as Henry IV., it came back to the Crown once more. All the successive earls and dukes of Lancaster habitually resided there; here " Crouchback " held his tournaments, and the blind Earl Henry kept the deposed Edward II. in custody, till Queen Isabella took him away and sent him to perish at Berkeley. But above all John of Gaunt, in spite of the many other castles and manors that he owned, was a very constant lover of Kenilworth. And, being a mighty builder, he refashioned a great part of the domestic structures of the inner ward, pulling down not only Norman work, but that of Henry III., in order that he might replace it by magnificent halls and chambers in late Decorated or early Perpendicular style. His greatest achievement was the banqueting hall, now, alas! roofless, and with shattered windows, which is reckoned the best thing of its kind after Westminster Hall. It was reared on a basement or cellar, well above the ground, measured 90 feet by 45, and had broad windows on both sides—one specially fine half-octagonal oriel towards the south end. There is a large fireplace, a raised dais for the high table, and a recess, obviously for a broad sideboard or buffet. Duke John also built the great apartments called Whitehall and the Presence-Chamber; also a new chapel in the outer ward, probably to replace a Norman chapel which was destroyed in his reconstruction of the inner ward. But it has disappeared no less than its predecessor, leaving the barest traces behind.

It was to be nearly two centuries before Kenilworth saw any more serious architectural additions. It had fallen to the crown by the accession of Henry IV., and was now state property, and no longer the abode of an individual master. It would appear to have been maintained, but not perceptibly altered, by either Lancastrian or Yorkist kings. But for reasons unknown, Henry VIII. set his hand upon it, and pulling down earlier work on the south side of the inner ward, built there the block called King Henry's Lodgings. Presumably it was in the Tudor style, with long galleries, fine chambers and much window space. But this unfortunately is the one part of the ward which has absolutely and entirely disappeared—there is now a missing side to the quadrangle, and we have only literary evidence to show that the gap represents the emplacement of this set of lodgings. Much Tudor work was somewhat scamped, and one can only conclude that King Henry's masons were jerry-builders, putting up the greatest possible extent of frontage with the minimum of solidity. There is no other way of accounting for the disappearance of such a comparatively modern structure, when the work of Lancaster alongside of it still stands. If deliberate destruction had been practised by some later owner, we may be sure that old sections would have been pulled down, rather than new and convenient ones.

This conclusion is corroborated by the fate of the main block of the other, and somewhat later, Tudor buildings at Kenilworth—those which belong to Robert Dudley, Earl of Leicester. These, as the first glance shows, are on their way to follow King Henry's lodgings, being only preserved from falling by elaborate propping and buttressing with timber balks. It cannot be many years before they will collapse.

The gift of Kenilworth Castle to Dudley by Queen Elizabeth, in 1563, was one of the many acts on the part of that magnificent and enigmatical lady, which filled her ministers with dread lest she might be inclining to marry him. It was followed in the next year by his promotion to the status of Earl of Leicester, a title to which he had no pretension by descent, though his elder brother Ambrose could put in a claim to represent through a female line the Beauchamps, Earls of Warwick in the fourteenth and fifteenth centuries. Elizabeth had, as we can now judge, never any real intention of jeopardizing her crown by a Dudley marriage. But she obviously admired the handsome, ostentatious and flamboyant Robert, and committed a thousand indiscretions with regard to him, ranging over a long series of years. At marriage she drew the line, as was made most evident when that unlucky accident at Cumnor Hall removed the favourite's rather elderly and quite unnecessary wife, Amy Robsart. Spanish ambassadors hoped, and English secretaries of state dreaded, that the widower would be too attractive—but the Queen never lost her head ; whether she had a heart in the popular usage of the word is quite doubtful. But she loved admiration and flattery, and Leicester had to be contented with the ungrateful and rather ridiculous rôle of *cavaliere servente* to a Virgin Queen.

Apparently he acquiesced in the position—at any rate he carried out its duties with zeal and apparent satisfaction, and consoled himself by a secret marriage with Lady Sheffield—if indeed there ever was a marriage. He spent the Queen's bounty with magnificence. He was the last great builder at Kenilworth, where he was regularly resident when not in London, or engaged on such distractions as his Dutch Expedition. He did a good deal to demilitarise the aspect of the castle. His most successful piece of building was " Leicester's Gate-house," the handsome pile with four hexagonal corner towers, which stands inside the north-east angle of the outer ward. It is rather a house over the gate than a gate-house, being a handsome and attractive Tudor residence, with some slight appearance of defensive attributes, though the mere size of its windows would, in fact, render it indefensible. More ambitious were the so-called Leicester Buildings, a very lofty block at the south-east corner of the inner ward, continuing the line of King Henry VIII.'s Lodgings. Like these last it has proved very perishable. The roof has long fallen in, great gaps have appeared, and long sections of the wall are only kept in the perpendicular by being shored up with timber. But the buildings were apparently composed of large and handsome rooms in the Tudor style, though there is little sign of that graceful luxury of outside decoration which often distinguishes manors and halls of this date. Elizabeth paid state visits to the man whom she delighted to honour on several occasions, but the one that is best remembered is that of 1575, described at length in Gascoigne's *Princely Pleasures of Kenilworth*. The queen stopped nineteen days in the castle, and the mere maintenance of the establishment is said to have cost Leicester £1,000 a day. There was one continual round of masques, plays, tilting, athletic sports, Morris Dancing, state ceremonies and miscellaneous pageantry. Elizabeth had all the flattery that she could desire. At her entrance along the narrow road across the dam she was saluted by the Lady of the Lake standing with attendant nymphs on a floating island, and Mars, Apollo, Neptune and Bacchus gave her appropriate gifts. On later days she was diverted by dances of "salvage men," fireworks, Italian tumblers, Latin orations, bear-baiting, and a play on the not very cheerful subject of the Massacre of the Danes on the day of St. Brice in 1002. Altogether Leicester was supposed to have spent the sum, incredible in his time, of £100,000, on these nineteen days of various delights. Truly the Tudor mind was insatiable in this matter of " pleasure."

Some years before this orgy of colour and noise Leicester had ventured to marry his second [or third, if Lady Sheffield counts] wife, Lettice Knowles. Their only issue was one little boy, deformed from his birth, who died before his father, aged only four. When the Earl's long life ended in 1588, just after the repulse of the Armada, his brother Ambrose, Earl of Warwick, inherited from him, to the vast disappointment of his son by Lady Sheffield, Robert Dudley, who failed to prove his mother's secret marriage, which indeed was more than doubtful, after much litigation. When Warwick died—he only survived his brother for a year—the disinherited man deserted his wife, fled abroad, turned Roman Catholic, and entered the service of the Duke of Tuscany.

WARWICK CASTLE: GUY'S TOWER

WARWICK CASTLE : THE RIVER FRONT

But Kenilworth was sold by Warwick's executors for £14,000 (much below its value) some years after, to James I., acting for his son Prince Henry, to whom he gave the great place. The prince, however, does not seem to have used it much, only occasionally visiting it for hunting, and his brother Charles I., on whom it devolved, did not care for it, and gave a lease of it in 1626 to Carey, Earl of Monmouth. It may have already been tending to decay at the time of the Civil Wars, when the Parliament ordered it to be "slighted." The north side of the keep was accordingly blown down, and breaches made in the outer walls in 1648. The castle and manor were then given to a Colonel Hawkesworth and certain other officers, by way of satisfaction for good service and arrears of pay. "They pulled down and demolished the castle, cut down the king's woods, destroyed his park, and divided the land into farms for themselves." Hawkesworth seated himself in the gate-house, cut the great dam, and drained the lake to make himself pasturage of water-meadows.

After the Restoration Hawkesworth and his comrades were expelled, and the crown resumed possession of the ruined castle. Charles II. ended by giving it to the Hydes, the family of his first minister, Lord Clarendon. They found that they could do nothing with it, and let it fall gradually to pieces, till it reached its present condition. It is still a majestic group of ruins, but the general effect is not that which it had in the Middle Ages, owing to the disappearance of the all-important lake, the absence of which changes the whole landscape.

Kenilworth Castle.   Leicester's Gate-house

Warwick

This very beautiful castle goes back in its origin to the first days of the Norman Conquest, but displays very little of its early structure, being in the main a picturesque fourteenth and fifteenth century *enceinte*, set with exceptionally lofty towers, enclosing a very attractive Jacobean residence, standing on the cliff above the Avon. We need not go back to foolish legends about King Guitolin, or the giant-quelling Guy of the romances—Warwick starts in 915 with Ethelfleda, the warlike Lady of the Mercians, who "timbered a burh" here, *i.e.*, ditched and palisaded one of those frontier fortresses against the Dane, which were destined to grow into the county-towns of the Midland shires. But she was the parent of the Borough, not of the Castle of Warwick. The town which she fortified was a prosperous place with over 250 burgesses when Domesday Book was drawn up, but the castle was placed outside it, between the burh and the river. Its foundation was decreed by King William as early as 1068, and the custody of it was given to Henry de Newburgh, son of the famous Roger Beaumont of Mellent, who was made by William Rufus the first Earl of Warwick, and became the founder of a dynasty. He was well endowed with the lands of Turchil of Arden, a great English thane in those parts.

Henry de Newburgh was the builder of a large "*motte* and bailey" fortress on the site of the present castle. His *motte* is still clearly visible, set in the western wall of the present *enceinte*, but is covered so thickly with trees that it is difficult to investigate. A tower of much later date is built upon its northern face. The bailey may very well have included the whole area of the existing castle, its *motte* being not central but set upon its western and highest side.

Henry de Newburgh was the trusted friend and councillor of King Henry I., for whose accession he had been largely responsible. He was favoured in every way, used as his master's representative, and enfeoffed by him with the Welsh March of Gower, which he planted and settled out with colonists. As he lived long, it is probable that he may have been responsible for the first stone buildings of the castle before his death in 1123, by converting the wooden house of defence on the *motte* into a shell-keep: and he or his son Roger (1123-53) probably replaced the palisading of the whole *enceinte* with a regular wall. But the shell on the *motte* is not now in existence, its stone casing having been completely removed at some date before the "North Tower" now visible on the *motte* was erected in the fourteenth century. Roger, the second earl, had his lot cast in the unruly days of Stephen, for which he was not well suited. Being an easy-going man (*vir mollis*) he did not join the rebels, but was a weak supporter of the king, and finally endeavoured to escape trouble by taking the Cross and going to the Holy Land—a most inadvisable voyage in a time of civil war. The lands of a crusader were supposed to be immune from war, and this may probably have been his reason for absconding. His sons, who followed in succession, William and Waleran, were loyal servants of Henry II.— the elder of them died on Crusade in 1184, having apparently inherited his father's

Newburgh

Beauchamp

Mauduit

Dudley

Neville

Greville

Plantagenet

Arms of the seven families which have held
Warwick Castle.

tendency to roam abroad. Waleran's son, Henry, second Newburgh of that name, was one of the few barons who supported King John during the troubles of the time of the Great Charter. In the next reign the house of Newburgh, having lasted for five generations, died out in the male line, like so many other of the comital families. The last earl, Thomas (*obiit* 1242) had a sister Margaret, whose husband, John du Plessis, one of the Poitevin favourites of Henry III., was allowed to call himself earl for the term of his life. But he had no issue, and on his death in 1262 the nearest heir was William Mauduit, the son of Margaret's aunt Alicia. The one earl of the Mauduit house was originally a Montfortian ; perhaps the fact that he had been kept out of the earldom for so many years by one of the king's foreign minions made him a nationalist. But in 1263 he fell away from the opposition, and submitted to the royalists. This brought on disaster : in April, 1264, Earl William saw his castle surprised and completely sacked and dismantled by John Giffard then commanding at Kenilworth as Montfort's lieutenant. He had to pay 1,900 marks ransom before he was released. It must have been at this time that the shell-keep was cast down, and other damage done to the original Norman buildings. Mauduit only survived this blow for a few years, and died in January, 1268, when castle and earldom went to the son of his sister, Isabella, who had married William Beauchamp, a small baron of Worcestershire.

Six Beauchamp earls followed in succession—a very vigorous and pugnacious race of high ability, each of whom in his generation was a leading man among the English baronage. As they must have taken over the castle in very bad order after the sack of 1264, it is not surprising to find that they completely rebuilt it, each earl adding his special contribution, and made Warwick into a fine castle with Edwardian features, but not of the " concentric " type. For the old *enceinte* of the Newburghs was preserved, and no inner ward added ; the shell-keep was not restored, but residential buildings were erected on the cliff above the river, where the present Jacobean mansion stands. This latter conceals much of the Newburgh's work, *e.g.*, the great hall—burnt out and reconstructed—and much more of the Beauchamps' buildings.

The great and special feature of Warwick, however, is the set of towers inserted in its outer *enceinte*, by one or other of the Beauchamps. Earl Guy, the "Black Dog of Arden"—who (as he threatened) "bit Piers Gaveston, so that he died" by the headman's sword, most illegally, on Blacklow Hill—has left his name to "Guy's Tower," but was not its builder, though he may have erected some of the minor and earlier towers in other parts of the walls. But the two great structures, "Cæsar's Tower" and "Guy's Tower," were really built by the two Earls Thomas, in the second half of the fourteenth century. The earlier Thomas, who commanded a wing at Cressy, and again at Poitiers, and was one of the most distinguished generals of Edward III., would appear to have been responsible for the massive gate-house and barbican, as well as for Cæsar's Tower. His son, the second Thomas, one of the " Lords Appellant," who tyrannized over Richard II., and were the victims of his revenge in 1397, built Guy's Tower.

Both of these are mural towers of quite exceptional height, far overtopping the rest of the *enceinte*. One is polygonal, the other cylindrical; both have projecting machicolations, which makes them splay out at the top story. "Cæsar's" has a small additional turret set upon the rampart-wall of the main tower. Guy's Tower is 128 feet high, Cæsar's no less than 147—their unusual loftiness makes them more like Continental than English work, and it is to be remembered that both the earls who built them had fought for many years in France.

Warwick the Kingmaker

From the tomb of his father-in-law, Earl Richard, in Warwick Church

Construction did not by any means cease at Warwick with the rearing of the great towers in the *enceinte*. The owners of the castle in the fifteenth century were men who made and played an even greater part in English history than did the two Earls Thomas. First came the great Earl Richard, the hero of the spirited series of biographical sketches in Rous's Roll, that most invaluable authority for arms, dress and ceremonial in the Lancastrian period. He served through the campaigns of Henry V. and Duke of Bedford across the sea, always in high command; he found time to visit the Holy Land as a pilgrim, and to joust before the princes of Italy; finally, he was regent of France in the time of oncoming disaster that followed Bedford's death, and died at Rouen in 1439, still keeping up the losing game of English domination. He figures—a not very sympathetic character—in Bernard Shaw's "St. Joan," as the astute warrior-statesman who cannot read the signs of the times. But to the men of his own day he represented the ideal of chivalry and loyalty, and they reared in his honour the most magnificent tomb in England. His only son is one of the pathetic "might-have-beens" of history—the lively and brilliant young man who captivated the fancy of that pious pedant Henry VI., who made him Duke of Warwick and—an odd freak—"King of the Isle of Wight." Just as he seemed destined to rule king and state he died—aged only 22 and a few months—in 1446. He was the last male Beauchamp—the earldom passed to his infant daughter, and after her death at the age of five, to his sister Anne Beauchamp, the spouse of Richard Neville, "the Kingmaker," always better remembered by his wife's title of Warwick than by his paternal title of Salisbury. For twenty years Earl Richard was the most prominent figure in the realm, the pillar

BERKELEY CASTLE : AERIAL VIEW

BERKELEY CASTLE : KEEP, AND ENTRANCE TO INNER WARD

of the house of York, soldier, diplomatist and administrator, one whose lot should surely have been to guide the steps of a feeble king like Henry VI., rather than to be associated with his cousin Edward IV., a man as capable in war as himself, and far more unscrupulous. The clash of rival wills ended on the field of Barnet, and in 1471, the Earldom of Warwick was once more without a male heir. The castle passed first to "false fleeting perjured Clarence," the husband of the Kingmaker's elder daughter Isabel, and then, after the not un-deserved execution and attainder of Clarence, to Richard of Gloucester, who had wedded Anne Neville, the younger sister of Isabel.

The Bear
Cognizance of the Beauchamps from Earl Richard's tomb in Warwick Church

Both Clarence and Gloucester left their mark as builders on Warwick—to the former we owe the Clarence Tower; to the latter, the unfinished Bear Tower [so called from the Beauchamp cognizance of the Bear] which flank on either side an entry to the northern side of the castle, which must have been intended to supersede Earl Thomas's great gate-house on the east side as its main access.

With the accession of Henry VII. there comes a break in the history of castle and earldom. Clarence's unlucky son lingered for fifteen years in prison and ended on the block: his sister Margaret Pole was never restored to the earldom, though she was granted that of Salisbury. And when Henry VIII. attainted and slew her in her old age, the Beauchamp dynasty might be supposed to have ended. This was not to be—among the king's most useful and unscrupulous tools was John Dudley Lord Lisle, the son of the equally useful and unscrupulous Edmund Dudley, the minister of Henry VII. John Dudley descended from Margaret Beauchamp, sister of Duke Henry, and daughter of the great regent of France. And in 1547 he got himself created Earl of Warwick, to the prejudice of all the surviving descendants of the attainted house of Clarence, and obtained possession of the castle no less than the title. This is the abominable intriguer who slew Protector Somerset, took the usurped title of Northumberland, and ruled the declining years of Edward VI. After the death of his ward he tried to be, if not a Kingmaker, at least a Queenmaker—placing his innocent daughter-in-law, Lady Jane Grey, on the throne. Hence came death both to him and to his unfortunate nominee on Queen Mary's scaffolds. But on the accession of Elizabeth Ambrose Dudley, eldest surviving son of Northumberland, was "restored in blood," and re-granted earldom, castle and estates—all the more willingly, perhaps, because he was the brother of the queen's favourite, Robert Dudley, who was soon to become Earl of Leicester and lord of Kenilworth.

Ambrose, a more steady and respectable character than might have been expected from the career of his father, was a trusted and competent servant of

Queen Elizabeth in peace and war, and somewhat of a Puritan. He married thrice, but had no issue, so that when he died in 1589, a year after his brother Leicester, the earldom once more disappeared. The castle having been restored in 1560 only to Ambrose and his heirs male, fell back to the crown. Sixteen years after King James I. bestowed it, in somewhat decayed condition, as we are told, on Sir Fulke Greville, a wealthy local magnate, long M.P. for the shire, who was also given the title of Baron Brooke of Beauchamp Court. With this Fulke and his nephew and successor, Robert, started the dynasty which still holds the place. But for a century and a half the title of Warwick and the buildings of the historic castle were divorced, for James I. gave the earldom to Robert Lord Rich, and Richs continued to hold it till 1759. Meanwhile the Grevilles were in possession of the castle: Fulke, their first representative, completely recast the residential block of buildings overlooking the river, into the pleasant Jacobean shape which it still preserves in the main, though George Greville in the time of George III. made many alterations in the style of his day. The second Lord Brooke, Robert, was the Puritan general whose troops ravaged Lichfield Cathedral, at whose storming he himself was slain by the ball of a " sniper " on the roof. The eighth baron, Fulke, was a Tory, but a personage of such importance that on the death of the last Rich in 1759, he was possessed of sufficient influence to get the title of Warwick given him within a few months, even by a Whig government. Thus earldom and castle were once more united, and have been so ever since.

Warwick is probably the best known and most visited, after Windsor, of all English castles. Its attraction lies in the combination of a very splendid Jacobean residence—containing some earlier features, such as the Great Hall—with a magnificent and impressive mediæval *enceinte*. Probably the interior decoration and the well furnished picture gallery, with its wonderful series of portraits, and the broad lawn and its peacocks, are the main delight of the tourist. But the antiquary will carry away in his mind the memory of Guy's and Cæsar's Towers.

Berkeley

This is a castle very interesting from the architectural point of view, and almost unique from the historical, since it is still in the hands of the descendants in the male line of the builder of the first stone fortress on the spot in the middle of the twelfth century. It has never since then passed through an heiress to a new family, though once, it is true, it was alienated from its rightful owners and remained in the hands of the king for sixty-one years. And on another occasion, in more recent times, it was diverted to an illegitimate branch of the house for eighty years. But in each case it reverted in the end to the lawful representative of Robert Fitz Hardinge, who in 1155 received the place from Henry II., and girt it with stone. We know more of its history than of that of most castles, mainly owing to the pious labour of an Elizabethan steward, John Smith of Nibley, who wrote a chronicle of the House of Berkeley, its battles and its buildings, in great detail, though not always with perfect accuracy.

In the great castle-building age just after the Conquest, there was no stronghold commanding the plain-land between Severn and Cotswold, till Earl William Fitz Osborne appropriated the revenue of five hides to build a " small castle " on the rising ground above the marshy lands about Berkeley Pill, which was held under him by one Roger of Coberley. This must have amounted to no more than the throwing up of a small *motte*, which is encased in the present keep, while the present inner ward may represent its bailey. In the third generation Roger's successor having followed Stephen in the Civil Wars, was dispossessed by Henry Plantagenet, who gave Berkeley to a valued partisan of the Angevin cause, one Robert, son of Hardinge, the reeve of Bristol, a man of English, not Norman, descent. In the charter giving the manor to Robert, his master covenants to build him a castle: "pepigi ei firmare ibi castellum, secundum voluntatem ipsius Roberti." This evidently means that the existing *motte* was not considered a castle by either Robert or Henry, and that the foundation of the stone-built fortress must not be put back earlier than 1155. The descendants of the original holder returned to their manor of Coberley, but Fitz Hardinge took the trouble to connect himself with them by asking for the hand of Alice de Berkeley for his son and heir, Maurice. His heirs continued to call themselves Fitz Hardinge for some generations, till the last of the old house died out, when the owners of the castle commenced to call themselves de Berkeley.

Robert constructed his castle in an odd way, turning the *motte* into a keep, not, as usual, by building a tower on top of it, but by cutting its slope vertically, and casing the whole of its exterior with masonry. Thus he got, not a shell-keep on a *motte*, but a shell-keep enclosing a *motte* in its core. It is about 50 yards in diameter, and 62 feet high, with three small half-towers or bastions projecting from it, and (what is very exceptional) a " forebuilding " on its inner face, *i.e.*, a small battlemented slip covering a staircase, which was the proper access to the whole keep. Generally, as at Launceston or Cardiff, the approach to a shell-keep was by a straight flight of steps, though square solid keeps, like those of Kenilworth or Newcastle-on-Tyne had forebuildings occasionally. Of the three bastion-towers of Berkeley keep, one contains an oratory, another has at its base the dungeon above which Edward II. is said to have been kept by his gaolers, in the hope that its insanitary conditions and darkness might kill him, and so actual bodily violence be avoided. His strong constitution withstood this abominable device, and in the end, as was generally known, he was put to a painful death in a chamber at the head of the forebuilding—so at least says Smith, the chronicler of the Berkeleys. The bed shown as his belongs to a later age.

The keep has one other tower, large and square, and obviously later than the rest of the original buildings, on its north side. Smith attributes it to the fourteenth century. It is the highest point of the castle, and looks out on Berkeley church and churchyard, which come all too close to the walls for safety or convenience. It has been suggested that this building—called Thorpe's Tower, from the name of a family who held a manor by the service of defending it in time of war—was thrown up to command the church. For the roof of the latter would have made a good position for archers wishing to incommode the garrison, and its yard would have been a natural place in which to put up military engines. In the siege of the Parliamentarians in 1645, this was the point from which the castle was successfully battered.

When the *motte* was turned, by Robert Fitz Hardinge, into a shell-keep, he undoubtedly also walled in the earthwork of the original bailey with a stone *enceinte*. And this now makes the inner ward of the castle. On its south and east sides this ward is at the head of a very perceptible and steep slope—looking over meadows which were no doubt morasses when the place was first fortified. The keep more or less protects the whole of the northern and western sides, lying towards the church and the village, which are on higher ground.

The late-Norman buildings which originally lined the inner ward have all gone, and were replaced by a fine set of domestic and residential offices, belonging to a later age, the work of Thomas the eighth lord, a notable soldier of the times of Edward III. To him is due the great hall, a fine room 61 feet by 32, with an open pointed roof, but with square-topped mullioned windows that were perhaps substituted for earlier ones in Tudor times. The chapel, dedicated to St. Mary, which abuts on the hall on the south-west, was also reconstructed, if not built [some of its walls seem to be twelfth century] by Thomas or by his son, Maurice, who obtained in 1376 a papal bull granting certain spiritual privileges to worshippers in it. On the other side of the hall are the kitchen and buttery, also apparently reconstructed in the fourteenth century by Thomas or Maurice, but with traces of original Norman masonry.

The whole courtyard of this ward, seen from within, gives an impression not unlike that of a college quadrangle—a remark which we have also to make in the case of Chirk, in a later chapter—due to the juxtaposition of hall, chapel, residential chambers and offices round an open central space. In one respect alone is there a marked difference—college quadrangles generally have a prominent gate-house, with rooms therein for the Warden, Provost or Master. At Berkeley there is no gate-house to this ward, but only a plain entry, 11 feet broad, cutting underneath residential apartments. The only gate-house of the castle is an insignificant one in the small outer ward.

The mediæval aspect of the inner ward is somewhat impaired by the many Tudor and modern windows that have been inserted at various times, especially in the upper-story living-rooms on the south side. But the present Earl of Berkeley is at work on replacing Georgian windows by something less inappropriate to their surroundings.

The outer ward of this castle is a comparatively small and insignificant thing—a triangular space with a one-storied gate-house at its front, and plain curtain walls trending back to the keep on one side and the western corner of the inner ward on the other. The gate-house is intact, but the curtain has mainly disappeared ; there are no buildings at all within the ward. As it would seem that its wall was never high or solid, the main defence here must have been the deep ditch which separated this outer ward from the village on one side and the church and churchyard on the other.

BERKELEY CASTLE : INNER WARD

EXETER CASTLE (ROUGEMONT): THE GATE-HOUSE

The history of the family of Berkeley is more interesting than that of the castle, which seems to have known only one siege, that of 1645. Robert the third lord was one of the barons who rebelled against John, but his successor made his peace with Henry III. when his tyrannical father was dead. Thomas the sixth lord was one of the favourite soldiers of Edward I., and always served in his Welsh and Scottish campaigns with a larger contingent than his small fief could have supplied. Maurice, his son, was one of the enemies of the Despensers in the troublous times of Edward II. His castle was occupied by those unrighteous ministers, and he himself imprisoned—he died a captive early in 1326. Naturally, therefore, his son Thomas was one of those who joined in the general insurrection of the following autumn : unluckily for his reputation and that of his castle, the victorious intriguer Mortimer and Queen Isabella selected Berkeley as the death-place of the deposed king. After he had been taken out of the custody of Henry of Lancaster at Kenilworth, he was hurried about secretly from castle to castle, till he reached Berkeley in the custody of those two villainous knights Thomas Gurney and John Maltravers. When Lord Thomas showed him courtesy, he was forbidden to see the ex-king again, and the gaolers took possession of the keep, which no one was allowed to enter. They first tried to destroy Edward by shutting him up in the dungeon tower below which carrion and dead beasts had been stowed. As he failed to die of the stench, and Mortimer complained that he was living too long, they finally murdered him most cruelly in his bed on September 21, 1327. Lord Thomas, disgusted at the insolence of Gurney and Maltravers, had gone off to his manor of Bradley, and was far away when the tragedy ended. Possibly he had some suspicion of what was likely to happen—but he was entirely free of responsibility, and when Edward III. raged against his father's murderers no one said a word against the owner of Berkeley Castle. Indeed Thomas was one of his most trusted commanders in the long French wars. The grandson and namesake of this distinguished soldier was a strong supporter of the cause of Henry of Bolingbroke, and was one of the peers who pronounced the deposition of Richard II. in the Parliament of September, 1399. Fortunately for him Henry chose Pontefract, not Berkeley, for the residence of his deposed cousin during the short remainder of his life.

When this Thomas died in 1417, his inheritance was disputed between his daughter and her husband, and his nephew, James Berkeley. The latter was awarded possession, but the claim against him was never forgotten, and fifty years after, in the middle of the Wars of the Roses, Thomas Talbot Lord Lisle, grandson of the daughter, and William Berkeley, the son of James, had a lively private war of their own, utterly unconnected with the affairs of York and Lancaster. It ended in a pitched battle at Nibley Green on March 20, 1470, in which Lord Lisle was routed and slain. The victor seems to have been a versatile but unamiable person—he commended himself to Edward IV., who gave him a viscount's title in 1481; to Richard III., who made him an earl in 1483, and to Henry VII., who created him Marquis of Berkeley and Earl Marshal of England in 1488. This last creation was part of an iniquitous bargain of doubtful legality

—William, who was childless, so hated his brother and natural heir Maurice, that in consideration of the marquisate and marshalship he gave the king an assignment of Berkeley Castle to him and his heirs male, with a mere remainder to the House of Berkeley.

In 1492 William died, and Henry VII. took possession; from that date till the death of Edward VI. in 1553, Berkeley was a royal castle. But the extinction of the male line of Tudor threw it back into the hands of the rightful heir, Henry, the great-grandson of the defrauded Maurice, a very young man, who possessed the family seat from 1554 till 1613, and outlived all his generation. He was succeeded by his grandson George, who was already an elderly person at the outbreak of the great Civil War of 1642, and who contrived to take no great part in it. But his castle suffered—it was occupied without resistance by the Parliamentarians in 1642, evacuated by them in 1643, when King Charles marched to besiege Gloucester, and then held for two years by the royalists. In 1645, after Naseby, Fairfax detached Colonel Rainsborough to besiege it. The governor, Sir Charles Lucas, made a haughty reply to a summons to surrender—" he would eat his horses first "—but only three days of battering by guns placed in the churchyard forced him to hoist the white flag—the wall of the outer ward joining the keep, and part of the keep itself had been brought down. So the garrison of 500 men marched out (Sept. 26, 1645), and laid down their arms. The usual " slighting " was ordered by parliament, but was carried out with some consideration for the owner, who was not greatly disliked by the victors. His residential buildings were left untouched, only the walls of the outer ward being destroyed and the breach in the keep enlarged. George Lord Berkeley died in 1658, his epitaph states that " he was eminent for the candour and ingenuity of his disposition, for his singular bounty and affability towards his inferiors, and his readiness (had it been in his power) to have obliged all mankind." This, obviously, was not the kind of disposition likely to shine in the time of Civil War. George's son of the same name took a prominent part in the Restoration of Charles II., was a man of great activity, and interested himself in the East India Company, and in trade and colonization generally. He was made an Earl in 1679, and the title still survives, though, owing to a strange family complication in 1811, the " Berkeley Peerage Case," the legal heirs refused to claim it for eighty-one years, and it was only after a full century that the owner of the title became the owner of the castle once more—a conjunction at which all lovers of ancient genealogies could not but rejoice—for it restored the connection of the castle and the old historic name, which had seemed for many years to be broken for ever.

DEVONSHIRE

NEARLY the whole interest of Devonshire for the seeker after castles lies in the south. To North Devon he need not go: and in the central tract which lies between Exmoor and Dartmoor, there is little to be seen, though it once boasted of two castles of considerable importance.

In mediæval days North Devon—a very isolated region—had one important castle, Barnstaple, the centre of a great "Honour" held by Tracys and then by Hollands. But when Leland made his great tour in 1540 he found only ruins and one piece of a donjon standing. When this was the state of things in the reign of Henry VIII., it is not surprising to find that no stone at all remained by the time of George I. The other castle of North Devon was Torrington, long the home of a family who took their name from it. But when Leland went by "their remained nothing standing but a neglected chapel."

North Devon, then, is a blank for the castle-hunter of to-day, and Central Devon, the strip of inhabited land between Exmoor and Dartmoor, will show him no more than poor remnants. At Okehampton—long the dwelling place of the earlier Courtenays, certain scraps of a chapel, a hall, and a tower can be detected among the trees which have overgrown a most lovely spot above the Ockment river. At Lydford, the other old castle of Mid-Devon, there is one big fragment of a keep "square and ruinous without picturesqueness," as Mr. Baring Gould observed. A local Elizabethan satirist remarked—

"They have a castle on a hill—
I took it for an old windmill,
The vanes blown off by weather."

And the description is not unfair for the effect of a mutilated Norman keep on the eyes of a somewhat ribald observer. This was originally a royal castle, given by Henry III. to Richard Earl of Cornwall, and neglected in the later Middle Ages, when the Duchy of Cornwall was an appanage of the crown, with (as a rule) no Duke of Cornwall alive, or requiring two (not to speak of ten) castles to live in. But we find, when we have arrived in South Devon, the land looking southward toward the English Channel, castles of which much still remains, and which are worthy of the attention of the archæologist and the lover of the picturesque. Here lie royal castles of the earliest Norman time, baronial strongholds of the twelfth, thirteenth and fourteenth centuries, and, to end the list, some of that long series of harbour-defence castles, built for the use of artillery, with which Henry VIII. lined the shore from Kent to Cornwall.

Devon was made an earldom in Norman days, not, indeed, by William the Conqueror, but either by his son Henry I., or at latest by Henry's contentious daughter, the Empress Matilda, in the early times of her war with Stephen. The comital family was that of the De Redvers; they start with Baldwin of Brionne, the Conqueror's sheriff of Devon, who held 159 manors in the shire when Domesday Book was compiled. His son Richard was the progenitor of seven Redvers earls, who endured till 1262, the line ending in an heiress, that Countess Isabella of masterful memory, who spoiled the harbour of her enemies, the citizens of Exeter, by throwing her weir across the Exe below their city, and blocking the tidal estuary. Hence the Exonians had to move their quay down to Topsham, and the Countess Weir remains as a landmark till this day. Isabella was wedded to William de Fortibus, Earl of Albemarle. Their only daughter and heiress, Avelina, was chosen by Henry III. as bride for his son Edmund of Lancaster, better known as Edmund "Crouchback." But she died young and childless, long before her mother the countess, who survived till 1293, when the lands of Redvers passed to a cousin, Hugh Courtenay, Lord of Okehampton, who descended, through females, from a son of the sixth earl. He was then a young boy, but long years afterwards, when he was a middle-aged man, Edward III. recognized him as Earl of Devon. From him came the ten earls of the second house of Devon, ending with that unhappy prisoner in the Tower, Edward Courtenay, who was unlucky enough to have a daughter of Edward IV. as his grandmother, and only escaped with his life because Henry VIII., when he executed the rest of his Yorkist relations, drew the line at beheading a boy of thirteen. After fourteen years spent in the Tower, Edward emerged on the accession of Mary, who did justice to the heirs of her father's victims. For one short year he was a leading figure in politics—spoken of as a fitting husband either for the queen herself or for her sister, the Princess Elizabeth. But he was a mean, spirit-broken creature, weak and false; he allowed himself to be involved in treason, and died an exile at Padua only three years after his release. Of the curious revival, after three centuries, of a title that was thought to be extinct at his death, we shall speak when dealing with the Courtenay castle of Powderham.

The Redvers and Courtenay earls, save this last degenerate descendant, were a race of fighting men, from Baldwin de Redvers, who made a desperate defence of Exeter Castle against King Stephen, down to John Courtenay, who perished at Tewkesbury Field in 1471. Their lands were scattered all over Devon, including the immense "Honour" of Plympton in the south-west of the county, the almost equally important lordship of Okehampton in the centre, Tiverton and its castle in the east, and lands along the lower Exe, to which were added, for a time in the fourteenth century, Powderham Castle and lordship, obtained by marriage with a Bohun heiress. But these were soon alienated to a younger son of the then earl, from whom started a minor branch of Courtenays. The Redvers family also held the lordship of the Isle of Wight, which did not, however, descend to the Courtenays after the death of the great Countess Isabella, like the rest of her lands, as she had sold it to King Edward I. But the Courtenay earls had, beside Okehampton and Plympton, and Tiverton, many outlying manors in Cornwall and Somerset, and even further afield, and were always among the greatest landed magnates of England.

The houses of Redvers and Courtenay, nevertheless, were not so entirely dominant in their own shire as some other earls—broad as were their estates

TIVERTON CASTLE: S.W. ANGLE TOWER

POWDERHAM CASTLE : AERIAL VIEW

there was room in the county for several other feudal families of importance, such as the Pomeroys, the Torringtons, and the Tracys and other heirs of Judhael of Totnes, one of William the Conqueror's most favoured grantees.

But since we are set on studying castles rather than the genealogies of their owners, we must turn to an inspection of the various castles of South Devon, which still survive in such a condition as to attract the interest of the traveller with historical instincts.

Exeter

This was one of the original royal strongholds set up by William the Conqueror to hold down a large and important town. Exeter had been one of the few centres of English resistance to the invaders, and had stood a siege in 1068. But the walls of a Saxon *burh* were not strong enough to resist a master of the military art, and the siege had lasted only eighteen days. William put Baldwin de Brionne, his sheriff of Devonshire, in charge of the place, with orders to build a castle therein. This Baldwin did by cutting off the northern angle of the city—its highest quarter—where there is a steep descent both to north and to west, and clearing out such houses as were to be found therein. Two sides of the castle were formed by the line of the former external wall of the *burh*, the other side (facing into the city) was originally, no doubt, no more than a ditched and palisaded earthwork. But before the century was out, stone must have replaced earth, for the important gate-house of Rougemont—the Red Hill, as the fortress was now styled—appears to be of the very earliest Norman style. The whole fortress constituted a very large shell-keep—there was no donjon or high tower in it. The most dominant building was the gate-house—about 30 feet square, with walls six feet thick: it was double, with an inner and an outer door, each formed by a twelve-foot arch. It was two stories high, and furnished with very small windows. It projects some twenty-four feet beyond the line of the *enceinte*, and must have had a drawbridge appended to it for the crossing of the ditch.

This gate-house, however, is not now the entrance to the castle—at some date in comparatively recent times its two doors were walled up, and a new and much larger gate was built immediately to the side of it, as shown in one of our illustrations. The new gate looks so indefensible, that one must suppose that it was built after any serious danger from the city side had become unlikely. Certainly it was not the entrance of the castle when it was defended in 1136 by Baldwin de Redvers—grandson of its original builder—who seized on it in the name of the Empress Matilda, and held it for three months against King Stephen in person, who had recovered the city, and so attacked the castle from its inner front. The king tried all the methods of twelfth century siegecraft, escalade, converging discharges of missiles against the ramparts, and finally, mining. Even the last, so often effective against castles on a dry site, failed, and the garrison only surrendered after three months, because their well had run dry and they were perishing from thirst. The king would have liked to make an example of the defenders; but he was compelled to let them march out with the honours of war by his barons, who thought more about the gallantry of the rebels than of their treason. Baldwin, not at all touched by this clemency, retired to his lordship of the Isle of Wight, and made himself a nuisance there by piratical attacks on merchant-men trading with Southampton and Portsmouth.

Exeter was several times besieged in later days, for example by Perkin Warbeck, and by the Catholic insurgents of 1549, but on each occasion city and castle were held by the same side, and the rebels tried to force their way in, not at the high lying castle walls, but on the weakest front of the city. In both cases they were repelled with ease, not having the artillery which would have made a twelfth century *enceinte* untenable.

The present condition of "Rougemont" is disappointing. While the outer walls and the gate-house are intact, the whole of the inner buildings have been swept away so thoroughly, that it is impossible to identify hall, chapel, kitchen, or any other locality. There are traces of fireplaces, flues, and party walls visible in the back of the *enceinte* in many places, but not a single perfect chamber. Vandals of the eighteenth century cleared every mediæval room away, and built in the centre of the enclosure a vast sessions hall of Georgian style, which stands alone in the centre of a broad grass-plot.

Tiverton

This was always the most important castle of Eastern Devon, and the centre of a great Courtenay holding. Its very considerable remains lie close to the magnificent "Perpendicular" church of Tiverton, at the north-west side of the town. The place must apparently have been a quadrangular fortress with round towers at each angle and a great gate-house in its main front. But only two of its sides now survive, and one of these is imperfect. On the western side are the remains of a large hall of the end of the thirteenth or beginning of the fourteenth century, joining on to the one surviving complete corner tower. On the southern side is a strong gate-house, looking like work of 1350, a little later than the hall on the west front, and much later than the surviving angle-tower: but its antique aspect is spoiled by a three-light Tudor window cut in its centre. There is a battlemented walk along all the surviving parts of the curtain wall. The south front has now been converted into a modern private residence, and most of its windows, therefore, have been cut square. This was probably done by the Giffords, its tenants in the days of Elizabeth and the earlier Stuarts. Tiverton stopped in the possession of the Courtenays till Henry VIII. slew the head of their house and confiscated their lands in 1539; the king gave the castle to Lord Russell, the ancestor of the Dukes of Bedford, whom Leland found in possession there in 1540. Russell exchanged it for other lands with Lord Protector Somerset. When Mary restored Edward Courtenay to the earldom in 1553, she could not get back for him all the spoils which her father's courtiers had obtained; but Tiverton was recovered and returned to him. On his death in exile in 1556, it was found that his nearest heirs were four great-aunts, who, having to divide his property, sold Tiverton Castle to one Roger Gifford. When this gentleman's estate was cut up among co-heiresses, and no single person wished for so large an abode, it was let out to farmers, who allowed the hinder parts of the castle to fall into decay, and lived in the gate-house and the adjacent front, which were rescued from agricultural uses, and made into a residential tenement in quite recent years. An engraving in Dunsford's history of Tiverton shows that in 1780 there was more surviving of the

Tiverton Castle.
The Gate-House and South Front

hall and the second angle-tower than is now visible, and that they were not so much overshadowed by trees as at present.

Powderham

This is one of the castles which has suffered from the point of view of the archæologist by having been in continual occupation since the Middle Ages, and therefore recast from time to time by residents who were desirous of light and comfort, after the days had passed in which military strength was the primary desideratum.

In Domesday Book, Powderham is found in the hands of William of Eu, one of the rebels whom William Rufus crushed and mutilated in 1196. It then became the home of a knightly family who called themselves after its name.

93

They built the original castle, probably in the thirteenth century, in an odd situation—in a rather low-lying position, less than half a mile from the broad salt-water estuary of the Exe. It neither commands the estuary nor occupies the highest ground of the neighbourhood, that being the adjacent hill, where an eighteenth century owner reared the " Gothic " Belvedere, which incautious passers-by have sometimes mistaken for the lower-lying castle.

John, the last of the Powderhams, was attainted in the reign of Edward I., and his manor was granted to Humphrey Bohun, Earl of Hereford, who gave it as a marriage portion to his daughter Margaret, when she married Hugh, Earl of Devon. But Earl Hugh did not incorporate it with his family estates, but passed it on as a separate holding to his younger son, Sir Philip Courtenay. Considering how rare is continuous male descent in the old landed families, it is worth noting that this knight's descendants have held Powderham in the male line from the time of Edward III. till to-day. From this Philip Courtenay, the son of Margaret Bohun, come, by a queer freak in a patent, the present earls of Devon. The story is worth noting. When Edward Courtenay, the prisoner in the Tower, was restored to his ancestors' honours by Queen Mary, in 1553, the document which set things right was drawn up in the form of the creation of a new earldom of Devon. Now nearly all Tudor patents were to heirs male, descending from the grantee, who was to have his peerage *sibi et heredibus suis masculis de suo corpore in perpetuum.* Apparently, by the error of a careless scribe, in this particular patent the words *de suo corpore* were left out. The restored earldom, therefore, was given to Edward Courtenay and his heirs-male simply, whoever they might be, and however distantly related. Edward died in exile only three years after, and the restored earldom was supposed to have died with him, no contemporary (as it seems) knowing of the abnormal wording of his patent. The title was unclaimed till 1830, though the exile had a very obvious heir male, Sir William Courtenay of Powderham, who descended direct from Earl Hugh (*obiit* 1337), the common ancestor of the fifteenth and sixteenth century earls and of the younger Powderham branch. But unless some one had chanced to look at the actual patent, there was no reason to suppose that this fact of relationship had any ulterior consequences.

The Courtenays of Powderham went on from 1556 to 1830 in a continual male descent, as important Devonshire magnates, obtaining first a baronetcy in 1644, and then in 1762 a viscounty. They never claimed the earldom, being, like the rest of the world, unaware that it had never ceased to exist. And the Cavendishes were given, by James I., the earldom, and by William III., the dukedom of Devonshire, under the idea that the title was at the disposition of the crown. In 1830 the third Viscount Courtenay was apprised of the extraordinary wording of the patent of 1553, it is said, by his cousin, who chanced to be assistant-clerk of Parliaments at Westminster, and so was accustomed to being consulted by persons searching through original documents for manifold purposes. He put in his claim to be heir male of Edward, who had died in 1556, and the House of Lords, on looking up the facts, decided that he and his ancestors had undoubtedly been earls *de jure* for the last two hundred and eighty years. Hence the emergence of the long-forgotten title, and the tiresome duplication of the names Devon and Devonshire in the peerage-roll of to-day. As the first restored earl died childless, his successor was his cousin, the Clerk of Parliaments, who had dug up the patent of 1553.

The long line of Powderham Courtenays (mostly Williams, a christian name perpetuated for generations by elder sons) are responsible for the present state of their castle, which—as mentioned above—is more gratifying to the occupant than to the archæologist. The main destroyer of antiquities would appear to have been the Sir William Courtenay of the days of George II., who in the words of a contemporary county historian, "from an old castle made Powderham a noble seat." Another admirer of the first Lord Courtenay, "whose taste deserved every commendation," notes that he had greatly improved and ornamented the house, and in particular had converted the chapel into "a very elegant drawing room," and done much else to change the ancient castle-like form of buildings, and, not least, had erected the beautiful towered Belvedere on the adjacent height, and replaced the original entrance-hall by a magnificent staircase "by Jenkins," luxuriously ornamented with plaster reliefs.

The general effect of the present castle, therefore, is that of modernization, despite the battlemented outline which has still been preserved. There are ancient walls to be discovered, but the arrangement within is eighteenth century, and without is eighteenth century striving to be a little Gothic. The general effect may be gathered from our illustration. Even the gate-house, the best looking part of the castle, is recorded to have been much altered in the restorations of 1750.

When artillery came into general use in the sixteenth century the castle was found to be so far from the shore that it did not command the estuary. A separate detached bulwark, or barbican, as Leland calls it, " to bete the haven," was therefore thrown up close to the water, and furnished with guns. But it seems to have disappeared entirely.

Dartmouth and Kingswear

This pair of castles, corresponding to each other like Portland and Sandsfoot, or Pendennis and St. Mawes, were the guardians of the entry of the broad estuary of the Dart, designed by Henry VIII. to protect a great centre of commerce and an important strategical point. The long tidal fiord running inland for eleven miles, as far as Totnes, and able to give anchorage for whole fleets, was almost as important as the Solent in the naval geography of England. Yet its entry is so narrow that it could easily be blocked by the cross-fire of such cannon as were known in Tudor times. Both castles are somewhat different in type from the normal low round tower, encircled by an embrasured battery, which is seen in the other haven-forts that we have quoted. Kingswear, standing low on the rocks and washed by every tide, is an adaptation of an earlier castle to the use of artillery. It is a square mediæval tower of three stages, whose lowest story has had embrasures cut in it on the side facing the water :

here King Henry was not the builder, but only the utilizer of what was already existing. Just at its side a small round Tudor tower stands, quite dwarfed by the old castle, and furnished with a few additional embrasures. On the opposite side of the haven-mouth stands Dartmouth Castle, on a small cliff, which rises well above the water. It is inconveniently sited, in the very yard of St. Petrock's Church, whose tombstones reach up to its walls. The main building consists of a square battlemented tower with a large and high look-out turret rising from it, and a casemented battery with embrasures at its foot. Separated from it by the churchyard, and at a lower level, on the water's edge, is a small round tower, with an embrasured battery adhering to it, exactly facing the similar addendum to Kingswear. Between these towers a chain could be, and was, stretched every night in time of war. The same precaution, as we shall see, was taken at Fowey. Leland, so often helpful in his descriptions, only mentions of Dartmouth that " there be two towers at the haven-mouth, and a chain to draw over."

Dartmouth town lies half a mile inside the estuary, strung along a hill-side in a picturesque fashion. It was the most famous of all the nurseries of Devonian seaman. Did not Chaucer's typical shipman in the Canterbury Tales come from Dartmouth? Its contingents for the Plantagenet navy were always large—31 vessels at the great blockade of Calais in 1346. Hence, when English fortunes ran low at sea, it was a favourite mark for French naval descents, like Rye and Winchelsea, and was twice surprised and sacked during the Hundred Years War. Probably the chain and towers at the haven-mouth were one of the many historical examples of the stable that is well barred after the horse has been stolen. During the great Civil War, Dartmouth and Kingswear Castles, and a new battery called Fort Ridley above the latter, were well defended against Fairfax and the " New Model " army in 1645, but fell in the following year after the final break up of the Royalist army of the West. A more picturesque combination than the two very dissimilar castles looking at each other across the strait it would be hard to find. Pendennis and St. Mawes—buildings quite as effective in themselves—are not closely juxtaposed, nor capable of being taken in at one glance like these two little fortresses, as our illustrations demonstrate.

Totnes

After surveying the very late castle at the estuary of the Dart, we find at the head of that broad water one of the oldest strongholds of Norman England, the great circular shell-keep of Totnes, which Judhael, the Breton, built with the leave of the Conqueror, long before Domesday Book had been compiled. To him William gave a very broad holding in South Devon, 103 manors in all, and Rufus, in return for his fidelity during the baronial revolt of 1193, added the great " Honour " of Barnstaple, forfeited by Robert Mowbray. With the exception of the house of De Redvers, Judhael was, in his later years, the most important landholder in the county. It was natural, then, that his chief

DARTMOUTH CASTLE

KINGSWEAR CASTLE

TOTNES CASTLE : EXTERIOR VIEW OF THE KEEP

BERRY POMEROY CASTLE : THE GATE-HOUSE

stronghold should be large, as well as strong, and being of the very earliest Norman type it was remarkably simple in plan.

Totnes town had been, in Anglo-Saxon days, the largest place in South Devon, after Exeter—it was a mint-town under Ethelred the Unready and Canute. It was built on a conical hill which marks the point where the Dart estuary ceases to be navigable. Judhael occupied the highest corner of the town—its north-western part—and there built a broad oval bailey about 80 yards in diameter : some two-thirds of its *enceinte* were protected by the steep slope of the hill, while the other third—that adjoining the town—was cut off by the digging of a deep ditch. On the northern side of the bailey Judhael threw

Totnes. Interior of Keep

up an enormous *motte* with almost precipitous sides, and on top of this was his inner house of defence. The way up to it was not, as in most *mottes*, by a straight flight of steps, but by a path cut into the mound and curling round it in circular fashion, so as to be commanded at every part of its ascent from some point of the strong building on the summit.

Presumably both the bailey and inner defence were originally walled with earthwork and palisading alone. But quite early in its history, apparently before 1150, the timber of Totnes was replaced by masonry. The outer wall became a broad stone structure with a rampart walk all around it. The building on the *motte* was turned into a small shell-keep, some 40 feet in diameter, well furnished with battlements, and with a good staircase leading up to them. All the masonry is of small and irregular stones—there is no good ashlar work— a sure sign that the construction was early.

97

The extraordinary feature of Totnes Castle is that it shows no sign of any building later than the twelfth century. It was apparently never reconstructed by owners of Plantagenet date either in *motte* or bailey. There must have been within the *enceinte* the usual fittings of a mediæval castle—hall, chapel, kitchen, and so forth. But of what date they were it is not possible to make any conjecture, for not a trace of them is left. The *motte* and its tower preside in solitary state over a large open grass-plot (now devoted to lawn tennis), and the clearance of inner buildings is as complete as at Launceston or Exeter. They existed once, for Leland, visiting the castle in 1540, saw them in decay: "the castle wall and the strong donjon be maintained, but the lodgings be clene in ruins." Of these ruins not a stone is now left: so much of the bailey enclosure as is not a grass-plot is all overgrown with ivy, and far too frequent trees.

Considering its size and strength Totnes Castle has little history. Judhael's son was the last male of his line, and the "Honour" was cut up—half seems to have gone to his grandson William de Braose, the other share is found in the hands of Guy de Nonant, whose connection with the original owner is not known—possibly he was only a grantee. But the castle, after the male line of Braose died out, went by inheritance through females to the Lords Zouche of Haryngworth in 1273. They held it for just two centuries : but John, seventh of that line, was a desperate adherent of Richard III., and was attainted and stripped of his lands after Bosworth Field. Henry VII. gave the castle to Richard Edgcumbe of Cotehele, the soundest Lancastrian in Devon or Cornwall, who had suffered many hardships in the days of Yorkist rule, and was entitled to lavish compensation. Piers Edgcumbe sold the lordship to Sir Edward Seymour of Berry Pomeroy, his neighbour, from whom it passed to the Dukes of Somerset, when the disinherited elder branch of Seymour obtained the ducal title, on the extinction of the younger and more favoured line as is explained in the next section. But which of the Seymours made the final clearance of the residential parts of the old fortress is not ascertainable.

Berry Pomeroy

About two-and-a-half miles from Totnes bridge, by a very uphill road, lies one of the best-known and quite the most picturesque of the Devonshire castles. Berry Pomeroy owes its name to one of the original Norman followers of the Conqueror, Ralph de Pomeroy, who appears in Domesday Book as lord of 106 manors in the county. Unlike his neighbour Judhael of Totnes, Ralph did not establish himself on an old site, but went out into the woods, and chose himself the most inaccessible spot that he could find, on a lonely knoll above a deep-sunk tributary-brook of the Dart. The ravine of this watercourse protects a good half of the *enceinte*: the exposed or southern side is covered by the main building of the old castle, a gate-house of exceptional solidity, from which rise two high hexagonal towers. This certainly does not belong to Ralph de Pomeroy's original castle, which (presumably) was a scarped and palisaded shell-keep, whose outline would have followed the contour of the summit of the knoll in a somewhat quadrangular fashion. But complete reconstruction in stone no doubt followed in the twelfth century, and most of the present buildings look even later.

The Pomeroys were among the most powerful of the early Devonian feudal houses, and had the unusual luck of continuing their lineal succession for nearly 500 years, during which they never lost their lands for a permanence, though they were more than once in danger of confiscation for treason. Henry de Pomeroy was a resolute supporter of John Lackland in his rebellion against Richard I., and when forced to fly from Berry seized the impregnable Cornish rock of Mount St. Michael, as will be told in the history of that fortress, and held it till all hope was gone. It would appear that he escaped forfeiture by committing suicide; having assigned his lands to his sons, he had himself bled to death by his surgeon, in the ancient Roman fashion. And Richard I., since he had never been tried or condemned, allowed the Pomeroy lands to escape confiscation. The local legend at Berry—quite unauthentic—gives Henry a still more lurid end—he is said to have blindfolded his horse, and then to have ridden him out of the postern straight down the precipitous north side of the castle, ending with a broken neck in the ravine below. Henry's grandson and namesake was deeply concerned in a more justifiable rebellion, having been a follower of Simon de Montfort in the Barons' War. He was lucky enough not to be present at the slaughter of Evesham, profited by the amnesty granted by the "Dictum of Kenilworth" to the surviving Montfortians, and got off with a fine instead of complete forfeiture.

The Pomeroys endured till the convulsions of religious war which marked the earlier years of Edward VI. The then head of the house, Sir Thomas Pomeroy, was one of the chief supporters of the old Catholic party in the West—when, therefore, we find him selling his castle to Lord Protector Somerset in the second year of the Protectorate, we are suspicious of undue pressure, or blackmail, on the part of that champion among land-grabbers. But the tale told to the effect that Pomeroy saved his head after the unsuccessful rebellion of 1549, by making over Berry to Somerset, cannot be true, since Somerset had been deposed, and was actually confined in the Tower of London (Oct. 1549), before the leaders of the western insurrection were tried and executed in January, 1550.

Somerset was released, and allowed two more years of life before he was attainted and executed by his jealous rival Dudley, Duke of Northumberland. It was during these last years of his life that he made over Berry to his eldest son, Edward Seymour, whom in other respects he had disinherited. For when he caused his own patent for a dukedom to be drawn up, in the first year of his protectorate, it included the astounding clause that his titles should pass to his younger son, the child of his second wife, Anne Stanhope, and not to his elder son, Edward, child of his first wife, Catherine Fillot. Only if all the male issue of the younger line should die out, were the elder line to have a reversionary right of succession.

The elder son, therefore, and his descendants for two hundred years, were lords of Berry Pomeroy and certain other Devonshire lands, and baronets after the time of James I., while the younger family enjoyed the earldom of Hertford and the restored dukedom of Somerset till 1750. It was this odd fact which gave Sir Edward Seymour, the first prominent Tory to join William of Orange after the landing at Torbay, an opportunity to vent a paradox. "I think, Sir Edward," said the prince, "that you are of the family of the Duke of Somerset." "Pardon me, your highness," replied Seymour, "the Duke of Somerset is of *my* family."

It was the earliest of the Seymour owners of Berry who cleared out part of the interior of the old castle of the Pomeroys in order to erect in the centre of the walls that magnificent Tudor building whose ruins strike the eye of the visitor so much more effectively than the ivy-smothered remnants of the

Pomeroy Arms
From a tomb in Berry Pomeroy Church

old *enceinte*. It is one of those mansions built for light and convenience, with enormous mullioned windows, which occupy more than half of its frontage, and with long galleries and spacious reception rooms, in which the period 1550-1600 is so rich. Apparently the interior decorations were elaborate almost to ostentation, mantelpieces of polished marble instead of freestone, fluted Corinthian pillars, cornices of wreathed fruit and flowers highly gilt, ceilings of curiously figured plaster, panelling of precious woods; the building is said to have cost £20,000—a great sum in Tudor days. "Yet the whole was never brought to completion, for the west side was never begun," says the author of the "Worthies of Devon," himself an eighteenth century vicar of Berry.

Here lived five generations of Seymours, knights and afterwards baronets, prominent among the noble families of Devon. But the great Civil War brought harm to Berry, as to so many other ancient castles; the walls were "slighted," and the residence somewhat damaged. It must still have been habitable in 1688, as Sir Edward Seymour (named above) brought William of Orange thither on his march from Torbay to Newton Abbot. But he would seem to have been the last resident, and himself spent his later years at, and died in, his manor of Maiden Bradley in Somersetshire. Tradition says that the roofs of Berry were fired by lightning in a storm, and that the owner, considering it a rather remote, if splendid, abode, would not go to the expense of reconstruction. Two hundred years of wind and rain have done the rest, and the once magnificent building is a picturesque skeleton, showing the sky through scores of mullioned ribs.

In 1750 died the last Seymour, Duke of Somerset, who sprang from the Lord Protector's younger son, and agreeably to the strange patent of 1547, the representative of the elder line, the Berry Pomeroy Seymours, succeeded to the dukedom, but not to the bulk of the estates, of his predecessor—there was a daughter left as heiress to the lands, if not to the honours of the younger branch. The title has again been the cause of much interesting historical enquiry in the very year in which this book was written—its succession in 1925 having turned on the validity of a marriage of 1770. Since 1750 Berry Castle is a ducal seat—but an uninhabitable one—perhaps the most ivy-covered of all ruins in Southern England. The fine gate-house of the original stronghold is particularly mantled over, and it is impossible to verify the statement of earlier antiquaries that above the portcullis-chamber is a fine carved shield with the lion rampant of Pomeroy—a bearing to be seen well displayed on the tombs of the parish church a mile outside the woods.

Of Plympton and other decayed Castles of South Devon

The "Honour" of Plympton was the most important of all the great feudal holdings of Devon, and the one most closely associated with the Redvers earls, who had it from their ancestor, Baldwin de Brionne, before the earldom was created. It was an immense unit—89 knights' fees or 185 manors, extending all over the south-west corner of Devon, of which Plympton was then the chief town, Plymouth being, as yet, no more than a fishing village.

Plympton Castle was early, important, and long inhabited, but unfortunately it has disappeared ; nothing remains but its mound. More might have been expected to survive, since Leland found it " a fair large castle with a donjon : the walls yet stand, but the lodgings within be decayed." But walls and donjon are now gone, and the archæologist will find nothing to repay a visit, unless he loves mental reconstruction of the non-existent from scanty indications on a bare site.

At Plymouth there was in Leland's day a haven-guarding castle, which he regarded as quite comparatively modern, but does not ascribe to his master King Henry's recent system of coast-fortification. " On a rocky hill hard by the south side of the mouth, where the shippes lyith, is a strong castle quadrate, having at each corner a great round tower. It seemeth to me no very old piece of work." This looks like a description of some late fourteenth or fifteenth century fortification, built in the days of the Hundred Years' War, when Plymouth (like Fowey and Dartmouth) had been suffering from French naval raids. Unfortunately this castle, whatever it was, was ruined, and completely superseded by the adjacent modern citadel. The description reads much like that of Bodiham—but to Leland Bodiham was an " old castle," while this was something newer—probably, therefore, fifteenth century and not of the time of Edward III. or Richard II. As we find that the townsmen of Plymouth, after a particularly vicious French raid in 1403, got leave to levy a toll on goods landed in their port, for the purpose of building a wall and tower, we may suspect that this was the date of the castle which was visible in 1540. The new and much larger citadel of Charles II. is immediately above the site of the old building, whose position is marked by the modern names of Castle Street, and the Barbican, on the very edge of Sutton Pool, the old town harbour. There is a scrap of wall in Lambhay Street, at the back of the Barbican, which may have belonged to it.

Another decayed castle of South Devon is Salcombe—one of the coastal fortresses of Henry VIII., set to guard the entry of the fiord which runs up to Kingsbridge. It was held in the Civil War by Sir Edward Fortescue, made a good defence for four months in 1646, against a detachment of Fairfax's Parliamentary host, and only surrendered on honourable terms when the royalist army of the West capitulated, and all its strongholds save Pendennis followed suit. It was then " slighted," and never utilized again as were St. Mawes, Portland, Pendennis, and others of the series, whose condition is so much more perfect, so that it is ruinous and not worth a visit from anyone who has looked over its more intact sister-fortresses.

Of other Devonian castles where even less survives—sometimes practically nothing but the name—it is unnecessary to speak, since we have laid down the rule that we are not concerned with sites and fragments, but only with buildings from which architectural information, and not merely historical reminiscences can be obtained.

BERRY POMEROY CASTLE : SEYMOUR'S BUILDINGS AND INNER WARD

LAUNCESTON **CASTLE**: THE KEEP

CORNWALL

VISITORS betake themselves to the Duchy for many reasons, ranging from the study of dolmens and cromlechs, and neolithic hut-circles, to the pursuit of a mild winter climate, or of cliff scenery, or of the pilchard. But it would be unusual to meet any one who had journeyed towards Land's End with the sole purpose of hunting for castles. Truth to say the very names of the Cornish castles are unfamiliar, save three—Tintagel, Launceston and St. Michael's Mount. Tintagel is known to everyone who has read the Morte Arthur and the Idylls of the King, or heard Tristan and Isolde sung. It is somewhat of a disappointment when visited—a few weather-beaten fragments of masonry, dating from Henry III., rather than from King Arthur, strewn over black precipices above a gloomy cove. Launceston is a good specimen of a Norman keep, surviving in an *enceinte* from which all other buildings have vanished in the course of the centuries. St. Michael's Mount, on the other hand, exceeds rather than falls below the expectation of those who have known it by pictures or descriptions alone. That the painter and the photographer have never done it full justice, is the first impression of those who see for the first time its towering outline silhouetted against an evening sky above the waste of waters at high tide. Of all the castles of the west that I have seen only Harlech and Caer Cynan approach it in majesty of site, and over each of these it has one advantage in the matter of picturesque placing—it rises directly from the sea on its pointed precipice, and is not separated from the water by golf-ridden sandhills like the rock of Harlech, or isolated among upland solitudes like Caer Cynan. This is undoubtedly the king among all west-country castles, and the journey to Cornwall would be worth making for the sole purpose of gazing on it.

The other surviving Cornish castles (some have vanished altogether, like Bottreaux and Tregony) are little known, and, when inspected, are interesting rather than impressive in the style of St. Michael's Mount. He who finds himself in Cornwall for other reasons than castle-hunting may well visit Trematon and Ince, the harbour castles of Fowey, Pendennis and St. Mawes, the lonely woodland fastness of Restormel, or the wonderfully perfect granite tower of Pengersick. Of these far the most important, from the point of view of historical architecture, is the small, late, but most shapely and decorative St. Mawes, the best preserved of all that long chain of fortresses to defend havens with which Henry VIII. lined the south coast from Kent to Cornwall. It shows a wealth of heraldry and versified inscriptions, no less than of artillery devices, with which none of the other Tudor structures that come within our scope can vie. And it lies on one of the most picturesque points of the long and lovely estuary which meanders down from Truro to Falmouth.

It may be asked why Cornwall is on the whole rather bare of castles, and why those which are to be found are either rather early—not later than the beginning of the thirteenth century—or else Tudor structures, belonging to the very last days of castle building. I am inclined to answer that the explanation is to be found in the existence of that curious institution, the " Duchy of Cornwall," which absorbed the greater part of the county, and swallowed up the lands of so many of that class of baronial families who were the great builders of castles. When an estate fell into the Duchy its castle was generally dismantled, or allowed to fall into decay by systematic neglect of repairs.

From the first the earls of Cornwall owned the greater part of the peninsula, and were semi-royal personages. William the Conqueror gave the earldom to his half-brother, Robert of Mortain, who built Launceston as the central stronghold of his domain, and other castles at Trematon, Liskeard and Restormel. After Henry I. had dispossessed the heir of Mortain, the lands were for many years in the king's hands, but went in the end to his illegitimate son Reginald ; he and his son Richard Fitz-Count held them, with certain interruptions, till 1220. The earldom was then recreated for a legitimate royal side-line, that of Richard, brother of Henry III. (1225), and he and his son Edmund held it till 1300. It was then given for a few years to Piers Gaveston (1307-12), and to John of Eltham, younger son of Edward II. (1330-36). At his death without issue, it was made into a duchy, and set aside as a permanent endowment for the king's eldest son—as the earldom of Chester had been in a previous generation. The Duchy fell back to the crown when a duke ascended the throne, and if (as was often the case) the new sovereign had, as yet, no son, it was not merged in the rest of the royal domain, but held ready to be handed over to the heir when he should come into being. The " Duchy of Cornwall," with its courts and revenues, has now existed for 558 years, but only for 323 of these years has a real live Duke of Cornwall been in existence ; and out of these 323 years, 118 belong to dukes who were minors, children under tutelage. Of the twenty princes who have borne the title, eight did not reach their majority or become kings of England. These facts sufficiently explain the want of castle-building enterprise in Cornwall in the fourteenth and fifteenth centuries : it was a department of the king's estate charged with the maintenance of his eldest son, when such a son existed, not a duchy under a continuous hereditary series of dukes, who could have a policy or require several competent residences. The only important castle-building after Edward III. was the construction of harbour-defences like those at Fowey, St. Mawes and Pendennis, which were dictated by the king's naval and military needs, not merely by those of Cornwall.

Now both the original dynasties of earls, and their successor the impersonal " Duchy," were great absorbers of land, and the large majority of the original castles of Cornwall gradually fell into decay from the moment that they ceased to be private property. So, for the matter of that, did most of the earls' own castles. A most interesting list of the Cornish fortresses was drawn up by the chronicler William of Worcester, after he had made a pilgrimage to St. Michael's Mount in 1478. He counted up to 28 in all, by dint of naming early Celtic hill-forts and other things that had never been really castles in any proper sense. But he noted that of the 28 no less than 17 were " *diruta*," and no longer existent, and of these 17 no less than six had been earls' property in the old days.

Of the 11 surviving castles, St. Michael's Mount, Launceston, Restormel, Trematon, and the granite cliff of Carnbrea, can be studied to-day, but Tregony, Liskeard, Bottreaux, Tregothnan, Lanyhorne and Binomy—near Stratton—have " gone under," either destroyed or rebuilt out of knowledge. In the half century between William of Worcester's pilgrimage and Leland's journey round the duchy about 1538, it is interesting to note that Lanyhorne had become " decaying for want of coverture," Bottreaux was now " a thing of smaul reputation," Liskeard was " all in ruin." It hardly required the ravages of the Civil War of 1642-46 to make an end of the Cornish castles as places of residence.

By the end of the day of the Tudors there would appear to have been no fortified dwellings of any importance* in private hands. St. Michael's Mount, which was destined to become private property by a Stuart grant, was in 1600 in the hands of the crown, and let out on lease to various heads of local families. The Bassetts and St. Aubyns had not yet come into possession. The oldest castles—Launceston, Trematon, Restormel—were standing, but tending already to decay, because they had got attached to that very impersonal entity, the Duchy of Cornwall, and no duke ever wished to live in them.

Launceston

This town and castle on the pointed hill were better known as Dunheved, " the fort of the headland," in the Middle Ages. The name Launceston, which is a corruption of Llan Stefan, the church of Stephen, only superseded the older title in Tudor times, and long after the sixteenth century its two members of Parliament continued to be designated in official rolls as the representatives of Dunheved.

The site is one equally attractive to the Celtic chief wishful to build himself a hill camp, to the Saxon who wanted good ground for a small walled " burh," or for the Norman set on erecting a castle as the central dominating point of a newly granted earldom. The Conqueror's brother, Robert of Mortain, made it his chief seat, and no doubt was responsible for the rearing of a typical " *motte* and bailey " fortress on the culminating hill-top. The ground is most favourable—the ascent from the plain is excessively steep—to this day motorists are denied the use of the breakneck main access which leads straight up to the town and castle, and are sent round by a road which negotiates the slope in a long curve. The castle, on the south-east side of the high-lying plateau, on which the town is built, has the town clustering at its back, and looks straight down into the plain. It is very simple in plan—there is a broad circular walled enclosure, with a mighty keep on a high *motte* in its eastern flank. There is probably nothing surviving of Earl Robert's work, which may

---

* The exceptions were Ince, near Saltash, and the granite tower of Pengersick which has an exceptional history—it is the defensive part of an early Tudor manor house, of which the merely residential wing has fallen into complete decay and vanished. But the massive tower has defied all Atlantic storms, stands intact, and is once again, after a couple of centuries of disuse, an inhabited dwelling.

very possibly have been no more than a mound, and an outer ward with ditch and palisade. The present castle looks like a structure of the twelfth and thirteenth centuries. The main *enceinte* is oblong, with two gates, one opening westward towards the town, the other toward the plain below : no doubt the wall must have been patched and repaired frequently, but its trace probably follows that of the original Norman bailey, though the western gate was rebuilt in the days of Henry VIII. But the great feature of the castle is the immense *motte*, with the fifty-seven steep stone stairs mounting up to the small plateau on top, where rises the circular stone keep-tower. The *motte* had a wall at its foot, cutting it off from the outer bailey, and there are the remains of a small barbican, which guarded the gate in this wall, from which the stairway started upward.

The keep on top of the *motte* is not a single tower, like the not dissimilar towers of Totnes or Trematon, but double, a tall narrow inner structure, 40 feet high, but only 18 in diameter, completely surrounded by a lower 35-foot outer circle of masonry, which follows the edge of the *motte*-plateau. The space between them is very narrow, not much more than a gangway in fact, and that it was roofed in, is shown by a series of beam-holes corresponding to each other in the outer and the inner circles. The walls are immensely thick— 12 feet at the lower levels. Unfortunately, both outer and inner circuits have lost their battlements, and all their internal fittings, so that, lofty though they are, they have a rather truncated effect. The whole looks like the work of Earl Reginald, or his long-lived son, Richard Fitz-Count, who died in 1220, rather than of any earlier Norman lord. It is certainly not advanced enough in style to have been built by the royal Plantagenet earls of the later thirteenth century.

There were many inner buildings of which all trace has now disappeared. Leland, itinerating in the days of Henry VIII., noted that the castle had three separate wards—the situation of the middle ward now requires to be looked for with care. He also saw a chapel, a common gaol for all Cornwall, and a " haule for syses and sessions." By the days of Mr. Tonkin (1740) there was no inner building left save the common gaol, and this seems to have been pulled down when the Cornish assizes were transferred to Bodmin in the time of William IV., a much stronger modern gaol having been built at Bodmin so far back as 1780. It is likely, however, that the mediæval buildings had vanished long before 1740, as the castle was " slighted " at the end of the great Civil War, after its capture by Fairfax and the artillery of the " New Model Army " in 1646. It had probably suffered severely from three previous sieges, for it had been twice in the hands of the Parliamentarians in 1642 and 1644, and recovered by the Royalists after a short leaguer on each occasion. Probably the buildings in the outer ward had been badly battered before the advent of Fairfax. Looked at as a fortress to be maintained against artillery, Launceston Castle had serious faults—the walls of the outer *enceinte* were not particularly strong, while the *motte* and keep are incapable of mounting heavy guns, owing to their extremely restricted area.

TREMATON CASTLE: THE GATE-HOUSE

RESTORMEL CASTLE: THE MAIN GATE

Trematon and Ince

These two strongly contrasted castles lie quite close to each other as the crow flies, both looking out on the broad waters of the great estuary into which the Tamar and so many other streams discharge themselves. But though they are distant from each other only some two miles upon the map, it takes a long circuit of five or six miles over very difficult ground to get from one to the other. Trematon is high aloft, on one of the summits of the rather chaotic group of hill-tops, which lie behind Saltash and its daring modern bridge. Ince is at the end of a long low peninsula, which projects into the tidal flats of the St. Germans' River. It is but a few feet above high water level, and was obviously built late in the Middle Ages to command the passage of the river and protect the low lying shore along it. Trematon on the other hand is one of the primitive Norman strongholds, placed on top of a steep hill for purposes of inaccessibility, and of the simple " *motte* and bailey " type, like Totnes or Launceston. As long as it was a baronial castle it was under process of improvement, but when it fell into the hands of the " Duchy of Cornwall " administration it suffered no further changes, and in the end was allowed to fall into decay.

Trematon, as we have said before, was originally founded by the first Earl of Cornwall, Robert of Mortain, but had been alienated in the twelfth century to the Valletorts, one of the few original baronial families of Cornwall, who held it under the earl as suzerain. It consists of an outer bailey with a large and important keep on one side of it, and a fine thirteenth century gate-house applied to its front access. The keep is on a big *motte*, apparently a rock-core overlaid with earth to make it regular : on three sides its slopes are almost precipitous. The tower itself is battlemented, and was clearly roofed in, and divided into residential stories ; the plaster surviving in patches within it, the beam-holes visible in two series on the inside, and the corbels at the top, obviously intended to support woodwork, prove that it was adapted to domestic as well as military uses.

The outer *enceinte*, on which the *motte* and tower look down, is fairly perfect and shows one round corner-tower : there may have been others, but the whole of the ruins are now smothered by trees and ivy. The gate-house at the main entrance is fine thirteenth century work, with a double system of portcullises, and with chambers still roofed in, above the archway. This and the keep-tower are the only marked features of the place.

Right in the middle of the outer bailey is the modern

Trematon Castle

house, apparently nineteenth century work, though it may have had an earlier predecessor. It has no structural or historic connection with the rest of the buildings.

The history of the castle would seem to be that Count Robert established the normal *motte* and outer bailey, and that his successors, the Valletorts, rebuilt the outer *enceinte*, erected the fine keep-tower on the existing mound, and finally added the gate-house. When they died out in the male line, and their collateral heirs, through female descent, ceded the castle and manor to Edward III., building ceased. In Leland's day it was " the king's round Castle of Trematon," but already in decay " though great pieces of it yet stand firm, and especially the donjon." Some part of it—probably the gate-house—was employed as a prison. The castle must still

Ince. View from Front

have been defensible—if somewhat decayed—for the Cornish Catholic rebels of 1549, led by Humphrey Arundel, thought it worth occupying, and we hear of it for a moment as garrisoned during the Civil Wars of Charles I. and the Parliament. Probably it was "slighted" along with so many other castles of the west, in 1646. Visitors are recommended not to approach Trematon from the side of the lower road along the Tamar, which leads up to the castle by a lane of breakneck steepness, but to go round by the higher ground at the back of Saltash town—a much longer route, but one which is comparatively easy for vehicles.

Ince, as observed above, is a complete antithesis to its neighbour Trematon. It is low-lying, comparatively late in foundation, small, and very simple in plan. Its name, which is a corruption of " Innis," the isle, sufficiently explains its character—it is on a long low peninsula projecting into the broad estuary of the Linher, the St. Germans' river, and watching all this backwater of Plymouth Sound. It was apparently built by the Devonshire Courtenays—who had an outlying patch of land here—presumably in the later fourteenth century, the plan being a regular quadrangle with a tower at each corner, somewhat like those of Shirburn or Bodiham ; but at Ince they are square, not rounded, as in the other two castles. The original building seems to have been much pulled about when it was in the hands of the Killigrews in the sixteenth and seventeenth centuries—they modernized all the windows, enlarging them and cutting them square, and clapped on to the main front, that which faces west towards the neck of the peninsula, a broad flight of steps and a classical pediment, so that the whole building has the effect of a house of the time of Charles II. rather than a mediæval castle. This is all the more the case because Ince, unlike all other Cornish castles, is built of red brick—probably in its flats brick-clay was easier to procure than the stone available in all the upland regions. Indeed, at a first glance, Ince might pass for a seventeenth century building, if it were not for its battlements and its four solid corner towers.

It was, perhaps, the isolated aspect of these towers which inspired the local legend of the eighteenth century which related that a Killigrew—it sounds like a story of Thomas of that name, the notorious Master of the Revels to " Old Rowley "—kept a mistress in each of them, so secretly, that none of the ladies was aware of the existence of the other three. " But," writes the old historian of the duchy, " I cannot believe in the tale of the towers having been constructed for a purpose in strict conformity, indeed, with Mahometan law, but at such complete variance from our own." There is a somewhat similar, and equally absurd, folk-tale of the same sort, with regard to a great Gloucestershire house.

Restormel

Each of the great tidal fiords which run up into the Cornish inland would appear to have had its own castle, in the days of the early Norman earls—and as Trematon looked over the Tamar estuary, so apparently the absolutely vanished castle of Liskeard guarded that of the Looe River. It was ascribed to Robert of Mortain, and was, no doubt, of the *motte* and bailey type, but it disappeared so early that Leland, in 1538, can only say that there once *was* a castle of the earls' here—" the site magnificent, and looketh over all the town : fragments and pieces of wall yet stond."

But the castle which dominated the valley which discharges into the Fowey estuary—the next fiord westward from the Looes—is in very tolerable preservation, no doubt owing to the fact that it is nearly two miles from a town, and in a rather inaccessible position. This is Restormel, a very complete specimen of a late Norman castle. It lies up-stream from Lostwithiel, the last place to which the tidal water reached, approached by a side-road (pleasantly free from motors and excursionists) under the edge of towering woods. The castle is at present completely surrounded by lofty foliage, and only comes into sight when the visitor has climbed the hill top. It is an almost perfectly circular shell-keep structure—110 feet in diameter—the summit of the height being encircled by a deep ditch, above which rises the double wall of the broad shell—which was destitute of a *motte*—the whole hill was its " *motte* " indeed. It would be exactly circular, but that the gate on the west side, and a chapel on the east, project some twenty feet, and impinge on the ditch. Beyond the latter there seem to be no outbuildings or external defences whatever.

The space between the two walls of the shell was divided up into chambers, in two stories, with the curious result that as both walls form parts of a circular structure, no chamber is square—each has its outer wall somewhat longer than its inner wall. In the upper story there are windows looking outward, whose shape—the transoms are all gone—seems to indicate late thirteenth century work. In the lower story all the rooms have their windows on the side of the inner court.

Leland says that Restormel had a fair donjon—it must therefore have shown, when intact, some sort of a dominating tower in its *enceinte*. Presumably this may have been above the projecting gate-house, and the section of the main ring-wall behind it, as at Kidwelly Castle in Wales. The other possible alternative would be that it may have been on the opposite side, including, as part of it, the chapel-building which still survives. Foundations in the *enceinte* here show heavier structure than in other parts of the circle.

There were battlements all round the ring wall, with a complete walk around them, at the level of the roofs of the upper story. The access to the gate-house was across a small stone arch spanning the ditch, not by a drawbridge. One road leading up to the castle was conducted by long curves up the hill side, which would be commanded from the battlements : another approached the gate-house on a long narrow ridge equally exposed to arrow-shot.

Restormel was completely smothered in ivy during the last century, but has just been freed from it by the wise activity of the Board of Works, with the result that inspection is now far more easy than it was ten years ago, when the whole was one mass of greenery, hiding all detail.

Restormel. Interior from Main Gate

This was originally an earl's castle — and the site was probably chosen by Robert of Mortain himself. But in the twelfth century it had been alienated to the Cardinhams, a family who in the time

FOWEY : BATTERY AND POLRUAN TOWER

ST. MAWES CASTLE : VIEW FROM THE LAND SIDE

of Richard I. were in possession of the neighbouring Lostwithiel town, and other adjoining lands. But it was back in the possession of the earls by the days of Richard of Cornwall, and while the general outline of the place is twelfth century, there is no doubt that it must have been largely reconstructed in the thirteenth, as is shown by the shape of arches, the windows of the upper story, and the three-cusped piscina in the chapel. Richard and his son Edmund are said to have lived here habitually, but there is no sign of any building later than their age. No doubt it ceased with the constitution of the Duchy of Cornwall. And of the state into which it was brought by its connection with that institution we have full evidence. Leland, in 1538, complains that the outer works are getting defaced: Carew, in 1600, puts up a bitter lament that the lessees under the Duchy were treating it abominably; they had stolen and sold the lead of the gutters and the roof, and were making away with the ornamental carving—a foul shame that private greed should be destroying a public building of princely origin. But the main walls must still have been standing in 1643, when some Cornish gentlemen of the Parliamentary faction seized it, and tried to hold it against Sir Bevil Grenville, with no success, for it was taken in a few days. And this was its last appearance in history, for in 1646 Hopton did not try to defend it against Fairfax. We do not know whether it was formally "slighted" or not, like the castles which actually resisted the "New Model Army." But by 1740 it was an ivy-clad ruin, in little better condition, apparently, than it is to-day.

Restormel. The Chapel

III

Fowey

Descending the river from Restormel and Lostwithiel, we reach the sea at the broad estuary of Fowey, where there is no castle indeed, but some not unimportant relics of fifteenth century harbour fortification—the earliest visible in Cornwall. For long before Henry VIII. began his great scheme of harbour castles, Fowey had begun to strengthen itself. Its enterprising and piratical seamen, who were always at feud with their rivals of the Cinque Ports, had found the loss of the control of the narrow seas during the Wars of the Roses very dangerous to them. French raids all along the Channel being rife, and one most disastrous raid having been made on themselves in 1457, they built two blockhouses at the harbour mouth to guard the ends of a chain, which was drawn across it every night. And higher up they erected a great square tower upon the opposite side of the haven, above the fishermen's houses of the suburb of Polruan. This tower stands to-day, firm but much mutilated. Of the small blockhouses which guarded the chain only scraps are left, but the tower is still a notable building. It is quite unlike the Tudor harbour-forts of Dartmouth or Falmouth, and is not (like them) built for artillery service, but only for passive defence.

When Edward IV. had made his peace with France at Picquigny (1475), the men of Fowey showed no signs of giving up their attacks on French merchantmen, though legitimate privateering had become, since the peace, piracy against the ships of a friendly power. After several remonstrances, which were ignored, the king sent a sergeant-at-arms, bearing writs, which summoned certain shipmasters to come to Westminster and answer for themselves before the royal courts. The townsmen rose in riot, burnt the writs, and cut off the ears of the messenger, who was hunted out of the town. Edward, much enraged, pretended to ignore the matter, but sent commissioners to Lostwithiel with directions to hold a session for the investigation of the naval resources of the Cornish ports. To this session came, most unwisely, many leading inhabitants of Fowey, who were surprised to find themselves arrested and indited for piracy, as well as for riot. One, Harrington, a notorious pirate, was hung, and many others fined or imprisoned, while, to mark his displeasure with the town, Edward sent ships from Dartmouth to unhook and take away the great chain which barred the harbour (1478).

When Henry VIII., half a century later, took up his scheme for building haven-protecting forts, heavily gunned, all along the south coast, Fowey was provided with a fort of the usual sort, at the western entrance of its harbour. But this building, St. Catherine's, has not survived like those of St. Mawes, Pendennis, or Dartmouth, or Calshot, or Hurst, but has been repeatedly rebuilt and modernized. Its present representative bears a large date of 1855, incised on it, and looks Victorian, wherefore we need waste no time on a modern battery. But the old fort of Henry VIII. had one lively day in its existence, on July 16, 1666, during the Dutch War, when the British "Virginia Fleet," 80 vessels small and great, ran into Fowey with the enemy in pursuit, and the leading

Dutchman, a 70-gun ship, exchanged many salvoes with St. Catherine's, before returning and warning his admiral that the passage was impossible.

Falmouth : St. Mawes and Pendennis Castles

The great estuary of the Fal, infinitely bigger than the sheets of tidal water by Looe and Fowey, and almost vying in size with the Plymouth fiord, was in early days unprotected at its mouth, but guarded high up by the castles of Tregony and Truro. Both of these were decayed by the time of Leland's itinerary, and the Tudor substitute for them was the building of the two beauti-

St. Mawes. The Battery

ful castles of St. Mawes and Pendennis on opposite sides of the entrance of the estuary. These were among the most important of the artillery-forts of Henry VIII., and while both are still visible and worthy of study, St. Mawes stands out as the most elaborate and decorative of all King Henry's buildings.

It is a large circular fort of no great height, with a three-lobed battery for eleven heavy guns applied to its seaward front, and ample provision for smaller shooting from those of its upper stories, which are not blocked by the battery in front. It is cut off from the hill-end on which it stands by a deep ditch, crossed by a bridge of two arches. That it was intended for harbour-protection, and not to serve as a self-sufficient fortress, is very clearly shown by the fact that it is completely commanded by the hill behind—unlike its sister, Pendennis, which lies on the highest ground to be found on the other side of the estuary.

The battery below is of immense solidity, pierced for three guns looking out to sea, five commanding the narrow opening of the estuary, and three more looking up into, and sweeping, the haven. The embrasures are sloped so as to show only a narrow opening, though there is a wider space to work the gun within. Behind them rises the round keep in four stories, the lowest, which is below the level of the battery, obviously the powder magazine (though wrongly styled the chapel), the second fitted for artillery with embrasures, the third and fourth living rooms for governor and garrison, but having loop-holes for " shot "—calivers or muskets. On top there is a flat roof surrounded with

St. Mawes. View from the Estuary

battlements, each pierced with a deep hole in which would be inserted the " crook " of a wall-piece or swivel, the heavy hand-guns of the sixteenth century, which were fired from a movable rest because they were too big to be lifted to the shoulder.

The most notable thing about St. Mawes is not its strength or its symmetry, but its lavish decoration. Not only is there over its main entrance a fine Tudor royal arms, similar to that at Pendennis across the water, but one long and four short ornamental inscriptions are carved on the outer circle of the keep. They were all, so Leland tells us, composed by himself at the request of Master Trewry, the king's architect. The large one has, over the royal arms, on a scroll sustained by two figures—

"HENRICUS OCTAVUS REX ANGL. FRANC. ET HIBERNIÆ INVICTUS
ME POSUIT PRÆSIDIUM REIPUBLICÆ TERROREM HOSTIBUS."

Of the four shorter inscriptions, carved in an arched shape, two glorify the king—

"SEMPER HONOS, HENRICE, TUUS LAUDESQUE MANEBUNT,"
and
"IMPERIO HENRICI, NAVES, SUBMITTITE VELA."

While the other two are in honour of the child Edward, Duke of Cornwall, heir of the realm—

"EDWARDUS FAMA REFERAT FACTISQUE PARENTEM,"
and
"GAUDEAT EDWARDO DUCE NUNC CORNUBIA FELIX."

114

ST. MAWES CASTLE : THE GATE-WAY

PENDENNIS CASTLE : EXTERIOR VIEW

On the external curve of the same story are five very large shields of arms, several feet in height, of which two show the usual blazon of England and France, while the others were either never completed or have lost their bearings by three centuries and more of wear and tear from the south-west wind.

St. Mawes was held for the king during the Civil War by Sir Richard Vivian, but surrendered to Fairfax in 1646 without making the desperate resistance offered by its twin sister Pendennis, on the other side of the water. But it must be conceded that its site is not nearly so favourable for defence.

Pendennis must always have been somewhat larger than St. Mawes, but its original shape must have been much the same, the round central fort, with outside batteries on the lowest level. Unfortunately most of its exterior, and many of its interior details have been altered in the course of ages, the original casemated batteries having been replaced by a much larger number of guns on several fronts and levels, in something more like a big outer ward than a simple battery. And inside the whole structure has not been left intact, like St. Mawes, but absolutely gutted. The lowest floor, where the powder magazine must have been, has been filled up, and the upper stories have been cut up into eighteenth or nineteenth century rooms for the use of the officers of the garrison. For Pendennis was occupied by one or more batteries, R.G.A., down to 1922, and behind the fort stands a large modern barracks, spoiling the landward view.

The round keep has no lavish decoration of inscriptions like St. Mawes, but one nice Tudor coat of arms over its main doorway ; this is its sole architectural ornament. Outside this entrance there has unfortunately been clapped on a little Victorian-Gothic residence for the porter of the castle.

Pendennis was one of the few places in England which in Tudor and Stuart times had a permanent garrison. During the Armada scare in 1588 it was reinforced up to 200 men, two companies under Sir Nicholas Parker, and a vast number of extra guns were planted in new additional batteries. But its famous slice of history was the defence in 1646, by Colonel John Arundel, an old gentleman of invincible courage, who had first girt on his sword in the camp of Tilbury in 1588, and yielded it up to the Parliamentarian besieger on August 17, 1646, only after six months close leaguer, and when every other castle in England, save Raglan (which held out two days longer), had already submitted, in consequence of the king's surrender in the preceding April. Though the royal army in the West had disbanded itself, this obstinate old gentleman held out until he had eaten his last horse and his last bowl of porridge, and then was allowed the " honours of war " by his admiring adversary, Colonel Fortescue. The garrison were so famished that many of them died of reaction after their first full meal, " like the captive Jews at Titus's taking of Jerusalem," as a Cornish chronicler observed.

The ground which John Arundel defended was not the mere fort of Henry VIII., but included the whole hill-top of the little peninsula, cut off by a ditch and palisading at the isthmus which joins it to the site of the modern Falmouth. The round Tudor castle was its innermost place of strength.

The besiegers won by means of famine alone, Pendennis being closely blockaded on the side of the sea by ships from Plymouth.

St. Michael's Mount

The westernmost of the castles of the British Isles is in some ways the most interesting and picturesque of them all. Essentially a water-fortress girt round on all sides by a natural moat, it differs from all others because its moat is the ocean. And it is not merely a fortress on an island — like Beaumaris or the Marisco's castle on Lundy—but rather an island which is a fortress in itself, a cliff-girt rock inaccessible save where man has hewn himself steps to reach the summit. And a sea-girt rock may be shapeless and unattractive to the eye—like the outer island of Tintagel—but St. Michael's Mount is gracefully shaped into a majestic cone, with its fantastic group of secular and religious buildings crowning the apex. These buildings are not so many nor so lofty as those of the more famous Mont St. Michel in Normandy, but they are bold and picturesque. The island fortress is not seen at its best at low tide, when the falling water exposes a narrow causeway, by which it may be

St. Michael's Mount.   Entrance

reached for three or four hours at the ebb. For the beach and scattered rocks, then visible, do not give such a fine foreground as the sea—whether the latter be placid or tempestuous. St. Michael's is seen at its best at high tide, completely water-girt, and best of all at evening with its black outline and crown of towers silhouetted against the glories of the sunset in the west.

A persistent local legend maintained that this wonderful rock had been part of the mainland, and had been separated from it by a comparatively recent cataclysm. The early Cornish writers tell us that its first name had been *Carreg luz en kuz*, the hoar rock in the wood, a forest having extended over the whole sweep of what is now Mount's Bay. But this is mere folklore, comparable to the story of "Lyonesse;" the supposed fertile plain which joined the Scilly islands to Lands End, and was engulfed by an earthquake in the sixth century. There can be no doubt that the coast lay much as it does now when Cæsar came to Britain, and that St. Michael's must have been an obvious stronghold for early Celtic tribes—perhaps a sanctuary also. The origin of its present name is as great a puzzle as that of the names of Mont St. Michel in Normandy, and Monte San Michele on the Apulian promontory of Mount Gargano in the Adriatic. The fame of all three goes back to the Dark Ages, and starts with a legend of the apparition of the Archangel to pious persons in trouble. The Apulian vision was vouchsafed to a bishop of Siponto, about 495—the Norman to Autbert, bishop of Avranches, in the early eighth century—the Cornish one, in 710, according to William of Worcester's note, taken down while he was on his pilgrimage to the Mount. Others said that the apparition was to St. Kenna, or Keyne, one of the innumerable local Celtic saints of Cornwall, whose *floruit* would seem to be a little earlier. But she is a vague personage, flitting across two centuries, and only remembered for her pleasant habit of turning snakes into fossil ammonites, and for her celebrated wishing well. But, as every reader of early papal annals knows, there was a still more famous apparition of the Archangel in 590, to Pope Gregory the Great, who, while he was praying for the cessation of a plague then raging in Rome, saw Michael standing on the great circular bulk of Hadrian's Tomb, and sheathing his sword. In commemoration of which the fortified tomb became ever afterwards the Castello Sant' Angelo, and the chapel of *Sanctus Angelus inter Nubes* was built on its summit.

Why St. Michael was such a popular saint in the Dark Ages is not quite easy to determine—perhaps because he was the victor over the "Prince of the Powers of the Air," who cast storm and pestilence on poor mortals. But there is no doubt that he enjoyed much of the worship, as the combatant protector of Christians, which devolved on St. George in later ages, and that he was often seen in lofty places was appropriate for a wearer of wings, who could well perch aloft.

Our particular Cornish shrine of the Archangel was known, like the Norman mount, as *Sanctus Michael in periculo Maris*—either because his lofty crag had served as a useful landmark to storm-tossed sailors, or (as others thought) because the isle was in danger of being swept away by the ocean like the fabled land of Lyonesse.

117

Probably there was a shrine of St. Keyne or some other local worthy on the Mount from the Dark Ages onward, but it is certain that Edward the Confessor, that great founder of religious houses, started the existing group of buildings when in 1044 he founded, on the summit of the hill, a priory of Benedictine monks, " in the place which is called St. Michael *Juxta Mare*," and endowed it with the port dues of Romney and certain lands. Forty years later the church duly appears in Domesday Book, in the hands of one Treiwal, and rated at two hides, " which have never paid tax." Count Robert of Mortain,

St. Michael's Mount. Sentry Box and Entrance to Outer Ward

the first Norman Earl of Cornwall, is recorded to have appropriated one of these two hides—but he gave other and larger lands instead, and annexed the foundation to the abbey of St. Michel in Normandy, so that for the next three hundred and fifty years it was an " alien priory." The imperfect list of thirteenth and fourteenth century priors shows that they were often Frenchmen, sent over from the patron-house, and with Norman names like de Carteret and de Cherbourg.

Not a stone can be surviving, so far as the eye can judge, of the church of the eleventh century monks. There is nothing Norman in the buildings on the hill top. Nor, probably, is there any original stone left of the first walls which turned St. Michael's into a building not wholly ecclesiastical. Its military strength was so obvious that Henry de Pomeroy, a desperate supporter of John Lackland, in his rebellion against Richard I., when his patron's cause was collapsing, and he himself had been driven out of his Devonshire estates, seized on St. Michael's isle as a last refuge, and threw up works to cover and block

PENDENNIS CASTLE : TUDOR ARMS ABOVE GATE-WAY

ST. MICHAEL'S MOUNT : AERIAL VIEW

the stairway and the few other accessible points by which the summit could be reached. When John submitted to his brother, Richard ordered the justiciar and the sheriff of Cornwall to lay siege to the Mount, which Pomeroy surrendered, and submitted to the king's mercy (1194). Cornish legend told that he immediately after committed suicide, by causing his arteries to be opened, in order that his estates might escape confiscation by his death before trial or sentence. The king restored the Prior and monks to their home, but seeing the military importance of the place, appointed a castellan and put him in charge of the Mount as a royal castle. St. Michael's thus became at once sanctuary and fortress, and so remained till the dissolution of the monasteries under Henry VIII.

But the Mount, on its ecclesiastical side, changed owners before that date. When Henry V. and Archbishop Chicheley fell upon the alien priories, and gave them to English houses or colleges, in order to prevent their revenues going abroad to the king's enemies, the Priory of St. Michael's was severed from its connection with Mont St. Michel, and finally, many years later, was annexed by Edward IV. to Syon Abbey in Middlesex. That its military purpose was not forgotten appears from a patent of the time of Henry IV. (1404), which orders repairs " because this priory is said to be, in time of war, the fortress of the whole adjacent region."

The most stirring incident of the whole history of St. Michael's fell eleven years after it had been made over to Syon Abbey. After the battles of Barnet and Tewkesbury (1471) it appeared that the Lancastrian cause was crushed for ever, its heir being slain, and well nigh all its leaders. Yet conspiracy against Edward IV. was intermittent, and in 1473, on the rumours of widespread discontent in the realm, John de Vere, Earl of Oxford, the most desperate of the Lancastrian exiles, executed one of the boldest and most futile enterprises ever known. Having got two ships from Louis of France, he came to anchor in Mount's Bay, having with him an insignificant following, variously estimated at from 80 to 300 men, exiles and adventurers like himself. Leaving their ships, he and his followers disguised themselves as pilgrims, with broad hats, and cloaks and gowns over their body-armour, and their swords muffled up in their cloaks. They walked over the causeway and presented themselves at the lower gate as a party of palmers, who had come by sea to make their offerings at the shrine. They were admitted without suspicion, and on coming to the upper court threw off their gowns, drew their swords, and caught and expelled the monks and the few men-at-arms of the garrison [Sept. 30, 1473]. They then swept the neighbouring parishes for food, and endeavoured to raise insurrection, in which they failed utterly. But Oxford recruited a few broken men to swell his force, and had time to fill his storehouse, before the king heard of his escapade, and ordered Sir Henry Bodrugan, the most notable Yorkist of these parts, and Sir John Arundel, Sheriff of Cornwall, to reduce the Mount with the men of the *posse comitatus*. The sheriff tried to break in at low tide by escalade, having no cannon, but was beaten off with ease, he himself being slain on the sand at the foot of the stairway, and many of his followers with him.

The king appointed John Fortescue sheriff in Arundel's place, and sent him guns, four ships, and ultimately a force of 900 paid archers, to stiffen the raw shire levy. But repeated attacks on the outer *enceinte* failed—it was difficult indeed to conduct regular siege operations when the causeway was under water more than half the day, and so communications cut between the mainland and any body of besiegers who might have established themselves on the small foothold at the foot of the rock. At last the siege dwindled down to a blockade by land and sea. Efficient gunfire was impossible, when the object aimed at was 230 feet above the battery below. The earl held out for no less than six months, but was forced by famine to surrender late in February, 1474, obtaining no better terms than that he and his followers should not suffer in life or limb. This much the king conceded because the blockade was expensive, and the resistance of the fortress injurious to his prestige. Oxford was sent to prison in Hammes Castle near Calais, from whence he only escaped after nine years' captivity. His followers got off with shorter imprisonment. So ended a most daring but most ill-advised adventure—which never had a moment's prospect of success.

It is curious to find that the Mount was again taken by surprise within 30 years of the siege of 1473-4—this time by an adventurer as reckless, but less courageous, than John de Vere. The impostor Perkin Warbeck, expelled from Scotland, came with three ships and his miserable following of 130 men, to Mount's Bay, in September, 1497, hoping to take advantage of the after-swell of discontent caused by the Cornish rebellion, which had just been put down at " Blackheath Field." He gained admission into St. Michael's, as Oxford had done, not without suspicion of treachery on the part of the monks, who, like most of their neighbours, were in a disaffected mood. Perkin then proclaimed himself king under the name of Richard IV., and found himself joined by several thousands of the rebels of the last summer. He placed his unlucky wife, Catherine Gordon, in the Mount, with a small garrison, and started on that wild march eastward which ended in the unsuccessful siege of Exeter, the dispersion of his army, and his surrender at Beaulieu Abbey. The Mount was yielded, without a shot fired, to Lord Daubeny, and the pretender's wife forwarded to the king, who treated her kindly, and kept her about his court— where, after Perkin's subsequent execution, she found three successive husbands of good estate and reputation.

Despite of these turbulent incidents, St. Michael's was at the height of its prosperity as a place of pilgrimage during the last century before the Dissolution of the Monasteries. The number of visitors was great, and their liberal contributions sufficed to pay for the rebuilding of the whole church, most of which is pure fourteenth-fifteenth century Perpendicular in style, though there are scraps of the earlier decorations surviving. Of the original Norman nothing remains. On the stone lantern of the tower there was constructed the famous Chair of St. Michael, a rather dizzy seat in which the pilgrim who climbed so high might flatter himself that he reached the exact spot where the " vision of the

ST. MICHAEL'S MOUNT : VIEW FROM SHORE

PENGERSICK CASTLE

guarded Mount," the figure of the Archangel, had appeared.   The Elizabethan songster could ask—

> "Who knows not Michael's Mount and Chair,
>   The Pilgrim's holy vaunt,
>   Both land and island twice a day,
>   Both fort and port of haunt."

On the eastern flank of the quadrangle, of which the church forms one side, there was, when Leland visited the place about 1538, another smaller chapel dedicated to St. Mary, which was used by the garrison, during the days when the monks had the greater place of worship. William of Worcester, writing 50 years before Leland, distinguishes between the "ecclesia," which was 90 feet by 36, and the "capella nova edificata," which was 90 feet by 30. The lodgings of the captain and the priests were side by side on the south of the main structure. The rest of the monastic buildings were lower down in the "outer ward."

At the Dissolution of the Monasteries, St. Michael's was valued at £110 per annum, which is credited to the Abbey of Syon. The crown proceeded to lease the buildings to a series of Cornish magnates, who were also appointed captains of the Mount from the military point of view. The first of these lessees would appear to have been Humphrey Arundel of Lanhern, a

St. Michael's Mount
Chapel Door

121

kinsman of the sheriff slain in 1471, who, though a holder of confiscated church property, distinguished himself by heading the Catholic rebellion of the West in 1549, and paid for his treason with his life. He was succeeded by Millatons and Bassetts in Elizabethan days, while James I. granted the whole in fee to his prime minister, Robert Cecil, Earl of Salisbury. When the second earl joined the Parliamentary party in 1642, Charles I. seized the Mount into his own hands, and regranted it to Sir Francis Bassett. Probably the earlier lay holders of the Mount pulled the monastic parts of the buildings to pieces—and it is recorded that there were wholesale clearances and reconstructions when the Mount was put in a regular state of defence in 1642 by Sir Francis Bassett. While the "New Model Army," under Fairfax, overran Cornwall in the spring of 1646, this officer made a creditable resistance to a besieging force under Colonel Hammond. The island was still found impregnable, but when the news of the king's surrender got about, Bassett yielded it on terms which permitted him and his garrison to depart by sea to the Scilly isles. The Parliament resumed St. Michael's as state property, but at the Restoration, Charles II. returned it to the Bassetts, a family who had served the crown loyally.

They were, however, in such an impoverished position, that they at once sold the island to Sir John St. Aubyn, whose descendants still possess it, and reside on its lofty summit. They have, as was inevitable, made sweeping alterations—the church remains and the refectory is still a dining room, known as "Chevy Chase Hall," from the hunting scenes portrayed on its walls. But there was much additional building in 1751, and again in 1878, as tablets inserted in the walls show. The former was in the style of the day—the latter in Victorian Gothic, calculated, perhaps, to deceive incautious antiquaries when time shall have worn it to the same hue as the mediæval walls. The whole is effective, if somewhat incongruous. The military character of the island's tradition is still preserved by a battery of old eighteenth century six pounders, mostly bearing the St. Aubyn arms, which stand on a little plateau outside the main entrance, and are fired on occasions of high ceremony.

The steep staircase of ascent from the little port below winds through thick brushwood of semi-tropical evergreens, giving an occasional point of view towards land or sea, and when the top is reached the seascape from the Lizard to Mousehole Cove forms one of the most striking coast-views in the whole realm.

Pengersick

This fine tower, five miles east of Marazion, and half a mile from the sea, has preserved the name of castle, and is so markedly military in aspect, as it now stands, that it would be wrong to deny it the title. It is, in fact, the sole surviving part of an early Tudor mansion, built for residence, but presenting strong defensive features. The rest of the house has disappeared, but the very solid tower of defence remains wonderfully intact, standing aloft above a group of farm buildings. It is large enough to form a good residence, and is—after a gap of some centuries—being once more used for that purpose.

Pengersick was, in the sixteenth century, the home of the Millatons, and the earliest holder of the estate from that family is credited with the building of it in the early years of Henry VIII. Local legend declares that this John Millaton, having slain a man in London, disappeared, and was never arrested, but had in fact reached home and secluded himself in a top room of his tower, where he remained immured for many years, till his death, his son and family denying any knowledge of his existence. Be this as it may, the Millatons endured for three generations, but their estate was split up among six co-heiresses in the end of the reign of Elizabeth, and the manor was sold to the Godolphins, who had many other abodes, and did not much need this one.

Pengersick

When Lord Treasurer Godolphin's estates passed to his son-in-law, the Duke of Leeds, Pengersick, already in a state of decay, was thoroughly neglected, and the residential parts of the house were pulled down after their roofs had fallen in. But the astonishing white granite tower of defence defied the force of the ages, and stood up proudly over the scene of ruin. On its northern front may be seen, high up, the gable-mark of the much lower range of buildings, which formed the domestic part of the original manor house. Their stones have gone to make the farm-cottages and walls below.

Pengersick, therefore, consists now solely of this splendid granite tower, in three stories, served by a broad and light newel-stair contained in a separate turret built against one angle of the tower. It loses somewhat in effect from its situation, which is at the bottom of a combe, sheltered by hills against the north and east winds—and commanded by them on two sides. The site is one which the original builder clearly chose for amenity, and not for military strength. But the tower itself is well-equipped for defence, battlemented, and furnished all round with gun-holes, not with archery-slits, a fact which demonstrates its Tudor date. There is a slanting gun-hole covering the front door, and a slit above, from which boiling water or similar unpleasant surprises could be dropped on an unwelcome visitor. All three stories have good Tudor fireplaces, and there is a pleasant look-out place on the roof. Probably the tower and the vanished domestic buildings beside it, were once surrounded by a slight outer wall, and a ditch, which the stream in the farm-yard may have supplied with water.

Tintagel

The bare breezy and rock-girt north coast of the Duchy was thinly peopled and ineligible, compared with the attractive lands along the great southern estuaries of the " Cornish Riviera." And it was specially handicapped by the absence of good harbours, Bude and Boscastle being mere death-traps in stormy weather, and Newquay and Padstow not much better, small and inconvenient. Hence we get on the north coast none of the fine haven-defending castles with which Henry VIII. lined the south. The only fortress worthy of notice is Tintagel—and that rather from its legendary fame than from the extent or detail of the fragments scattered on its black slate headland. Of the other early castles of the region, Bottreaux, the home of the baronial family of that name, had become of small account, by Leland's time, "unworthe the name of castle," and has now entirely vanished. Few know that the modern name of Boscastle is a syncopated form of Bottreaux Castle. Of Binomy Castle near Stratton, mentioned by William of Worcester, as in 1478 still inhabited by the Colshill family, Leland, sixty years later, speaks not at all, and its very memory is gone.

The fame of Tintagel goes back very far—always connected with the name of King Arthur, and in the days of the later Romances with those of Tristram, Iseult of Ireland, and the venomous King Mark. No one can deny that the bleak peninsula, joined to the mainland only by a narrow spine of rock, would be a natural place of refuge for prehistoric chiefs—Celtic or even pre-Celtic. But Dun-dagil, " the impregnable hill-fort," starts its record with the legend of King Uther Pendragon, Prince Gorlois and the Lady Ygerne, though it may have harboured Dumnonian, Ivernian, or neolithic heroes long before their day. Modern historic opinion is inclined to accept the fact that an Arthur—Artorius— a Romano-British general or prince—not a king of all Britain—really existed in the later years of the fifth century, and the early decades of the sixth, and that it was he who stayed for a time the Saxon invasion of West Britain at the battle of Mount Badon, somewhere about 516 A.D. But it would be hazardous to accept any other information about him, whether supplied by Nennius, the Welsh Triads, or the far too voluminous record of Geoffrey of Monmouth, who rearranged a farrago of Celtic legends, amplified by his own shameless and inexhaustible imagination, and imposed them on the literary public of the twelfth century with lamentable success. Only Giraldus Cambrensis dared to call him an inventor: chroniclers for five centuries swallowed him whole, and falsified all early British history, while the writers of romances battened still more freely on his lurid tales of war and lust.

As Geoffrey tells the tale, Uther Pendragon, King of Britain, brother and successor of Aurelius Ambrosius [who happens to be a real personage], cast eyes of lawless love on Ygerne, wife of his vassal, Gorlois of Cornwall, and provoked the prince—who was no simple Uriah but a suspicious husband—to not unjustifiable rebellion. Gorlois shut up his wife in the impregnable Tintagel, and took the field against his lord. By treacherous slight and the art-magic of Merlin, Uther got entry into Tintagel in disguise, and wrought his will on the princess—Gorlois fell in action that same night, many miles away, and the king took Ygerne as his lawful wife. Hence came their son Arthur, conceived and born at Tintagel. Into his fabulous history we need not go—it includes in Geoffrey not only the hunting of the Saxons out of Britain, but the conquest of all France, and the slaying in battle of a Roman emperor, with the not very plausible name of Lucius Tiberius! But during Arthur's reign Cornwall was held under him—so the later romances tell— by his cowardly and spiteful kinsman, King Mark. It was at his castle of Tintagel that occurred the tragedy of Tristram, the king's nephew, and the beautiful Queen Iseult of Ireland—the Paolo and Francesca of Celtic legend. Their lives were entwined by the fatal love-potion which they drank unwittingly on King Mark's ship, and ended together when the furtive king clove Tristram's head from behind with a glaive as he sat harping to the queen, who forthwith "died fawning upon his corpse," as the *Morte Arthur* tells.

Tintagel looks gloomy enough to be the proper setting for any amount of scenes of lawless life and death. But though it may have been the stronghold of countless chiefs of the Dark Ages, there are none of its present ruins which can possibly be attributed to any earlier date than the twelfth century. It consists of two parts—a sea-girt isle of black slate surrounded by cliffs on all sides, and a lodgment upon the mainland, on equally precipitous ground severed from the isle by a cleft or chine, which has at its bottom one spur or spine of rock which joins them. The waves wash right up to this spine, and often through it, for there is a curious hole by which the sea water, at high tide, percolates from one side to the other. The isle must have been the original Celtic fortress, with the entry "which three men may hold against an army": but on the cliff opposite, Robert of Mortain or some other early Norman lord built an outer ward, forming a considerable castle in itself, which served as an additional protection. There is more of this left than of the buildings on the isle, but both began to perish early: John of Eltham, when Earl of Cornwall, is recorded to have pulled down the great hall about 1330. And the present aspect of Tintagel differs little from that which it presented to Leland in 1538.

"The residue of the buildings of this castle," he writes, " be sore weather-beeten and in ruine, but it hath been a large thing. . . . . Belike it had three wardes, but two be worn away by the gulfing in of the sea, insomuch that it has made almost an isle, and no way to enter into it now but by long elm trees laid for a bridge. So that now without the isle remaineth only a gate-house, a wall, and a *fausse braye* digged and walled. In the isle remain old walls and in the east side of the same, the ground being lower, remaineth a wall embattled, and men alive remember thereyn a gate of iron. There is in the isle a pretty chapel, with a tomb on the left side. Also there remaineth in the isle a ground quadrant-walled, as it were a garden plot, and by this the ruines of a vault. The isle now nourisheth only shepe and cowys."

The chapel of St. Julitta on the isle is now gone—tomb and all—only the square of its foundations is left. But the remainder of Leland's description may serve to-day—the embattled wall and the quadrangular enclosure on the isle are all that remain of what must have been the inner fortress. Of the outer works on the mainland there survives a little more, but it is all shapeless rubble, fragmentary walls rising to no great height, and on the south-east side the sea is still making incursions on the cliff and the ruins. There are two levels, probably representing the two outer wards of which Leland speaks, and in the higher level some courses of what may have been a large tower. But only the eye of faith can reconstruct any ground-plan of the works. All is very ruinous and depressing—fragments of ugly black slate, with no remains of architectural detail or ornament visible. One wonders not that the earls, after 1300, deserted the castle and let it crumble, but rather that the original Norman builder ever settled on a spot which has so few attractions save inaccessibility. Well suited enough for a primitive Celtic chief in constant danger of his life, it would seem to offer little advantage to an earl already possessed of such far more eligible abodes as Launceston, Trematon, or Restormel Castles. Conceivably it may have been intended as a last desperate hiding place in times of trouble. The buildings, scanty as they are, look too late to be attributed to Robert of Mortain's rebellious son William—conceivably Earl Reginald, the bastard of Henry I., may have started them in the anarchic years of Stephen, but the time of King John's temporary occupation of the earldom in the days of Richard I. would suit rather better. Documentary evidence is, unfortunately, wanting. The one thing certain is that the castle cannot have had more than 250 years of residential occupation, and probably had much less. For the state in which it was found by Leland shows that it must have gone to complete ruin in the fifteenth century, if not in the fourteenth. At present it can only be said that of all the British castles of ancient fame it is, perhaps, the most disappointing to the visitor— "STAT MAGNI NOMINIS UMBRA."

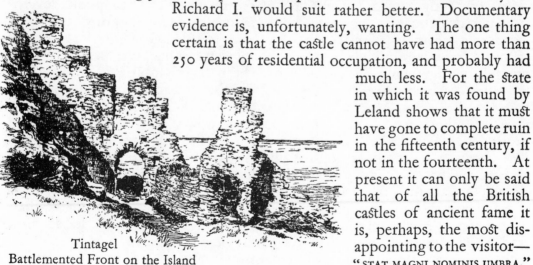

Tintagel
Battlemented Front on the Island

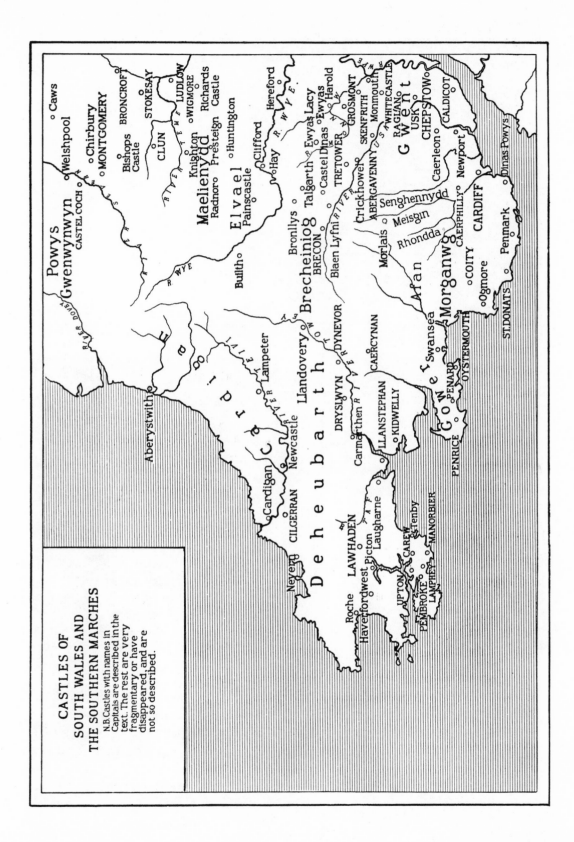

CASTLES OF
SOUTH WALES AND
THE SOUTHERN MARCHES

N.B. Castles with names in
Capitals are described in the
text. The rest are very
fragmentary or have
disappeared, and are
not so described.

Caws

Welshpool

Powys
Gwenwynwyn
CASTEL COCH

Chirbury
MONTGOMERY

BRONCROFT

Bishops
Castle
Richards
Castle

STOKESAY

LUDLOW
WIGMORE
Knighton
Radnor o Presteign

CLUN

Huntington

Clifford

Hereford

Maelienydd

Elvael
Painscastle

R. WYE

Hay

Ewyas Lacy

Talgarth
Castel Dinas
Ewyas
Harold
GROSMONT

Bronllys

Brecheiniog
BRECON

TRETOWER
Crickhowel
ABERGAVENNY
SKENFRITH
Monmouth
WHITECASTLE
RAGLAN
USK
CHEPSTOW

Gwent

Caerleon

CALDICOT

Bullth

Blaen Lyfni RIVER USK

Mortais
Meisgin

Newport

Dinas Powys

Senghennydd

CAERPHILLY
COITY
Penmark

CARDIFF

Rhondda

Aberystwith

Lampeter

Newcastle
Llandovery

DYNEVOR
DRYSLWYN

CAERCYNAN

Morganwg
PENARD
OYSTERMOUTH

Ogmore

ST. DONATS

Cardigan

Ceredigion

Afan

Gower
Swansea

CILGERRAN

Deheubarth

Neyern

Roche
Haverfordwest
Picton
LAWHADEN
Laugharne

Carmarthen RIVER

LLANSTEPHAN
KIDWELLY

UPTON
CAREW
Tenby

PEMBROKE
LAMPHEY
MANORBIER

PENRICE

OBVERSE

represents Owen crowned and enthroned, with the Welsh red dragon at his feet. On the drapery behind him is the coat of arms of the principality—quarterly gules and or, four lions rampant countercharged.

REVERSE

represents Owen horsed and armed, charging to right. On his helm is the Welsh dragon. His shield reproduces the coat of arms seen on the obverse; the lions may also be detected on the housings of his horse.

GREAT SEAL OF OWEN GLENDOWER, from the only existing specimen, attached to a letter addressed by him to Charles VI. of France, now preserved in the Archives Nationales at Paris.

PART II

Castles of Wales and of the Marches

THE first impression on the mind of the student who sets to work to master the history of the border of Wales, is that it is surprising that such a small country could have maintained its independence for six hundred years and more after the Anglo-Saxon invasion of England. The second impression, of a wholly different sort, is that it is most astonishing that the conquest of the greater part of Wales, which the Old English kings had left unsubdued, should have been achieved in the thirty years between 1090 and 1120, not by the kings of England at the head of the national forces of their realm, but by a handful of Norman adventurers, whose resources in men and money were most limited. For even the earls of Hereford, Shrewsbury, and Chester, who led the first assault, were no better than newly arrived adventurers, leading bands of adherents collected in the most casual fashion, and much of the early conquest was achieved by men like Bernard of Neufmarché, Robert Fitz Hamon, and Roger Mortimer, who were not even earls, but only lords of a few manors.

The comment to be made on the first impression is that the Anglo-Saxons, who conquered the Midlands and swept up to the Welsh border in the sixth and seventh centuries, were settlers and not seekers for empire. They stopped short at the foot of the hills, after occupying the eligible valleys: and the greatest of their kings contented themselves with taking homage from the Welsh princes, to whom they left the wild West. They did not aim at annexation, and Edward the Elder, or Edgar, were well satisfied if the Celtic chiefs attended their Witan and signed their charters. Edgar is said to have had three royal oarsmen from Wales among the eight kings who rowed him in that oft-quoted excursion on the tidal waters of the Dee. He did not ask for their lands, but only for their allegiance.

The greedy, restless, capable, Norman swarm, which settled down on England after 1066, were a very different sort of people. Their only conception of social organization rested on land-holding—the feudal system— and they were essentially land-grabbers of the most ruthless sort. When all England had been lotted out into fiefs, there were still hundreds of adventurers who craved land, and many of them achieved their object in Wales, though many perished in the quest. Just in the same way did their brothers and cousins deal with Naples and Sicily.

The Norman, as we have seen in our second chapter, was essentially a builder, and his *motte* and bailey castles, followed soon by his stone shell- or square-keeps, were the devices by which he held down England. The same system was applied in Wales—the ditch and palisade appeared the moment that the invader had pitched upon his chosen site. And his sons carried out with trowel and mortar what the father had begun with spade and axe. But the task of holding on to what had been seized was infinitely more hard in Wales than in England: the Celt for many generations was untameable, and the record of castles burned or cast down is lengthy. Hence came the enormous number of fortresses, small and great, in the newly won Marches. Instead of there being six or eight castles in a whole shire, as in England, the Normans in Wales had to build them very thick: Gwent had as many as the broad Somersetshire, Glamorgan more than Hampshire. And since, in time of insurrection, every Marcher was a friend, and every Welshman a possible enemy, they were placed so as to give each other strategical support, in the way of blocking routes and cutting off valley from valley. Some of the early ventures like that of the earls of Shrewsbury and Chester to settle up North Wales, and of the de Clares to hold down Cardigan, failed completely. More were successful—the grip of the invaders on Glamorgan, Pembroke, Brecknock and Gwent was, in spite of many vicissitudes, made firm. With the details of the history of each group of castles we shall be busied for many a page.

But how came it that the venture was on the whole successful, and ended with the incorporation of all Wales with the kingdom of England, when Edward I. made up his mind that the constant bickerings on the Marches must come to an end? The answer to this is that the Welsh were a most divided people. Local hatred between kingdoms, and dynastic rivalry between their ruling houses, is the only sort of politics that we can discover in Wales before the Norman Conquest. And internal politics within the several states were quite as depressing from the moral point of view. Succession in a Welsh principality was by the simple method of the survival of the fittest. The princely families were generally large—Nature (as is well known) generally provides for the survival of a species that is exceptionally liable to destruction by making it very prolific. It was quite impossible for even the most successful usurper to exterminate *all* his kinsmen. There was always some uncle, brother, or cousin, a refugee in a neighbouring state, or in Ireland, or in England, who was waiting for a snatch at the princely diadem, when its present wearer should have made himself unpopular, by losing a battle, or exacting too heavy contributions from his subjects. The Welsh liked to stick to their old dynasties, and bitterly resented any attempt of a neighbour from another state to win dominance over them. But provided that a pretender was one of the right royal stock, he could always find supporters who were discontented with the existing régime. Princes and pretenders slaughtered each other indiscriminately: the Welsh, indeed, fulfilled Tennyson's conception of Nature—

> " So careful of the type she seems,
> So careless of the single life."

They were loyal to the stock, but rather indifferent to the fates of individual members of it. It cannot be said that the constitution was "despotism tempered by assassination "—for a mild and well-disposed prince, who was anything but a despot, might easily perish, from his neglect to use the proper means of self-defence against unscrupulous relatives, much sooner than a tyrant who took those measures.

Inter-state feuds, and hatred within families, were so bitter that there never was a rising against the English intruder so general that *no* local prince adhered to the cause of the stranger, out of hatred for his neighbours. And, if a prince took the patriotic side, the pretender-in-ordinary of the moment would be forced to adhere to the side of the English king, who could give him his brother's or his cousin's lands when the rising should have failed. Normally a Plantagenet king had a selection of Welsh pretenders living at his court, whether as honoured guests or as prisoners, who would be let loose against their reigning relative when he gave trouble.

These pleasant Celtic foibles must be borne in mind when we study the history of the Welsh and the Lords Marchers. In Wales, as afterwards in Ireland, the external invader could always find guides, helpers and partisans among discontented kinsmen of the occupant of the throne. And it was rare that he should fail to find also the assistance of one of the states against the others. On a smaller scale each Marcher Lord could count on Welsh dependents, who had sought refuge with him from their enemies, and had become his bailiffs, his sub-tenants, or members of his band of archery.

Seal of Fulk Fitzwarine II. from his Charter to Abberbury Monastery, now in All Soul's College, Oxford.

THE ENGLISH MARCHES

SHROPSHIRE AND HEREFORDSHIRE

THE western border of England, in the early Middle Ages, had, along its whole front, a double, sometimes a triple, line of castles —there was a front line on Welsh soil, newly won, a second line along the old border of Mercia, and, behind these, three great fortresses which had been the bases from which the first attack on Wales had been made—Chester, Shrewsbury and Hereford. The northern section of the Marches does not come within the scope of this book : we are not concerned with Chester, nor with Hawarden and Malpas, and the other castles which lay as a screen in front of it, nor with Rhuddlan or Flint, Denbigh or Mold, and the other outposts established on the Welsh side of the border. Our survey takes in only the strongholds of Shropshire and Herefordshire, which originally faced the Celtic Kingdom of Powys, and the smaller principalities, more or less dependent on Powys, which lay to the south of it. There is no good single name for this last-named group, the land which the Welsh (as Leland records in the topographical table annexed to his Itinerary) called *Rhwng Gwy a Hafren*, "Twixt Wye and Severn." It must be noted here that the modern frontier between England and Wales, in this part of the Marches, by no means coincides with the mediæval. Henry VIII., when he created the new Welsh shires, cancelled many old boundaries. For example the castles of Montgomery and Radnor were reckoned English down to his day, while on the other hand Llanthony and its valley, now in Herefordshire, were counted Welsh.

As we have already said, the original Norman attack on Wales started from three bases—Hereford, Shrewsbury and Chester, each of which was in the days of William the Conqueror the abode of a restless and ambitious earl— William Fitz Osbern, Roger of Montgomery, and Hugh Lupus, the nephew of the king. Of Fitz Osbern's early advance into Gwent, and of his fortification of Chepstow and Monmouth on Welsh soil we speak later on. He died early (1071) and the lands and title of his son Roger were forfeited for rebellion in 1074. The king created no Earl of Hereford in his place. Exactly similar was the fate of the House of Shrewsbury. Roger of Montgomery engaged along with Hugh of Chester, not only in encroachment on North Wales, but in a bold scheme for its entire conquest. But the great adventure was foiled by the defeat and death of the second earl, Hugh of Montgomery, at the battle of Menai Strait, and the third earl, Robert (more often called Robert of Belesme than Robert of Montgomery) saw his earldom confiscated for persistent treason and rebellion by Henry I. in 1102. Copying the policy of his father with regard to Hereford, Henry made no new Earl of Shrewsbury. The title was not resuscitated till 1442.

LUDLOW CASTLE : FROM THE RIVER

LUDLOW CASTLE: INNER WARD AND ROUND CHAPEL

After 1071, in South Wales, and 1102, in Central Wales, there were no great earls to lead the assault on Welsh territory. But the assault continued : we shall see presently how Bernard of Neufmarché and Robert Fitz Hamon won Brecknock and Morganwg. Further north there was no such conquest on a large scale, but perceptible encroachment on the unconquered Welsh lands by the smaller Marcher lords, who had inherited the ambitions, if not the power, of the great house of Montgomery. The early adventurers were Braoses of Radnor, Corbets of Caws, Says of Clun, Fitz Alans of Oswestry, and Lacys of Ewyas, already settled in the Middle Marches, and new men to whom Henry I. had distributed some of the forfeited lands of Robert of Belesme, such as Baldwin of Bollers, who got the newly-built castle of Montgomery. Most important of all were to be the Mortimers of Wigmore, destined to become, three centuries later, Earls of March. But ere they came to their greatness in the thirteenth and fourteenth centuries, it had seemed likely that the Braoses had an even greater future before them—Philip de Braose of Radnor conquered the big cantref of Builth, and when his son William married the grand-daughter of Bernard of Neufmarché, and got with her Brecknock and Abergavenny, and much more, he had a breadth of lands which many an earl might have envied, though the title of earl never came to him. The Braose main line failed in 1230 —that of the Mortimers had a much longer endurance, and only passed on its possessions with the hand of its sole heiress to the house of York in 1424.

Though there were conquests, such as that of the Braoses in Builth and the Cliffords in Llandovery, over and above the first subjection of Brecknock by Bernard of Neufmarché, yet on the whole the frontier against Powys fluctuated far less after the first Norman invasion than did the frontiers against North and South Wales. This was partly due to the fact that the Marchers—always excepting the Braoses and Mortimers—were lords of comparatively small holdings, but partly also to the general policy of the Princes of Powys. The dynasty of Bleddyn ap Cynfyn, which ruled mid-Wales all through the period of the great wars, nourished so desperate a hatred for the house of Rhodri Mawr, which held North Wales, that it quite surpassed in intensity any feeling against the English. Again and again the princes of Powys threw in their lot with the Plantagenets when the latter were attacking Gwynedd. This did not mean that they were not ready to fight the Marchers if provoked, but that when not attacked themselves they were willing to help against their hated northern countrymen. They were comparatively—only comparatively—Anglophil, because the main anti-English party in Wales was always led by their rivals from Gwynedd. And this persisted to the end, so that alone among the Celtic princes, the lords of Powys survived the complete subjugation of Wales by Edward I. : they became important English barons regularly summoned to Parliament, till in the fourteenth century, in the reign of Edward II., the last male of the house of Bleddyn, left only a sister, who had married a Cherlton—a small Marcher baron. To their issue the main principality of Powys, including nearly the whole of the modern county of Montgomery, passed for a hundred years, afterwards to go through another heiress to the Greys. The more northern part of the land, Powys Fadog, as it was called, which had fallen to minor branches of the house of Bleddyn, got involved in the annexations of Edward I., because its owners had sided with the last Llewellyn of North Wales in his rebellions. But the main bulk of the principality, Powys Gwenwynwyn, passed by regular lineal succession through all the centuries of the Middle Ages, and the owner of Powys Castle under the Tudors could show a complete title by inheritance going back to the ancient royal line.*

The minor principalities south of Powys, Elvael and Maelienydd, in the modern county of Radnor and its neighbourhood, which did not belong to the house of Bleddyn, were the part of the mid-Welsh border where possession was most fluctuating in the twelfth and thirteenth centuries. In times of English aggression the Mortimers were usually its owners—in times of Welsh reaction its old princes returned, and the Mortimers were driven back to Wigmore. When Llewellyn the last was at the height of his power, about the time of the Barons' War, the English seemed to have lost them for good (1264-1276). But on Lleweyllyn's overthrow the Mortimers got back Maelienydd by force of arms, and the Toenys of Pain's Castle conquered Elvael.

All this land of "Rhwng Gwy a Hafren" is full of the traces of castles— but they are traces only. As in Brecknock, so here the hand of time has fallen with special severity—there is not a single surviving remnant of real architectural importance on either side of the March—English or Welsh. Old Radnor shows the remains of a *motte*, Knighton and Cefn Llys those of a *motte* and bailey, at Presteign only "the Wardens' Walk" marks the area of the vanished fortress. The most historically famous of the castles in this region was Pain's Castle, very close to the Herefordshire border, built by Pain de Quercy about 1130, in the usual *motte* and bailey style, and the centre of much fighting. It was defended with success in 1195 by Maud of St. Valery, wife of its absent owner,† whence the English often called it Maud's Castle, but taken by Rhys ap Griffith of South Wales in 1196. William of Braose had got it back by 1198 when it stood a third siege within five years, at the hands of Gwenwynwyn of Powys. But the justiciar, Geoffrey Fitz Peter, came to its aid, beat the Welsh prince in a pitched battle, before its walls, and relieved the garrison. In the next generation it was rebuilt in the new thirteenth century style by Henry III., when he made it his base during his campaign of 1231, against Llewellyn the Great, of North Wales. Simon de Montfort, in his hour of distress, before Evesham, ceded it to the last Llewellyn in 1265, along with Hawarden, as part of the price for the Welsh prince's assistance against the insurgent royalist party. This was one of the acts for which the great earl was never

---

*Powys Fadog and Powys Gwenwynwyn mean the parts of the Principality which fell respectively to two relatives, Madog and Gwenwynwyn, in the late twelfth century. The former got the lands along the Dee, the latter the lands along the Upper Severn. The descendants of Madog split their holding into several minor lordships, became very small people, and fell under the supremacy of the Princes of Gwynedd. They were annexed by Edward I. for joining in Llewellyn's rebellion. The house of Gwenwynwyn wisely kept its land undivided, and were almost consistently Anglophil.

†This was the Maud de Braose, whom King John starved to death in the vaults of Corfe Castle in 1214, along with her eldest son, when he had failed to capture William de Braose, her husband, who was a fugitive and a rebel.

forgiven by any of the Marcher lords. It is curious to find that Pain's *motte* is now far more in evidence than King Henry's stonework.

But this survival of the primitive work, and disappearance of the later masonry, seems to be the general rule on this March. Take, for example, Richard's Castle, near Ludlow, one of the very first castles built in England, for its founder was Richard Fitz Scrob, who was in Herefordshire even under Edward the Confessor. He reared a *motte* of portentous size, 70 feet high, with a 30-foot platform on top for his wooden house of defence, and a deep ditch around its base, with a palisade outside it, and a second and smaller ditch encircling the palisade. Richard's Castle came to the Says of Clun, who built a stone tower to replace the original wooden structure on the *motte*, and drew stone walls down the sides of it, and round half of the line of the palisade below, thus creating a perfectly semi-circular stone castle. Leland found it in 1541, " with keep, walls and towers yet standing, but going to ruin." But now, while the *motte* and ditches are perfectly clear, the stone has mostly gone. On the top of the keep is a mass of debris overgrown with brushwood, and though a part of the walls which descended the *motte* towards the outer circle is standing, the lower curtain is only marked by fragments of masonry lying among trees and nettles.

So is it also at Bishop's Castle—on the other side of Clun from Richard's Castle—the old stronghold of the bishops of Hereford, which Leland described as " well maintained, and a castle of good strengkth." But now only the *motte* remains, with no keep upon it, or walls below.

SHROPSHIRE

Leland, summing up, as was his wont, the lists of castles, abbeys and market-towns in each shire, credits Shropshire with no less than 26 castles, though he notes that several are " decayed this many a day," or " very ruinous," or are " places like a castle." And Montgomery and Wigmore, which he names among them, are not now reckoned to be in Shropshire at all. Nevertheless, it is surprising to find how few of these twenty-six now show any surviving military architecture worth inspection—putting aside the original Norman *motte* and ditch which outlive stone.

It may give some idea of the present melancholy condition of the castles of Shropshire if—leaving out the few of which it is worth while to give full notice—we set forth Leland's list of what existed in his day, with appended to it the short analysis of what Mr. Auden's excellent guide to the county gives as the present condition of each place :—

BISHOP'S CASTLE. Motte only surviving.

BRIDGEMOUTH. A leaning tower, a fragment of the keep, is all that remains of Robert de Belesme's great stronghold.

CAWS. Now represented only by earthworks, scarcely a stone being left.

CHERLTON. A mound only remains.

133

CHIRBURY.   A mound only.

CORFHAM.   Well defined earthworks and a double moat, no masonry.

HOLGATE.   Lower portion of one tower left, built into a farm house.

HOPTON.   A small square Norman keep, among traces of ruined enclosures.

KAYNHAM.   " Clene down," says Leland.   Is really a British camp.

KNOCKYN.   Stones all removed to build a bridge in 1818.

MORTON CORBETT.   " Jacobeanized " in 1606, and now a ruin.

MYDDLE.   Only a staircase-turret and fragment of wall left.

OSWESTRY.   Only a few stones left in a public recreation ground.

REDCASTLE.   A few remains of broken walls and turrets among earthworks.

SHRAWARDINE.   Castle " slighted " in 1646, and stones carted away to make a bridge.

SHREWSBURY.   Converted into a private house for Sir W. Pulteney, 1790.

SHEPTON CORBETT.   Its interesting features hidden by a new Georgian front.

WHITCHURCH.   The castle, of which there were still remains in 1760, has now entirely disappeared.

WHITTINGTON.   Two drum-towers of the twelfth century gate-house, and some scraps converted into a modern dwelling.   Complicated earthworks outside.

These excisions leave us only Ludlow, Acton Burnell, Clun, Broncroft and Stokesay.   The fate of Shrewsbury Castle is particularly exasperating to the archæologist: after being one of the great royal castles of England for several centuries, it was found by Leland " a strong thing, but now much going to ruin."   The eighteenth century handed it over to the architect Telford, to turn into a Georgian private residence for Sir William Pulteney.   It has just been rescued, and is at present under process of " restoration " as a public edifice.   It is said that the " Great Hall " can be reconstructed, and will be used for public functions: and the Norman doorway still stands.

Ludlow

This is by far the most important castle of the whole Welsh border, surpassing Chepstow in size and Raglan in historic interest.   It is splendidly placed for effect, on the culminating point of a hill, which, though not so precipitous as those of Harlech or Caer Cynan, commands the whole country round, and is a landmark for miles.   The river Teme curls around its base on the steep side, the fine church and the picturesque streets of Ludlow town are grouped outside its more accessible front.   Its history is interesting, and alone among all English castles it has its own mediæval Romance surviving, the Geste of Fulk Fitzwarine, the only long tale of the life of an adventurous knight of the twelfth century, written out for the benefit of his admiring descendants, which has come down to us.   It is more precious than many chronicles for those who wish to realize castle life in its prime.   The whole of the incidents of its first half centre round Ludlow, and the very chequered fortunes of its owners during the troublous times of Stephen and the earlier years of Henry II.

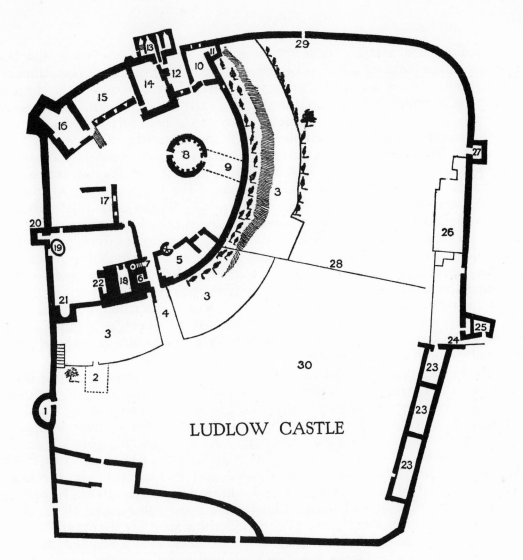

DESCRIPTION OF THE PLAN

No.
1. Mortimer's Tower.
2. Formerly used as a Magazine, now an Ice House.
3. The Moat.
4. Stone Bridge of two arches which occupies the place of the ancient Drawbridge.
5. Buildings erected during the Presidency of Sir Henry Sydney.
6. The Porter's Lodge.
7. A Newel Staircase leading to the Keep.
8. The Norman Chapel.
9. Site of the Choir of the Chapel.
10. Apartments occupied by the two Princes sons of Edward IV. Supposed tower of Pendover.
11. A small Room.
12. The Armoury.
13. A Watch Tower.
14. The State Apartments.

No.
15. The Hall, or the Council Room.
16. Prince Arthur's Room.
17. The Kitchen.
18. The Original Chapel, afterwards converted into a Prison.
19. The Well, now about 85 feet deep.
20. A Tower, called the Lion's Den.
21. Small Norman Tower and Oven.
22. The Black Hole.
23. The Stables.
24. The principal Gate-way leading to the Castle from the Town.
25. Offices where the Fire Engines were kept.
26. Barracks.
27. A Beacon Tower.
28. Iron Palisades across the Outer Court.
29. A Sallyport.
30. The Castle Yard or Outer Court.

Ludlow was a small border town in pre-Norman days, about the last inhabited place held by the English toward the side of Wales. The Palmers' Guild, whose history is recorded in the fifteenth century windows of the church, was specially proud of its connection with Edward the Confessor. Domesday Book shows that William the Conqueror gave it to Osbern Fitz-Richard, the son of Richard Fitz Scrob of the neighbouring Richard's Castle, which is only four miles off. But Osbern enfeoffed as his sub-tenant at Ludlow a person of somewhat greater importance than himself, Roger de Lacy of Ewyas, and seems afterwards to have ceded all his rights to him. The Lacys, though in trouble for rebellion against William Rufus, continued to hold the castle intermittently for many generations, and were undoubtedly the builders of the original castle. It was presumably at first a *motte* and bailey fortress, though whether the bailey of 1100 included all the present outer ward, or only the inner and middle wards, is not certain. The great width and depth of the ditch which separates the two inner wards from the outer suggests that it was originally the main line of defence, and that the outer ward was an afterthought of the later twelfth century. There is plenty of room for an average Norman castle of early date if we take the keep and its immediate appurtenances as the original point of strength, and the middle ward as its original bailey.

Be this as it may, the replacing of palisades by a stone *enceinte* evidently came earlier at Ludlow than at many places, and its great square keep probably belongs to the time of Henry I., while the outer ward is not later than that of Henry II., if it be not contemporary with the inner buildings. In the anarchical reign of Stephen the castle was to see much fighting. At the death of Henry I. it seems to have been out of the hands of the Lacys ; the second of them had left his sister's son as heir, having no child of his own, and the king had claimed it as an escheat, and had intruded one Pain Fitz John, to the great wrath of Gilbert the nephew aforesaid, who had assumed his uncle's name and claimed all his heritage. Fitz John was slain by the Welsh, and soon after his death, at the outbreak of the general insurrection of the western barons against Stephen, in 1138, Ludlow was seized by Gervase Paganel of Dudley, one of the leaders of the revolt, and was besieged by the king, who failed to take it on this occasion, but was luckier on a second attempt, when he gave the castle to one of his few trusty followers, Josse (or Joyce) de Dinant, probably a member of the Northamptonshire family of Dinants, in which this queer Christian name was prevalent. Josse held the castle against all comers, till his death in or about 1166, his enemies being primarily the Lacys, Hugh, son of Gilbert, who was now dead, and Walter his heir, who held themselves entitled to the place ; secondly, Hugh Mortimer of Wigmore, head of the party of Queen Maud in those parts, and thirdly, the Welsh. For Owen Kyveiliog of Powys, and Jorwerth ap Owen of Gwynedd, were well aware that times of English civil war were favourable to Welsh reaction.

The romance of Fulk Fitzwarine falls into the twenty troublous years during which Josse de Dinant was holding Ludlow against various foes. The hero of the tale was son of Warine de Metz, lord of Abberbury, from whom

LUDLOW CASTLE: GATE-WAY OF CHAPEL

STOKESAY CASTLE: THE COURTYARD

came the family name, and was the first of no less than nine successive Fulk Fitzwarines, for the house was lucky in preserving its male descent from the reign of Henry I. down to that of Henry VI. Warine of Metz sent his son, as was the custom in that age, to serve as a page in the household of Josse de Dinant and there to learn courtesy and knightly exercises. His long stay at Ludlow was to be full of adventure. The first event of note that he saw was the capture by Josse of Hugh Mortimer, who was taken by an ambush, confined in the tower in the outer ward, which still bears the name of Mortimer's Tower, and released only on paying an enormous ransom. If the romance speaks true, this would prove that the outer ward had been built in stone by 1150. Some years later it was the Lacys who were most in evidence. They beset Ludlow intermittently and once committed themselves to a pitched battle under the walls. Fulk was then a stripling, and not permitted to go out to the combat. But as he watched it from a tower in company with Josse's wife and daughter Hawise, they saw the castellan beset by Walter de Lacy and three other knights, well in sight of the walls. Fulk ran down, snatched up an axe, put on a rusty helm, and supervening unexpectedly, just as Josse had been beaten down and dismounted, slew two of his assailants and captured Walter and the fourth knight, both of whom had already been severely wounded by Josse before he fell. After this exploit Fulk was naturally admitted to bear arms with his patron, whose life or liberty he had saved, and was very much in the good graces of Josse's daughter.

But disaster was impending over Ludlow. Arnold de Lisle, the knight who had been captured along with Walter de Lacy, won favour with Marion de la Bruyére, a damsel of good family who was being reared in the castle by Josse's wife. She was cajoled into furnishing him with a rope of knotted linen, by which he and Lacy let themselves down from their prison and escaped. After some time " the neighbours"—not the king whose peace was being broken— negotiated a pacification between the rival claimants for Ludlow. All seeming quiet, Josse proceeded to give the hand of his very willing daughter to Fulk ; they were married in the castle chapel, and then accompanied by the old Warine, Fulk's father, went off on a long journey to " Hartland "—wherever that may have been—it hardly seems likely to be Hartland in Devon.

Tragedy followed on the absence of the lord. The damsel Marion de la Bruyére, who was absolutely besotted on Arnold de Lisle, sent him a secret message that she was almost alone in the castle, and that Josse and his train were far away. He might visit her without danger, and she would let him in by the same window by which he had escaped before. De Lisle was more of a traitor than a lover : he pointed out to de Lacy that they had a unique opportunity of surprising the castle. Accordingly he came by night to the rendezvous, apparently alone, but with some hundreds of men-at-arms following at a discreet distance. He was admitted, left his ladder hanging from the window, and went off with the lady to her bower. While they were pleasantly employed, a hundred Lacy retainers mounted the ladder with vast precautions, and while some stole to the dormitory of the garrison, others descended to open the

137

fortress, slew the watchman and admitted the main body. Without delay the sleeping garrison were murdered in their beds, as well as many menials. The screams of the dying roused Marion in her lover's arms, she ran to the window, saw and understood what had happened, and before de Lisle realized her purpose ran him through with his own sword, which was lying on the table. She then leapt from the window and broke her neck on the rock below.

Thus de Lacy got possession of the much-desired heritage of his family, but he had soon to stand a siege from Josse and Fulk, who returned in haste on receiving the horrid news. They gathered all the men they could, established themselves in the British camp at Kaynham, three miles away, and beset the castle. After much fighting outside the walls the besiegers got in close on the side of the town, and attacked the outer ward. They ultimately broke in by using the primitive device of heaping burning brushwood and faggots against the gate, and throwing grease upon it till it was charred through, and a storming party burst in over the burning embers.

Walter de Lacy, pent up in the inner ward, was soon in such desperate straits that he sent a message to Jorwerth ap Owen of Gwynedd offering to take him as lord and secure him many lands, if he would drive off the besiegers. This was contrary to marcher etiquette—but proved a successful device. The Prince of Gwynedd came up, and Owen Kyveiliog of Powys with him, bringing tribal levies in great force, and fell upon Josse's base-camp at Kaynham. The siege of Ludlow had to be raised, the garrison joined the Welsh, and between them they beat the host of Josse and Fulk, taking the former prisoner, while the latter, badly wounded, escaped only by the speed of his horse.

Then only, and not before, did Fulk go to the court of King Henry, and plead his cause. Evidently, in the mind of a marcher baron, it was almost as bad to call in the king as to call in the Welsh. The results were not altogether satisfactory : even the first of the Plantagenets was not a perfect *deus ex machina*. Henry ordered de Lacy to release Josse de Dinant, and to get rid of his Welsh allies. The former command was carried out at once, but as Josse died very soon after, the Lacys were allowed to keep Ludlow. But to dismiss the Welsh was another matter : they overran the whole march, and though Fulk was made constable of an army sent against them, it took four years to clear them out of Shropshire, and even then the king had to bribe them to peace by ceding the border district of Maelor and the castle of Whittington.

Here we dismiss the Romance, which goes on to tell the story of Fulk II., the son of Fulk I., and his rebellion against King John. The restored de Lacys, who had much to suffer from that unpopular monarch, kept Ludlow in the end. Their house died out in the male line in 1240, and its scattered lands were parted between two co-heiresses—Matilda de Lacy took Ludlow to her second husband, Geoffrey de Geneville, one of the South-French favourites of King Henry III. : Margaret took Ewyas to John de Verdun. But the Geneville line only endured for two generations : Joan, the grand-daughter of Matilda, was left the sole heiress, and married Roger Mortimer, the wicked Earl of March, the murderer of Edward II. Through this wedlock Ludlow got swallowed up in the immense holding of the Mortimers, "not kings themselves, but the ancestors of many kings."

Five generations of Mortimers lived at Ludlow, which was almost more the centre of their power than their ancestral Wigmore, for it was a larger and a stronger castle. How to divide the thirteenth and fourteenth century additions to Ludlow's architecture between Lacys, Genevilles and Mortimers is somewhat of a puzzle. It is complicated by the fact that the Romance of Fulk Fitzwarine, written in the later thirteenth century, speaks of many towers, chambers and walls of the castle by name as existing in *circ.* 1160, which appear to be somewhat later date, *i.e.*, it may be describing the Ludlow of 1250 rather than that of Fulk's day. Be this as it may, the keep at least is probably of the time of Henry I., and there are traces of Norman work in the much-rebuilt corner towers of the middle ward which overhang the river. Late Norman also is the very curious round chapel of St. Mary Magdalen, which stands in the middle of the ward, and displays a particularly fine entrance door with zig-zag moulding, and another arch opening into the place where the now-vanished chancel stood. The interior, now open to the sky, was once very elaborately decorated with woodwork of armorial designs, which was standing perfect in the late eighteenth century.

The interior of the keep has been at least twice remodelled, the last changes having been made as late as Tudor times, when Sir Henry Sydney, the great Elizabethan President of the Council of Wales, built the now existing gate-house adjacent to the keep, and put on it his own and his mistress's coats-of-arms, and the curious inscription—"*Hominibus Ingratis Loquimini Lapides.*" But its dominating character in the line of defence of the inner ward has always been the same.

Far the most imposing ranges of building in Ludlow Castle are undoubtedly the great five-storied blocks of the north front, from the tower of the Two Princes [Edward V. and his brother] on the north-east, to that of Prince Arthur on the north-west. These look like the Mortimers' work, with the interior pulled about by fifteenth and sixteenth century successors. For while some of the fireplaces and the lines of the windows are in good "Decorated" style, others are undoubtedly Elizabethan. The Great Hall in the centre of the block is a magnificent room, 60 feet by 30, with a roof 35 feet high. And the State Apartments to the right of it contain spacious and highly decorated chambers.

Ludlow was kept in good repair, and inhabited, down to a date far later than that at which most of the castles of the Marches had gone to decay. When the last heiress of the Mortimers married Richard of Cambridge, and passed on her ancestors' wide lands to the House of York, the castle became more important than ever, as the chief abode and stronghold of a royal line with strong aspirations to the crown. It was the place at which Anne Mortimer's son Richard, Duke of York, mustered his army for his abortive insurrection in 1459, and the rout of Ludford Bridge, which wrecked his hopes, took place before its walls. Richard's son, Edward IV., prized Ludlow greatly, and made it the regular abode of his two much-cherished sons, the princes after whom the north-east tower is named.   It was from there that they set out on that unhappy journey to London in 1483, which led them to a secret grave in the Tower.   Notwithstanding these sinister associations, Henry VII. gave it to his son Arthur as his abode, when he had married Catharine of Aragon, and had started an establishment of his own.   Arthur left his name to the north-west tower, in which he died in April, 1502, only a few months after his marriage—thereby ensuring the succession of his formidable younger brother Henry VIII.

Ludlow was never again a royal residence, but it was made the site of the " Council of Wales " after Arthur's death.   This important local delegation

Ludlow.   Sydney Monument

of the king's own Council, which had as its parallel " the Council of the North " at York, had charge of the principality and the March right down to the Civil War of 1642-46.   It had even a nominal—but only a nominal—restoration after 1660, and was only abolished in 1689.   The Lord President of the Council was almost a Viceroy, and lived in great state at Ludlow, with a great body of clerks and officials, who occupied the whole of the buildings.   Many of the Presidents were bishops, but the most notable and long-lived of them was a layman, Sir Henry Sydney, a great favourite of Elizabeth, who held the post from 1559 to 1586, and has left traces of his work all over the castle, and a magnificent tomb in the adjacent church.

The Whigs of the Revolution abolished the Council of Wales as one of the engines of royal bureaucracy—if not a very effective one of late.   Ludlow was left for a few years theoretically a garrison—with a retired colonel as governor, and a skeleton company, whose barracks may be seen in the outer ward.   Only

STOKESAY CASTLE: VIEW FROM THE POOL

STOKESAY CASTLE: SOLAR ROOM

a small part of the castle was occupied, and in the reign of George I. the crown (or Sir Robert Walpole) came to the conclusion that to keep up such a vast place was an unjustifiable extravagance. The lead was stripped from the roofs and sold, and the castle was allowed to moulder. Visitors as late as 1768 and 1774 reported that many of the floors and some of the roofs were still standing, and that the woodwork of the chapel was wonderfully preserved. But by 1800 all had fallen in, and things were apparently much as they are to-day. Finally, in 1811, the ruins were sold to the Earl of Powys, the greatest landowner of the district—a guarantee that no wilful dilapidations would follow.

Clun

Twelve miles north-west from Ludlow, on the edge of what was once a waste land, the Forest of Clun, lies one of the original Norman castles of the time of the Conquest—the stronghold of Robert of Say, a follower of the great Earl Roger of Montgomery. Just three miles on the English side of Offa's Dyke, the immemorial boundary against the Welsh, are a cluster of three well-marked knolls, round which the river Clun runs on three sides. Robert chose the highest of the knolls, built a *motte* upon it, drew a palisade around its contour, and scarped the sides—two towards the river could be made quite precipitous— the third was cut into a ditch, which separated this knoll from that lying south-west of it. This second and lower knoll was probably used as an outer bailey, as it was scarped and has traces of an earthen parapet around it—presumably the base of a palisade. This bailey never seems to have had any further fortifications given it, but the main castle on the northern and higher knoll went through the usual vicissitudes of a Norman fortress. At some time in the twelfth century a stone *enceinte* replaced the palisading, and a big stone keep was constructed. But this did not stand on the site of the original small *motte*, but to the east of it, and partly outside the knoll. For its foundations start at the level of the ditch, and it covers the whole east end of the eminence, three of its five stories overtopping the level of the summit, but the other two rising from the ditch and being actually below the curtain wall. It has been suggested that this curious scheme was adopted so as not to throw the whole weight of such a vast structure, 80 feet high, on the artificial earth at the top-level, but rather on the solid rock of the lower stratum. It thus projects into the ditch in a very curious fashion. This great mass of stone is fairly perfect, but the rest of the defences of the castle have gone entirely to ruin. There remain a fragment of the north-western wall, with two bastions, and a smaller one on the south. The latter is in front of the small circular mound, which probably represents the original *motte*.

The Says of Clun do not seem to have made any great advance against Wales—it was their neighbours the Mortimers of Wigmore who overran Maelienydd, the region to the west of Clun Forest. The family did plenty of fighting—Helias, the third of the line, slew two princes, Howell and Cadogan,

141

in 1142. But his son Ingelram left no male heir, only a daughter, Isabella, who married a Marcher baron of somewhat greater importance than her father, William Fitz-Alan, Lord of Oswestry. The two marches remained permanently united, and as Oswestry was larger and richer than Clun, which was mainly forest, it is probable that the Fitz-Alans resided more within it, and paid less attention to Clun than if it had been their main holding. There seems to be no definitely thirteenth century or fourteenth century architecture at Clun, or anything later than the great keep. The absolutely ruinous condition

Clun Castle. The Keep

of the castle makes it dangerous to state that nothing was built by the Fitz-Alans : at any rate nothing is visible. An interesting *inquisitio post mortem* made after the death of John Fitz-Alan in 1272, reports Clun as small though well-built, but the roof of the tower, and the bridge connecting the castle with its outer bailey were in need of repairs.

The position and status of the Fitz-Alans had been entirely changed in 1243, when the death without issue of William of Albini, last Earl of Arundel of the old creation, caused the castle and manor of Arundel to devolve on his nephew, John Fitz-Alan, the child of his sister Isabella. The Fitz-Alans thus became the greatest landowners in Sussex, and began to have other interests than those of a marcher baron : the Albinis' old title of earl was conceded to them by Edward I., and they ranked for the future among the most important subjects of the crown. While the Earls of Arundel were leading armies or insurrections, marrying the daughters of kings and princes, or going to the block, it would be natural that the less important of their two march-lordships should be neglected.

Leland, passing by in 1540 or thereabouts, found Clun "somewhat ruinous, though it hath been both strong and well builded."

An Arundel heiress took Clun in 1580 to the Howards of Norfolk. But the attainders to which that ducal line were so subject under the Tudors brought Clun to the crown, and James I. in 1604 gave it to the rightful heir's great uncle, Henry Howard, Earl of Northampton, who left it by will to his nephew the Earl of Suffolk. In 1646 the Parliamentarians "slighted" it, and for centuries it has been going slowly to decay. Only the enormous bulk of its curious projecting keep makes it worthy of a visit.

Stokesay

The Says of Clun have left their name associated for ever with this pretty little place "builded like a castle," as Leland cautiously says, when he reckons it, with some little doubt, among his twenty-six castles of Shropshire. But there is no doubt of its right to enter the list, though its entry was late. Walter de Lacy of Ewyas had a manor called Stoke, on the Onny River, seven miles north of Ludlow, on which he enfeoffed, for three knights-fees, Thierry de Say, a cousin or younger brother of the lord of Clun, somewhere about 1150. This branch of the Says died out early in the thirteenth century, and the Lacys came back into possession. When (as we have seen while dealing with Ludlow) the Lacy lands were split up in 1240, Stoke, now regularly called Stokesay, after its 50 years' tenancy by the Says, fell into the portion of Margaret, the younger Lacy co-heiress, wife of John de Verdun of Ewyas. Margaret and John alienated Stoke, which, in 1281, passed by sale to John de Ludlow, one of an official family of Shropshire, who had been sheriffs and castellans under Henry III. Laurence de Ludlow, son of the purchaser, got from Edward I., in 1290, a "licence to crenellate," and made Stokesay from a manor into a castle. This meant that the already existing residential buildings of Stokesay were surrounded with a moat and curtain wall, and strengthened by the building of a very fine and lofty tower, which would serve as a final place of defence if the outer *enceinte* should be pierced. Laurence also added a second and smaller tower, at the opposite end of the west front of the square of buildings enclosed by the moat and wall.

The present general aspect of Stokesay is prevented from recalling the conditions of 1290 by the fact that the *enceinte* wall is almost entirely gone, as is the original gate, and the moat is mostly dried up, while the interior buildings have survived—exactly the opposite to that of the very similar castle of Farleigh Hungerford, where the *enceinte* and gate have survived almost intact, but the buildings within have mostly perished.

The outstanding features of Stokesay are its two towers, the great hall which lies between them, and the picturesque black and white Elizabethan gate-house, which has superseded the original thirteenth century entry. The great tower is a double octagon, with narrow windows toward the outside, and large battlements, one of which, in a corner, is fitted with a small look-out turret. It stands above the pool from which the now waterless moat used to be supplied, very dominant and picturesque. Connected with it by a passage are the buildings of the hall—obviously a civil and not a military structure, and therefore looking somewhat inappropriate in the outer front of a castle. This is thirteenth century work, but evidently existed before the towers of 1291 were built, and must have been the work of Laurence de Ludlow's predecessors. It is lofty, lighted by three large mullioned windows, and furnished at both ends with large chambers, which must have been solars or withdrawing rooms. They are neither on a level with the hall, nor (as in some castles) above it, but are approached by wooden staircases of some height. One of them, on the side leading to the tower, has been decorated in Jacobean times with good panelling, and a handsome overmantel with grotesques and armorial bearings.

Stokesay was built too late to share in any of the historical events of the old Welsh wars : its only touch with military events was during the great Civil Wars of Charles I. and the Parliament. By this time it had changed owners—the Ludlows, its founders, died out in the male line in the reign of Henry VIII., and a daughter of the last of them took the castle to Thomas Vernon, who was dwelling there when Leland passed by in 1540. But the Vernons died out in 1607, and Stokesay passed by sale through several hands, till it came into those of the Lords Craven, who let it to a family named Baldwin. These last were in occupation when the Civil War turned them out of house and home—the Royalists made it a garrison, which was besieged and taken by the Shropshire Roundheads in 1645. This provoked the governor of Ludlow and the Herefordshire Cavaliers to make a desperate attempt to recover it, but their leaguer was beaten up by a hostile force from Shrewsbury, and a pitched battle on a small scale took place before the castle. It ended in a complete rout of the Royalists, who lost their two guns, 300 prisoners, and 100 slain, among whom was Sir William Croft, " the best head-piece and activest man in Herefordshire."

In 1647 the Parliament ordered Stokesay to be " slighted," but the damage done was, fortunately, no more than the blowing down of the walled *enceinte*, and the Baldwins were able to return to a still perfectly habitable abode. The last of them died in 1706, after which Stokesay ceased to be a gentleman's house, and was handed over to farmers, who lived in a corner of it, and turned the hall into a cart shed, the great chambers into granaries, and the basement of the tower into a smithy. But on the whole, this beautiful place escaped fairly well from the vandals of the eighteenth century, and is now well kept and maintained as an " ancient monument."

Acton Burnell

This interesting place is very much of the same date as Stokesay, and has a history parallel to that of the other thirteenth century addition to the list of Shropshire castles, for it was also an early manor converted into a military building under a " licence for crenellation " given by Edward I. Unlike Stokesay, however, but like Rotherfield Greys in Oxfordshire, it owes its

STOKESAY CASTLE: EXTERIOR OF NORTHERN TOWER

ACTON BURNELL : THE GREAT HALL

ACTON BURNELL : S.W. ANGLE

BRONCROFT CASTLE

origin to a wealthy and ambitious ecclesiastic. Robert Burnell, Bishop of Bath and Wells (1275-92) was long Chancellor to King Edward I. : he was a great builder, as his magnificent reconstruction of the castle-palace of his See has already shown us. And he was also a great acquirer of land, not (as some bishops had been) in order that he might become the founder of an abbey or a college, but for the purpose of endowing his own family. Chances of un-expected deaths had made him, though a cleric, the head of his own rather obscure knightly house, which had been for several generations seated at Acton Burnell, six miles south of Shrewsbury. If he could not be the father of a baronial line himself, he intended that his younger brother, Sir Hugh, should be, and after Sir Hugh, his nephew Philip. It was for this object that he gradually bought up twenty-one manors in Shropshire, and more across its boundary, and started his nephew as a much-landed man and the owner of a comely castle. He got " licence to crenellate " his existing manor house in 1283, and received King Edward I. there in state during that same year, when the celebrated " Parliament of Acton Burnell " was held in its hall, and passed the *Statutum de Mercatoribus*. It seems clear, however, from the dates that the parliament cannot have sat in the existing hall, which could not have been built in a single year, and it probably assembled in the older hall of the unfortified manor, which may be represented by two ruined gables standing in the park, at some little distance from the bishop's own buildings. As these gables indicate a chamber 150 feet long, there would have been ample room in it for a large muster of peers, knights of the shire, and burgesses. But the date of the gables is rather uncertain.

The bishop's " crenellated " fortress consisted of a great gate-house, shielding many other buildings, of which by far the most important is a long and magnificent hall, with good " Decorated " windows ; some of their transoms are still surviving. The castle shows a military character only by its large and strong battlements, and the small but stout square towers at its angles. Being quite in the flat, it was protected by a ditch only : if there was ever a good *enceinte* wall, as in Burnell's other moated building at Wells, it is completely gone. The whole is red sandstone, pleasing to the eye, but very fragmentary at the back, where there are traces of almost vanished annexes running out toward the park. The gate-house and the hall are the only parts of which the main walls are still standing almost intact.

Robert Burnell's attempt to start a baronial family was not over successful. It is true that his nephew Philip was called to Parliament as a peer, but he was a notorious waster, and dilapidated the great estates which his uncle had left him. Moreover, he left no male issue, so that his sister's son, Nicholas Handlo, in-herited the castle and what was left of the lands. But the second Handlo owner, Hugh (*obiit* 1420), left only grand-daughters, among whom the estates were divided ; and the peerage flickered out into abeyance.

It would seem that the castle of Acton Burnell was alienated by the co-heiresses, as Leland says that it was in the second half of the fifteenth century held by the much-estated Lovells—and this is quite likely, as the Lovells had a

Burnell descent by females.   After the attainder of the last of them in 1487, Acton got into the hands of the Dudleys.   It was apparently habitable in 1540, as Leland does not speak of it as ruinous or decaying : but it was probably " slighted " (like Stokesay) by the Parliamentarians in 1646.

Broncroft

This little red castle, under Wenlock Edge, in the long valley of Corvedale, is not a ruin like Acton Burnell or Clun, but has suffered the other lot to which mediæval strongholds are subject, that of frequent reconstruction.   It is now a modern residence, but as one half of its original front remains, with the most

Broncroft

prominent buildings of the old house intact, and the new section only juxtaposed, it may (like Upton in Pembrokeshire, an exactly similar case) be admitted into our list of castles worth visiting.   It lies well within the English border, and is not one of the earlier line of strongholds reared to keep out Welsh raids, but is, like Stokesay and Acton Burnell, an Edwardian castle, built by a family desirous of asserting its right to stand high among its neighbours.   The manor was held under the lords of Corfham by Tyrrells throughout the thirteenth century, and well into the fourteenth.   But they parted with it late in the time of Edward III. or early in that of Richard II. to the Burleys.   Sir Simon Burley, the well-known companion of the Black Prince, and the tutor of his son, the young Richard, was a great getter of lands, and (like Bishop Burnell at Acton) had only a nephew to be his heir.   He appears to have settled Broncroft on this nephew, Sir Roger Burley, before his death, for when he was judicially murdered by the Lords Appellant, in 1388, and his estates forfeited, Roger was not disturbed, and his son and grandson were sheriffs of Shropshire under the early Lancastrians.   They ultimately had all Simon's estates regranted to them.

The first Burley owner was probably the man who built the castle, in the days of his kinsman's great prosperity under Richard II. He designed a small square castle, with a great battlemented tower at its south-eastern angle, a somewhat smaller one at its south-western, and a hall between them. All these survive, but the other buildings and offices on the west and north sides of the square have disappeared, or are buried under the modern house. The hall has a good fireplace of fourteenth to fifteenth century style, and two rooms above it, with Tudor dormer windows.

The Burleys endured till 1470, when their heiress, Joan, took the castle to her husband, Sir Thomas Littleton, a lawyer of fame, the author of the Treatise on Tenures, better known by its commentary "Coke upon Littleton." By Leland's day Broncroft had passed to the Talbots, Earls of Shrewsbury, but they cannot have held it long, as by the time of Elizabeth it was owned by a family named Lutley, who kept it till about 1805. In the time of the third and fourth Lutley owners, both ardent royalists of the great Civil War period, Broncroft went through many troubles. It was garrisoned for the king in 1642-44, but in 1645, when the royalists had taken up the policy of abandoning small garrisons, they evacuated Broncroft after "slighting" its wall—presumably by blowing in part of the curtain or destroying the gate-house. The Parliamentarians then inspected it, and judging it still tenable, threw in a garrison under " the Lord Calvin," *i.e.*, Lord Colvill of Culross, a Scottish peer then serving with the Shrewsbury local forces. By him it was repaired, and held against the royalists of Ludlow, till the war flickered out in the following year, by the surrender of all the king's strongholds in the Marches.

Broncroft must have been left in a somewhat battered condition, but was not "slighted," and remained inhabited by the Lutleys, who restored the ruined parts in the time of Charles II. This reconstruction and a second and more drastic one by an owner named Johnstone (*circ.* 1840-50) left the place in its present condition—one-half almost undisturbed Richard II. architecture—the other showing a front of obvious Victorian type.

It is curious that no traces seem to survive of an outer ditch, which one would have supposed that a castle of 1380 would have been certain to possess. But Broncroft does not display one, even on its most exposed side. In the garden are the remains of a circular dovecote of red sandstone.

HEREFORDSHIRE

The County of Hereford was, from the twelfth to the fifteenth century, as well provided with castles as Shropshire, and is at present even more disappointing to the visitor of archæological tastes, unless he be one of those who care more for primitive *mottes* and ditches than for the stately military architecture of the later Middle Ages. For here, even more than in Shropshire, the destroyer has been abroad ; and the remains of castles which we know to have been as interesting for their structure as for their history, are scanty and fragmentary. Some of the most famous of them have absolutely disappeared—

for example, the Castle of Hereford itself, which Leland saw, in 1540, " with as great a circuit as Windsor," high and strong, with two wards each with a wet ditch, " a great thing but it tendith toward ruin." The fact that the Royalists in 1642 furbished it up with bulwarks and platforms for batteries, sealed its fate when their enemies conquered ; and it was " slighted " with more completeness than any of its neighbours. A rectangular embankment and a corner of the moat are all that the visitor can detect in a public garden. Hereford Castle has shared the fate of the equally noble strongholds of Bristol and Gloucester.

There is nothing left in the shire that can vie with Harlech or Raglan, Pembroke or Caerphilly—everywhere we see green mounds and half-obliterated ditches ; we think ourselves fortunate when we can detect a fair scrap of masonry. There is only one fine second-class castle surviving in Herefordshire, Goodrich, one of the original homes of the family of Talbot. Wigmore, the first seat of the Mortimers, from which they went out to conquer Radnor and Builth, is certainly to be remembered for its eventful annals, but presents to-day little that suggests that it was once as important as Chepstow or Ludlow. The first Mortimer pitched his castle on a narrow ridge with a steep fall on either side, and with a deep depression at one point in it, which cut off the chosen site from the higher ground beyond its western side. He piled up a thirty-foot *motte* and palisaded the contour east of it, an oval area of 100 feet by 50 or thereabouts. Some early successor turned the palisade into a stone *enceinte*, built a keep on the *motte*, and so produced an inner ward : later on an outer ward was added on the lower slopes to south and east ; but the inner ward formed part of the outer defences to north and west, where the slope was too steep to allow of additional building down hill. So much can be made out ; but Wigmore is a heap of ruins, showing original Norman work much built over with thirteenth century " Early Decorated." There is barely one portal arch, and a few windows, the stumps of a tower or two, and here and there a fragment of curtain, in evidence. The general impression produced is that the later Mortimers, the partisan of Henry III., and his grandson, the murderer of Edward II., completely rebuilt the whole Norman castle.

But fragmentary as is Wigmore, it shows far more masonry surviving than most of the Herefordshire castles. As we have already done for Shropshire, we may produce Leland's list of castles in the county, and write opposite each its hapless condition to-day. Goodrich is the only stronghold which deserves careful investigation. We omit from the list many of Leland's castles which are not really situated in Herefordshire at all, some owing to changes in boundary, others to misinformation on the great itinerist's part.

BRADWARDINE. Of masonry only a few fragments of foundations remain.
CLIFFORD. The base of a round tower and a few fragmentary walls.
DORSTONE. A mound only, of some 30 feet high.
EWYAS HAROLD [MAPHARALD]. Only a lofty conical mound remains : no masonry.
HEREFORD. Only a platform and a piece of ditch left.
KILPECK. Little remains but earthworks.

GOODRICH CASTLE: CORNER TOWER

GOODRICH CASTLE: THE KEEP

LYONSHALL.   A few vestiges of masonry, belonging to a circular keep.
LONGTOWN [EWYAS LACY].   A mound, with remains of a cylindrical keep.
SNODHILL.   Only earthworks and a fragment of keep remain.
WEOBLY.   Extensive earthworks in a public park.
WILTON.   Destroyed by fire and is now a ruin.
WIGMORE.   As described above : fragmentary.

Goodrich

This castle alone, in the whole shire, has remained fairly perfect, and shows some fine towers and walls.   It lies on the Wye, between Ross and Monmouth, in the second rather than the first line against Wales, since it was covered by an advanced line the moment that the invader had taken possession of Monmouth, and the " Three Castles " to the north of it.   It appears to have been built by the de Clares of the Pembroke branch, early in the twelfth century, and to have followed the lot of the other great castle which they owned in this region—Chepstow—passing to the Marshalls.   But on the division of the Marshall estates among co-heiresses, in 1240, Goodrich went to the daughter who had married de Valence, not (like Chepstow) to the daughter who had married Bigod, Earl of Norfolk.

The buildings visible show Norman origins, and lavish thirteenth century improvements and alterations.   Presumably the first were the work of the de Clares, and the last—that of the Marshalls.   The castle is placed on a bold bluff overhanging the Wye, whose steep banks make two sides of it precipitous and inaccessible.   It is a magnificent and impressive building when seen close—less so when looked at from a distance, because the down-slope of the bluff, on which it stands, hides many buildings from a spectator who approaches by the only feasible road.   It is mostly red-sandstone, only the keep in the inner ward being grey.   The castle is rectangular, with an inner and an outer ward.   The main entrance has outside it, and protecting its gate, which lies in its east front, a quite exceptionally deep ditch cut in the rock, only passable by means of a drawbridge. Behind this the gate-house shows two drum-towers and between them a double set of portcullises, with machicolations above them in the upper story.

The keep, the oldest part of the castle, and going back to the days of Henry I., is a good example of a square Norman tower of the earlier type.   It stands out in the courtyard, and is not built into one of its walls, as keeps generally are.   It is not of the monstrous size of Colchester, or the Tower of London, but is still a large and impressive building.   It was three-storied—the original entrance (as in the Tower of London) was not in the basement, but on the first floor, and to be reached only by wooden steps.   But some fourteenth century owner has opened a new door in the basement, and turned the old one into a double-lobed window.

On the east of the court is the chapel, with a basement below and a small third floor above.   The interior looks like fourteenth century work, with fifteenth century windows inserted : there are angels bearing shields as interior decoration. A staircase in the wall shows that there must have been a rood screen—not a common thing in castle chapels, which are usually too small to allow of such a structure. On the west side of the court is the great hall—60 feet by 30—with the kitchen in a corner hard by, and the two arches of the buttery hatch still perfect. The hall has windows of a good size, looking like late thirteenth century work—presumably of the time of the Valence earls.

A notable feature in the external defences of Goodrich is the finishing off of the corner towers with " spurs," projecting triangular buttresses applied to the foot of the wall and splaying out from it, so as to give extra strength to the most exposed angle. This can also be seen in the south-east corner tower of Chepstow.

After the extinction of the house of Valence, Goodrich came in the fourteenth century into the possession of the Talbots, then still more of a Herefordshire than a Shropshire family—best known as lords of Archenfield, and not yet destined for many a year to get the title of Earls of Shrewsbury. It was in their hands in Leland's day, but unfortunately he did not visit or describe it, so that we have no record of its condition in 1540. Probably it was pretty good, as Goodrich was held as a royal garrison throughout the Civil Wars of 1642-46, and was maintained by Sir Henry Lingen till all the other castles of Herefordshire had fallen. He only yielded to compulsion, when the Parliamentarians had brought up cannon, and thoroughly well breached his south wall. There is a large pile of seventeenth century shot in the office now attached to the castle, and with it a few specimens of large stone balls, which look like the missiles used for thirteenth century *trébuchets* or mangonels. As we have no knowledge of any mediæval siege of the place, these may be relics from the mediæval magazine, and not projectiles thrown by an enemy.

Goodrich Castle. S.W. Tower with Spur

SOUTH-EASTERN MARCHES

MONMOUTHSHIRE AND BRECKNOCK

AS we saw, in our general survey of the military history of the Conquest of Wales, the first assault of the Anglo-Norman adventurers on the faction-ridden princes of the Celtic states started in the south, with William Fitz Osbern's advance into the lands of the Wye and the Usk, where he built the first line of "*motte* and bailey" castles on land which the Saxons had left untouched, or at least unoccupied. The great scheme for the conquest of the whole of North and Central Wales, which was framed by the Earls of Shrewsbury and Chester, came a little later. So did the separate adventure of Bernard of Neufmarché and his fellows, the smaller lords of the Middle Marches, for the conquest of the lands which now form the shires of Brecknock and Radnor. So also did the quite distinct enterprise of Robert Fitz Hamon in Glamorganshire, which was not (as might have been expected) a mere continuation of the original forward movement of Fitz Osbern across the Wye, but an independent raid from the side of the sea starting from another and a different base.

When the advance of the Norman lords of the southern marches began, South-eastern Wales was divided into two small principalities, Gwent and Morganwg—roughly, but not exactly, represented by the modern counties of Monmouth and Glamorgan. North of them beyond the highlands of the Brecon Beacons and the Black Mount was Brecheiniog (Brecknock), a land belonging to the larger South-Welsh Kingdom of Deheubarth, but owing a very precarious allegiance to its suzerain. Gwent and Morganwg were twin states, ruled by branches of the same princely house, but seldom united. Each consisted of a fairly broad and fertile coast land, with wild hills behind. The shore and the inland were absolutely different, the former most desirable for the invader, the latter poor and difficult of access. The history of the two states before the coming of the Normans had been mainly the story of a struggle to keep off at all costs annexation by the larger and more powerful Kingdom of South Wales [Deheubarth] which lay behind them : local and dynastic antipathies are the key to all early Welsh annals. The salvation of the two minor states had been their rough inland—the ravines and gorges of what is now the great South-Welsh coalfield but was then one series of fastnesses—from Aberavon in the west, to Pontypool in Gwent in the east. This was a most inaccessible region, and one not attractive to invaders— the names of Rhondda and Rhymney, of Merthyr Tydvil and Ebbw Vale, only suggested, in the eleventh century, passes susceptible of defence against a multitude, and upland valleys the home of impoverished mountain chieftains. Nothing can show a greater contrast than that between Upper and Lower Gwent, that is, between Gwent above and below its central forest, or than that between the coast plain of Morganwg and the southern slopes of the bleak Brecon Beacons.

William Fitz Osbern, the great Earl of Hereford, the first invader of Welsh land, worked by castle-building on the largest scale; his scheme was to throw out line after line of fortresses upon his border: the base line to protect the settled land which had always been English, then advance lines carrying the border forward into new and hostile territory. To his short four years of rule on the border (1067-71) must be attributed the building of castles at Wigmore, Clifford-on-Wye, Richard's Castle, and Ewyas, which were inside the old frontier, but also at Chepstow and Monmouth, which were on the other side of the Wye and on Welsh soil. These two served as bridge-heads for the conquest of the whole eastern part of the principality of Gwent, and Domesday Book shows it as settled and organized land. The head place of the invaders was undoubtedly Chepstow, a narrow dominating triangular rock, placed between the high cliff over the Wye and a ravine running down to the river. No doubt it was merely palisaded, and Wigmore, Clifford, Ewyas Harold, and all the earlier castles, were mere " *motte* and bailey " structures also.

Fitz Osbern was slain in 1071, when absent abroad on a foreign campaign, and his son Roger (who instead of devoting himself to Welsh conquest, joined in the celebrated " Conspiracy of the Earls " in 1075) was disgraced and imprisoned for life. William the Conqueror made no new earl in his place, and the attack on South Wales was for the present carried on by minor families—Mortimers, Toesnis, Lacys, Fitz-Baderuns and Says, the lords of Cleobury, Clifford, Ludlow, Monmouth and Clun. There were three separate lines of attack by which three different groups of Norman adventurers fell upon Brecheiniog, Gwent and Morganwg. Somewhere about 1088, the barons of Herefordshire, led by Bernard of Neufmarché, Ralph Mortimer, and Philip de Braose, began to encroach upon the lands which form the modern shires of Brecknock and Radnor. The details of the struggle are lost, but it terminated with the death in battle of Rhys ap Tudor, the last generally acknowledged King of Debeubarth, near Brecon, in 1093. This was the actual deed of Bernard of Neufmarché, who therefore assumed the lordship of Brecon, stockaded a great castle there, and established knightly vassals at Crickhowell, Talgarth, Tretower and other places. They all built castles of the simple " *motte* and bailey " type. The lordship of Brecon only remained for one generation with the family of the original conqueror: his daughter Sibylla married Milo of Gloucester, and when this pair again had no male issue, their heiress, Bertha of Gloucester, wedded William de Braose, whose father had conquered Radnor at the same time that Bernard of Neufmarché overran Brecknock. By the union of these two lordships the Braoses were for several generations the leading Marcher-power on the central border—a position which they in their turn—male heirs again failing—passed on to the Bohuns, Earls of Hereford, in 1230. The Braoses, had also in the twelfth century, got possession of the northern part of the old principality of Gwent, round

CHEPSTOW CASTLE : FROM THE RIVER

CHEPSTOW CASTLE: GATE-HOUSE OF UPPER WARD

Abergavenny, and later of the outlying peninsula of Gower on the south coast. But in 1230, when their main line died out, while one daughter took Brecon to the Earl of Hereford, another took Abergavenny and North Gwent to her husband William de Cantilupe, and a third Radnor to Roger de Mortimer, Lord of Cleobury.

GWENT

Chepstow

Chepstow, alias Striguil, was the earliest and the most important of the original bases from which the Normans conquered South Wales, the first foothold occupied beyond the old Anglo-Saxon border. It is a lofty but very narrow castle, occupying the whole backbone of a rocky spur which has the precipitous cliffs above the Wye on one side, and a deep and steep ravine on the other, separating it from the hill on which Chepstow town stands. It may be taken for granted that the original fortress of William Fitz Osbern was on the central summit of the spur, where the present Norman keep stands, and that the keep itself was built some fifty years later, either by Walter de Clare, to whom Henry I. gave the lordship of Striguil about 1119, or by his nephew and successor, Richard de Clare, Earl of Pembroke, the famous " Strongbow," the conqueror of Ireland. This keep no doubt replaced the original wooden " tower of strength," put up by Fitz Osbern. The present middle ward, sloping down from the keep toward the Wye, would represent the outer bailey of the first castle. There are traces of a deep-cut ditch between it and the much later outer ward: while on the other side of the keep, to the north, the present upper ward probably represents a second and smaller " bailey." It is separated from the platform of the spur northward by another very deep ditch. Presumably, then, the keep with a bailey on each side of it, was the castle as it existed when Walter de Clare dwelt there in the days of Henry I. Walter lived long, died in 1138, and passed Striguil on to his nephew " Strongbow," who held it till his death in 1176. The Conqueror of Ireland, as everyone knows, died not long after his installation as Lord of Leinster, leaving only one daughter, Isabel, by his wife Eva, the heiress of Dermot Macmorrough. The child was but three years of age, and it was not till thirteen years after that Richard I. gave her hand to William the Marshall, one of his companions of the Crusade, who assumed in her right the title of Pembroke, and became lord of Striguil, as well as of Pembroke and Strongbow's Irish lands. The Marshall, the victor of Lincoln, and the saviour of the crown of the infant Henry III., dwelt much at Chepstow, and undoubtedly he or his sons stand responsible for the enormous extension of the castle downhill, toward the river, and uphill, along the top of the spur, beyond the small original northern bailey. Downhill the extension consisted of the present lower ward, running quite close to the bank of the Wye, and presenting a tremendous front of defence, the heavy gate-house, with its two drum-towers, and the portcullis chamber between them. This sufficiently formidable work was strengthened later, by the

153

throwing out of a round corner tower, with a " spur " at the exposed south-east angle of the ward.

At the other, or upper, end of the castle, the thirteenth century builder— one cannot be sure which of the Marshall earls it was—fortified the original smaller bailey with good walls, so as to make it an integral part of the fortress, and threw across its outer ditch a "fore-building" or barbican, only to be reached by a drawbridge. This was the castle's back door into the open country; it was no mere trifle, with a strong and lofty gate-house of its own.

Such large additions having been made to the fortress, it was possible to alter its internal arrangements. The keep, which must originally have contained most of the living-rooms, was turned into a single great dining-hall, with a " solar " or retiring room for the lord and his family at its upper end. The boundary between this chamber and the main hall devoted to the retainers, is obviously indicated by a decorative arch four-fifths of the way up the hall. Meanwhile the new lower ward was given spacious living-rooms and dormitories, of good thirteenth century architecture, with a kitchen suite on its river side, and a large square tower, containing a chapel and many good chambers, on its inland side.

On the death of Earl Ambrose, last of his line, in 1245, the vast Marshall possessions in England, Wales and Ireland, were divided among his four sisters. Maud, the eldest, got Striguil and its " Honour of Nether Gwent " as her portion, and also took the dignity of the Marshalship of England to her husband, Hugh Bigod, Earl of Norfolk. Severed from all the other Marshall lands, and united to those of a great earl whose main interests lay in East Anglia, Striguil ceased to be the centre of a principality, and became only an outlying possession of the Bigods. A couple of centuries were to pass before it became again the chief residence of its master.

From the Bigods Chepstow passed to Thomas of Brotherton, the younger son of Edward I., whose heiress took it to the Mowbray dukes of Norfolk. In 1468, Duke John, last of that line, feeling, as it would seem, no great interest in the place, disposed of it by a great exchange of lands to William Herbert, first Earl of Pembroke of that name, the favourite of Edward IV., who was busy in accumulating South Welsh estates on every hand. Earl William perished for the House of York—beheaded by the rebel " Robin of Redesdale," after Edgecot Field. His son and successor left an only daughter, Elizabeth Herbert, who was married by Henry VII. to his only male kinsman on the mother's side, Charles Beaufort, alias Charles Somerset, the one Beaufort who came alive through the Wars of the Roses. Charles was illegitimate—the son of that Duke Henry who perished after Hexham Field. But his cousin, the king, made much of him, and gave him the hand of this great Yorkist heiress. He repaid these bounties by much good service, as soldier, admiral and diplomatist. Henry would have liked to have given him the title of Earl of Pembroke, but this had to be returned to its old Lancastrian owner, Jasper Tudor. So he was given, instead, some years after, the title of Earl of Worcester, with which

CHEPSTOW CASTLE: MARTIN'S TOWER

CALDICOT CASTLE : AERIAL VIEW

Striguil (and Raglan also) have been ever since connected, though it is now swallowed up in the dukedom of Beaufort.

The Beaufort-Herbert line seem to have dwelt indifferently at Chepstow and at Raglan, in their earlier days, and the founder of the family, Earl Charles, is buried in Chepstow Church. It is probable that the modernized parts of the castle, especially the handsome Tudor-windowed chambers which are imposed upon thirteenth century walls in the lower ward, are of their construction. But Chepstow, despite of modern improvements, could not compare with the spacious and sumptuous Raglan, and the family tended more and more to reside in that magnificent building—where the great Earl of Worcester, *temp*. Charles I., held his almost regal court.

But Chepstow becomes prominent in history once more during the Civil Wars of King and Parliament. It was of high strategic value as covering the little port from which, despite of Parliamentary garrisons in Gloucester and Bristol, Charles I. kept up his communications between Oxford and South Wales. As long, indeed, as Bristol was held for the Parliament, it was the only way in which this touch could be maintained. This was the reason why Sir William Waller made a successful dash at it in 1643, hoping to cut the line completely. But Waller's success was transitory, and only a few months later Prince Rupert stormed Bristol, and opened the communications again. From July, 1643, to the end of 1645, Chepstow was a most important base, by which royalist supplies and troops passed freely by water to the east. After the fatal Battle of Naseby, Fairfax ordered Colonel Morgan, governor of Gloucester, to reduce Chepstow at all costs. This led to its first siege under modern conditions. Morgan brought up heavy guns and mortars, and battered the lower ward with success. A great breach was made in its curtain, whereupon the Governor, an Irish Colonel Fitzmorris, surrendered without standing a storm.

But Chepstow was to see a second siege in that "flash in the pan" called the Second Civil War, of 1648. South Wales was one of the main centres of revolt against the Parliament, and an

Chepstow Church. Tomb of the first Earl of Worcester

155

enterprising royalist gentleman, owner of the neighbouring estate of Caldicot, Sir Nicholas Kemmis, seized the place by surprise, and held it against Cromwell, when the latter swooped down to suppress the insurrection (May 11). Oliver had come in haste, without artillery, and was more anxious to beat the enemy in the open field than to take isolated castles. Accordingly he handed over the siege to Colonel Ewer, and marched on into the west. The last siege of Chepstow lasted a fortnight only : having got heavy guns from Gloucester, Ewer breached the south-western side of the lower ward, apparently the same point where Morgan had broken in three years before. Kemmis, after a vain attempt to abscond by boats on the Wye, began to treat for terms. But he haggled too long, and Ewer, knowing that such a proposal meant that the governor was despairing of further power to resist, would grant nothing but unconditional surrender. He broke off the negotiations, and ordered a storm. When the assailants reached the breach, the greater part of the rank and file of the garrison flung down their arms ; but Kemmis threw himself in the way of the enemy and was slain (May 23).

Despite of the easy way in which Chepstow had been twice taken by the force of artillery, the Parliament did not " slight " it, like so many other castles, but repaired the breach, and kept it as a permanent garrison, and incidentally as a state prison. In that capacity it endured many years—Jeremy Taylor was shut up there by Cromwell, and Henry Martin, the regicide, by Charles II. The latter was so long a prisoner in the rather comfortable apartments in the lower ward, that his name has stuck till this day to " Martin's Tower."

Chepstow ceased to be a garrison in 1690—but its old owners, the Beauforts, had little use for it ; the place was simply neglected, and its buildings, which were still in good order, were let out as warehouses, workshops and meeting-rooms to townsmen of Chepstow. An eighteenth century *entrepreneur* turned one block into a glass-factory, and another into a smithy. As no proper repairs were ever made, dilapidation ensued. The roof of Martin's Tower fell in about 1803, and in the other chambers wind, weather and ivy roots, those destroyers of masonry, worked their united will till Victorian times. For the last fifty years the castle has been kept from further decay. Its whole outline remains intact ; one can still walk round the entire circuit of the ramparts, and Strongbow's keep, Martin's Tower, and the great gate-house are still externally strong. Though roofs and interiors are gone, Striguil can still be studied as an epitome of Marcher history and architecture.

Usk and Caldicot

The " Honour of Striguil " or the Lordship of Nether Gwent, to use its alternative name, as held by the de Clares, and the Marshalls, had two minor castles over and above the central strength of Chepstow. These were Caldicot and Usk. The former lies in the coast zone, in the absolute flat of the marshy " Caldicot Level," only two miles from the sea. Though much pulled about, and at present inhabited only in one section, it shows its history in its architecture.   It is in essence a " *motte* and bailey " castle of the time of Henry I., whose bailey-enclosure has been turned into a very large ward by the substitution of stone walls for the original palisading.   The primitive " house of defence " on the *motte* is now represented by a small circular stone keep in one corner of the large enclosure, which appears to be of late twelfth century work. A large square gate-house, projecting from between two square towers, has been inserted in the *enceinte*, in the fourteenth century.   Caldicot passed from the Marshalls to the Bohuns, and then by a female descent to the Stafford Dukes of Buckingham.   On the attainder of the last Duke in 1521, it fell to

Caldicot Castle.   Gate-House Front

the Crown, and was ultimately alienated.   The gate-house, modernized in the sixteenth century, when the craving for light and space had prevailed over that for military efficiency, contains some fine and large rooms with good carving. This was probably the work of the family of Kemmis, who tenanted the house in Stuart times, and were prominent royalist partisans in the great Civil War.

The other castle of Nether Gwent was Usk, on the river of the same name, some twelve miles from the sea, at the point where the plain has ended, and the foot-hills of the interior have begun to rise.   It is a shell-keep on a precipitous shoulder of the eminence which rises above the little market town below. The east curtain is fairly straight, but for the rest of its circumference the walls follow the rounded contour of the hill-top.   The *enceinte* is strengthened by one round and one square tower in its north-eastern and north-western sections, and by a third and larger round tower on its southern front.   There are traces of a hall with a large fireplace on the west wall.   Outside the straight eastern curtain, on a lower level of ground, the remains of an outer ward or bailey are visible, separated by a ditch from the main building.   The gate was on the

157

Usk. Interior of the Keep

north side between the north-east and north-west towers. The whole castle is in such bad order, so much overgrown with trees and ivy, that it is hard to get any general view, or to draw certain conclusions.

Usk was one of the Marshall castles which Henry III. beleaguered in vain during the rebellion of Earl Richard in 1233, before his final defeat at Grosmont. At the general breaking up of the Marshall inheritance in 1245, it fell to Isabel, one of the younger sisters of Earl Anselm, who took it to her husband, Gilbert de Clare, Earl of Gloucester. That its fortification was not quite up to date in 1265 is shown by the fact that Simon de Montfort took it after a very short siege, during his South-Welsh campaign before Evesham. When the last de Clare earl fell at Bannockburn in 1314, Usk went to Elizabeth, one of his five sisters and co-heiresses. She married a minor Marcher baron, Theobald de Verdun, Lord of Ewyas, but brought him daughters only, so that in the next generation Usk and Ewyas were divided up into small fractions. The castle seems to have been neglected, and not used as a residence, from this time onward: there is no late Plantagenet building visible in it. It was, however, still strong enough to serve for defence in the days of Owen Glendower. When that restless rebel was besieging it in 1405, Henry, Prince of Wales, the future victor of Agincourt, won his first military success by relieving the place and routing the Welsh—slaying Owen's brother Tudor, and taking his son Griffith prisoner. After this we hear little of it, and it seems to have been " slighted " by the Parliamentarians in 1646.

Monmouth and Over Gwent

If Nether Gwent is reasonably flat, Over Gwent (the northern half of the modern County of Monmouth) is quite the reverse. Its eastern half is formed by the picturesque valleys of the Monnow and Usk, and is a pleasant dappled country of hill and dale, not destitute of good agricultural land. But the western half, to the left-hand from Pontypool and Abergavenny, is a region of ravines and gorges. Hence a complete difference in their history—the east half of Over Gwent was part of the original conquest of William Fitz Osbern, one of whose most important castles—Monmouth—was placed on the Welsh side of the Wye, at its junction with the Monnow. But the western half remained unconquered till the thirteenth century, and was the haunt of the dispossessed princely families who had once held the plain below. Whenever there was trouble in Wales, the men of North-west Gwent were always prominent movers of mischief, raiding southward toward Caerleon and Newport, or eastward toward Abergavenny and Monmouth.

The section of Over Gwent occupied by the early invaders falls into two parts. To the east was the "Honour of Monmouth," a lordship which in the twelfth and early thirteenth centuries belonged to the house of William Fitz-Baderun, a companion of Fitz Osbern. This family was prominent in the Marcher history for some 170 years: they changed their name to "de Monmouth" in the twelfth century, and ended with a John de Monmouth, who was a strong Montfortian partisan in the Barons' War. After Evesham his lands were confiscated, and in 1267 Henry III. granted them to his younger son, Edmund "Crouchback," Earl of Lancaster. They, therefore, became part of the immense Lancaster inheritance, and passed ultimately to John of Gaunt and his son Henry IV. The chance that Henry V. was born in Monmouth, in one of his grandfather's innumerable castles, has probably done more to keep the place in memory than any of the stirring historical events which there took place.

Monmouth Castle is a sad disappointment to the archæologist. It now consists of a large residential house of the style of Charles II., a number of shabby buildings connected with the depôt of the South Wales Borderers' Regiment, and one poor remnant of the old castle. Facing the modern mansion, on one corner of the little plateau, which was occupied by the stronghold of the Fitz-Baderuns, are a number of angular fragments of red sandstone buildings, obviously ranging over several centuries in style. There is one imperfect tower in the west angle, but the whole is a mere wreck. And indeed the only interesting thing in Monmouth is not the castle but the fortified bridge over the Monnow, perhaps the best specimen of a road-blocking bridge tower in the whole realm. The castle owed its present state (like so many Welsh castles) to a "slighting" by the Parliamentarians in 1646. It had earned distinction by holding out for some days against the "New Model" army, after the town below had been stormed (Oct. 24, 1645).

The "Three Castles"—
Skenfrith, Grosmont, Whitecastle

Monmouth was, so to speak, in the second line of defence of the long front of Marcher castles, as it was completely covered to the west by three strongholds which always occur together in military history, and are often called in documents simply "the Three Castles," as they were marked together as a unit. Skenfrith and Grosmont are on the Upper Monnow, six and ten miles respectively from Monmouth; Whitecastle is on the hills above them, covering the important mountain pass and road from Monmouth to Abergavenny. All three served together as a guard against the unruly Welsh who, driven from the plains, had taken refuge in the network of ravines and gorges which is now covered and blackened by the coal mines of Tredegar and Ebbw Vale, and Rhymney. Though surrounded on all sides by Marcher holdings, in Brecon, in Glamorgan, and in Eastern Gwent, they were still untamed, joined in both the risings against Edward I., and more than a century later in the formidable rebellion of Glendower.

The origin of the " Three Castles " is rather obscure. Presumably they were built as " *motte* and bailey " strongholds by companions of William Fitz Osbern. A certain Hamelin was lord in these parts by 1106, and was followed by Brian Fitz-Count, a natural son of Alan of Brittany, a very strong supporter of Queen Maud in the Civil Wars of Stephen's day. Brian's two sons were lepers, and Henry II., rejecting the claims of the Braoses as next of kin, to succeed to all their possessions, seized on the administration of the three castles. In his day they appear as royal fortresses in the charge of the Sheriff of Hereford. But John gave them away to Hubert de Burgh, for good services rendered, and the great justiciar held them for many years. When Hubert fell from power, undermined by Peter des Roches and the Poitevins, in 1232, the castles were again confiscated, and remained crown property till Henry III. gave them—as he did the neighbouring Honour of Monmouth—to his son Edmund of Lancaster. They followed henceforth the fortunes of that house—Henry of Lancaster the first duke, and father-in-law of John of Gaunt, was born at Grosmont, and was always known as " Henry of Grosmont."

The three castles differ from each other in situation and character. Skenfrith, the smallest of the three, and the one which was least pulled about by its later owners, lies low, at a point where a lateral depression opens out into the main valley of the Monnow. The builder did not take advantage of any one of several neighbouring knolls, but chose a site in the trough of the valley, where he could use a stream to give himself the protection of a wet ditch. The little castle is a perfectly quadrangular enclosure, with four drum-towers at its corners and one more set in its south side. It has a large circular keep, standing isolated on a very low *motte* in the centre of the court. All the inner buildings, which must have existed, are gone, save this keep, which still dominates the whole valley—it is some 40 feet high, and must once have been higher. The castle is much neglected : it is overgrown with ivy and trees, and the interior of the keep serves as a refuge for cows, and was in a filthy state in 1924. On two sides the outer wall is still protected by the wet ditch formed by the running stream : on the other sides there is a dry ditch. Obviously this was a " *motte* and bailey " castle of the time of Henry I., which received a stone keep and a stone *enceinte* for its single ward some time in the reign of Henry II. Probably the drum-towers may have been inserted by Hubert de Burgh in the early thirteenth century, but since his time the castle seems to have been neglected. The Lancasters, its later owners, had far better and stronger castles in Monmouth

SKENFRITH CASTLE

GROSMONT CASTLE : THE GREAT CHIMNEY

WHITECASTLE : THE GATE-HOUSE

RAGLAN CASTLE : MAIN GATE-WAY

on one side and Grosmont on the other. By Tudor times it was described as " ruinous and decayed time out of mind."

Grosmont, four miles further north, and, like Skenfrith, placed close to the Monnow, differs in every detail from the smaller castle. It does not lie in the trough of the valley, but occupies the culminating point of a very steep hill, rising 200 feet above it. The descent to the bridge on its further side is absolutely precipitous, hardly suitable for wheeled traffic. The plateau on which Grosmont stands was once occupied by a small town with a very fine cruciform church, obviously the " *burgus* " which grew up under the shelter of an exceptionally strong castle. Local tradition maintains that it was once the third largest centre of population in South Wales, only Carmarthen and Abergavenny having surpassed it in size. But now it is a small and scattered village, a few houses on the summit and slopes of the level hill-top, and the whole parish does not contain more than 700 souls. The castle occupies the western part of the high lying plateau, of which the town must have covered the eastern and northern part. It is cut off from the rest of the place by a very deep and formidable ditch, which must have been crossed by a drawbridge. Its site seems to indicate that a very large, more or less quadrangular, earthwork, was its foundation—this may have been a Celtic stronghold before it became the bailey of a Norman castle. Outside of the ditch, to the east and south, there are traces of another bailey, probably added when the original outer enclosures became an integral part of the castle, and more accommodation for the residents was required. This supplementary work shows some traces of walls upon its earthen rampart, but they do not seem to have been strong or lofty.

The castle within the ditch is an irregular roughly polygonal structure standing on a quadrangular mound, of which the diameter is about 150 feet. There is a large square keep in the west side of the curtain, and a very fine and solid building, evidently a hall, in the north-east corner, some 80 feet long and furnished with a good fireplace. One prominent isolated chimney stands up against the sky from a room which may have been the " solar " or retiring room of the lord—it is octagonal and ends up in an elegant pierced lantern for the escape of the smoke. As all the neighbouring roof and wall has perished, this chimney catches the eye more than any other feature of the castle.

The gate of Grosmont—in its western curtain—is not of the ordinary type with the two drum-towers and the portcullis-room between them, but merely consists of two splaying-out rounded walls, and a recess with a pointed arch in the middle.

The whole castle, as it now stands, is obviously the work of Edmund of Lancaster and his immediate successors, who were holding the place from 1267 onward, and no doubt resided there habitually till the marriage of the Duchess Blanche to John of Gaunt drew her descendants to other and more eastern abodes. There is no clear indication of what the earlier twelfth century castle may have been, save that the great earthwork on which the present building stands hints at a large square palisaded enclosure with a keep somewhere within it. But all the present stonework is of a later date than 1267. What we know of the original history of the place has already been given under the name of Skenfrith—it was certainly in existence in the time of Henry I., formed part of the lordship of Brian Fitz-Count, was got somehow from his two leper sons by Henry II., and was given by John to Hubert de Burgh. Confiscated from the latter in 1232, it was for thirty years crown property, till Edmund of Lancaster received it as a gift from his father in 1267. Edmund's grandson, the hero of successful campaigns in Aquitaine under Edward III., was born there in 1299, and at his death it passed in 1345 to his heiress, the Duchess Blanche, and was absorbed in the vast holding of her husband, John of Gaunt.

Grosmont saw some stirring scenes beneath its walls. In November, 1233, Henry III., campaigning against the rebel Earl Richard Marshall, was surprised in his camp below the castle by Richard, and forced to abscond in haste. In March, 1405, the army which Owen Glendower had sent to conquer South Wales, and which had met its first check from Henry of Monmouth under the walls of Usk in May, was completely destroyed before Grosmont by the same prince, in October. Owen's chancellor, secretary and son-in-law were all taken prisoners. After this the rebels of the region threw up the game, and the royal archives of the following winter are full of pardons granted to gentry of Gwent and Glamorgan who had surrendered themselves.

White Castle, the third of the group, which passed from the Fitz-Counts to Hubert de Burgh, and from Hubert to the House of Lancaster, is not a residential castle, but had purely strategic ends, being set on the pass across the Skerrid Fawr Mountains from Abergavenny to Skenfrith and Ross. It lies very high, commanding the road, on the top of a well-marked hill. Unlike the sister castles below, it has no signs of a *motte* or keep, and would appear to have been a fortress consisting originally of a palisade and a very deep and wide ditch, and afterwards of a stone *enceinte* replacing the palisades. Its present aspect suggests a builder of the time of Henry III., but we know that the place was in existence a hundred years before his day, and can only suppose that it was thoroughly remodelled about 1230-1250. At present it is a sort of hexagon, with a drum-tower at each of its angles. But the shape is not regular, the north-eastern and north-western towers being so much nearer to each other than the rest, that they form the two sides of the entrance gate-house, the door being in the short piece of curtain between them, much recessed. This is by far the most striking point of the castle, though the other four towers are good pieces of work : they are lofty, at least 45 feet high. All of them seem to have contained chambers in several floors, but none of them contains a hall, solar or chapel. There must have been such buildings, so presumably they were reared against the inner side of the *enceinte* wall, with slight materials, and have vanished under stress of wind and weather. Stone-stealers, so frequent in every castle that was near a town, do not seem to have been at work here. The region is thinly peopled, and in consequence the thick external *enceinte* is still very nearly complete. One can only conclude that the garrison never had any very solid dwellings—the result, no doubt, of White Castle not having been a residential abode for its lords, but rather a fortress that had to be reinforced in time of war or raids, but was very slenderly held at other times.

White Castle has two outworks :—in front of the main gate was a large low base-court, with a separate ditch of its own, too big to be called a barbican, yet hardly self-sufficient enough to merit the name of an outer ward. Its entrance was carefully arranged so as not to face the gate-house of the castle, and any one approaching the latter was exposed to flanking fire before he got near it. This outwork was in stone; there was another, apparently of earth and palisades only, on the opposite side of the castle, that most remote from the gate-house, and only accessible by a small postern in the back of the curtain. As at Kidwelly, this back bailey or hornwork, or whatever we choose to call it, was evidently not considered of such importance as that which covered the front entrance, and would not have been capable of very long defence against a serious attack.

White Castle seems to have been on somewhat of a backwater, and is not mentioned nearly so frequently as Grosmont, nor, of course, Monmouth. But its capture is recorded when the Braoses rebelled against King John—they then took both it and Skenfrith—very probably by treachery from within, for their cause was popular—and the king's was not. There is no trace of any fourteenth century or fifteenth century additions or repairs in the whole building.

Raglan

Raglan differs from all the other castles of Gwent which we have been considering, in that it is of very late date, formed no part of the original Norman scheme for the holding down of a newly-conquered land, and owes its splendour entirely to the family pride of a noble house which only attained to importance in the fifteenth century. It covers no pass or ford, and dominates no valley, being situated in pleasant rolling ground, half-way between Monmouth and Usk.

It would seem that there was here, in the fourteenth century, a small defensible manor house belonging to a family named Morley. Its heiress took the estate to her husband, a Norman-Welsh knight, Sir Thomas ap Jenkin. Their son, Sir William ap Thomas, otherwise called Sir William Herbert, held the place *temp.* Henry V., and served in France with that king. His son was Sir William Herbert, first Earl of Pembroke of the new creation, of whom we have heard in connection with Chepstow. This hard-fighting favourite of Edward IV. worked himself up from small beginnings to the position of head of the Yorkist party in Wales, and profited on a large scale from his master's generosity. Though given confiscated Lancastrian estates all over the Principality, he retained a partiality for his ancestral home, and set to work to transform it to the most magnificent castle in the whole land. He had started rebuilding it on the largest scale, and made some progress, when he died at the hands of " Robin of Redesdale " in the rebellion of 1469, after his defeat at Edgecot

Field. King Edward naturally continued his liberality to the heir of such a faithful friend, more especially because the second earl had married his sister-in-law Mary Woodville, the sister of Queen Elizabeth—but oddly enough he made him change his style from Earl of Pembroke to Earl of Huntingdon—having conceived the idea that Pembroke was a royal title and should be given to his own son. William Herbert the third, now Earl of Huntingdon, lived well into the reign of Henry VII., but had no male heir. His daughter Elizabeth carried all his immense territorial possessions to her husband, Charles Beaufort, the illegitimate cousin of the first Tudor king—as has been already told under the story of Chepstow Castle. In 1513 Charles received the title of Earl, not of either Pembroke or Huntingdon, but of Worcester.

Both of the Herbert earls, and most of the Beauforts, had a hand in the building of Raglan, which started in 1465 or thereabouts, to be the last of the great military castles of England, but ended in being a splendid Tudor palace, with some remnants of its original design still clinging to it. In spite of its Tudor galleries and broad lines of mullioned windows, it was strong enough to stand a protracted siege in the Civil War of 1642-46. The first Beaufort-Herbert earls had still dwelt a good deal at Chepstow and elsewhere, but the later generations settled down at Raglan, in much more spacious and modern surroundings. The record of the sumptuous court—it was more than a household—kept up by Henry, the fifth earl and first marquis—a heroic supporter of Charles I.—recalls the Middle Ages. He had two knights as his stewards, and as pages " many gentlemen's sons of from £200 to £700 a year, all bred in the castle," who served him at his high table. What with masters of the horse, auditors, surveyors, gentlemen of the chapel, gentlemen of the chamber, masters of the wardrobe and armoury, ushers, clerks, comptrollers, chaplains, and keepers of the records, he had a retinue of 150 persons, when the minor ranks are counted in. And the fully developed Raglan could shelter them all.

The shape of Raglan is peculiar—projecting to its front is its most military feature, the great hexagonal keep called "the Yellow Tower of Gwent," five stories high, each of its six sides thirty-two feet long. It is set in the middle of a deep and broad moat, had no external approach—save by boats on the moat—but was connected with the main bulk of the castle by a stone bridge. The walls were ten feet thick, faced with good ashlar, and proved so strong that in the siege of 1646 they got little or no damage from 18-lb. cannon balls, though the battlements above were easily knocked off.

To the rear of the great Yellow Tower was the castle itself, disposed in two vast courts—one cannot call them inner or outer wards, since they are parallel in all respects. The north-east, or Stone Court, had the internal measurements of 120 feet by 58, the north-west, or Fountain Court, of 100 by 60, the depth of the buildings round them being in neither case counted. The main entrance was into the Stone Court, by a gate-house consisting of two four-storied pentagonal towers, very richly machicolated, joined by a battlemented portcullis chamber above the gate-arch. This gate-house is flanked to the right by the so-called Library-Tower, a solid building of military aspect, highly machicolated like the gate-towers. But on the left is a very domestic-looking and indefensible piece of front, with large Tudor windows and heraldic carving, which faces into the moat of the Yellow Tower. The moat might make it inaccessible, but it was obviously capable of being battered to pieces by cannon fire.

Round the four sides of the Stone Court were the kitchen—in one of the corner towers of the castle—and many other offices, store rooms and residential chambers. This court was separated from the other, or Fountain Court, by the largest buildings of the whole palace, the great hall, 66 feet long and 28 broad, with a large buttery at its northern end, and a panelled withdrawing room (or solar, as the earlier generations would have called it) at the corresponding southern end. On a floor above these was the earl's private dining room—50 feet by 20—an innovation since the days when the master feasted on the dais, and the retainers below in the same hall. Next to the dining room was the great

gallery—the pride of the Tudor builders, 126 feet long, "with many fair windows, but the most pleasant was that at the farthest end. All this part of the castle stood out like a tower, being about 60 feet high, and most pleasant of aspect." In its roofless and sadly shattered remains may be seen many vestiges of carving and sculpture. We are told that during the siege these splendid and lofty, but unmilitary, buildings, were a special mark for the Round-heads' cannon. "The fair and large compass window on the south side was beaten down by the enemy's great guns, and the two great windows at each end."

By a passage under the hall-block, there was a way into the second great court of Raglan, usually called

Raglan Great Hall Buttery Hatch
Main Stair in Distance

165

the Fountain Court, from a marble piece of waterworks in its centre, which spouted jets round the figure of a large white horse set on a pedestal. This typically seventeenth century piece of decoration was a device of Lord Herbert, son of the first marquis, who was greatly given to mechanism, and had contrived engines and wheels, and aqueducts, "which made fearful and hideous noises," when set going. The most sumptuous dwelling rooms of the owner, the "state appartments," were on the western side of the Fountain Court, approached by a fine flight of stairs in the north-west angle of the castle. Here Charles I. was lodged for some time, when, in his hour of defeat, he paid three separate visits between July 3 and September 15, to the old Marquis of Worcester, after Naseby, and heard some home truths from his loyal but free-spoken host, all of whose wealth had been lavished in his cause.

An arched gate in the south-west corner of the Fountain Court led to the bowling green, 270 feet long, which occupies that part of the eminence on which Raglan stands, which is not actually covered by the castle buildings. There is a sharp fall below it. Where the bowling green faced the Tower of Gwent was a slightly lower terrace, on which we are told that there was once a circular walk with statues of Roman Emperors: this continued all round the south front of the castle as far as the main gate-house. A little way out and to the south-east was an isolated outer doorway to the whole castle enclosure, called the White Gate. It was not flanked with defensive walls but apparently only by a light enclosure and a ditch, and rather marked a boundary than constituted a military obstacle.

Raglan's first and last siege, which ended in its ruin, lasted from May to August, 1646, starting eight months after the king's last melancholy visit to the place, and his departure from Wales, where he had vainly hoped to gather another army to replace that which had perished at Naseby. The operations were at first no more than a distant blockade by local Parliamentary forces under Sir Trevor Williams, Colonel Laugharn, and Colonel Kyrle. The garrison, 800 men, was able to make sallies for several miles outside the walls, and the old marquis was little impressed by several summons to surrender. But in July reinforcements from the "New Model" army came up, and Colonel Morgan was placed in charge of the siege. He drove the garrison within the walls, commenced regular approaches by trench-work, and brought up heavy guns, eighteen and twenty pounders. Raglan had not been built to resist such artillery, and ere long all the inner buildings had been damaged by mortar fire, from which no room was safe. Musketry fire was also kept up upon the windows: one ball entered the marquis' own chamber, ricochetted against a wall, and slightly injured him on the head. The main front of approach for the besiegers was on the east front of the Stone Court, where their trenches had got within sixty yards of the *enceinte*, and a good breach was established to the north of the Library Tower.

Things were looking hopeless for the defence when, on August 8, Sir Thomas Fairfax, commanding the whole Parliamentary Army, came up in person

RAGLAN CASTLE: CORNER **OF THE** FOUNTAIN COURT

RAGLAN CASTLE: THE TOWER OF GWENT, WATER-GATE

to finish matters. His summons, couched in very courtly and reasonable terms, moved the old marquis to open negotiations for surrender, which, after much haggling, ended in a set of terms being signed on August 17th. They were very lenient—the garrison marched out with the honours of war, and were then allowed to disperse, the officers being given safe conducts to their homes. Only the marquis himself was to be at the mercy of the Parliament. He was brought to London, and placed under custody of Black Rod in a private house in Covent Garden. There he died, aged seventy, in the following December, worn out by the stress and anxiety of the siege, no less than by sickness of heart at the ruin of the cause for which he had sacrificed fortune, house and liberty. The Parliament gave him a handsome funeral at the expense of his estates.

Before he died Raglan had already been "slighted." On August 26th the House of Commons had passed a resolution that " the house and buildings should forthwith be pulled down and destroyed, and the saleable material of it disposed of to the best advantage of the state. The lead stripped off the roof alone brought in £8,000. The carved timber was sold in Monmouth and Bristol, and gaps were blown in several sections of the outer walls. No later Marquis of Worcester cared to rebuild the ruins, and the chief residence of the family was transferred to Badminton in Gloucestershire. After the Revolution the title of Worcester was merged in the new Duchy of Beaufort, which perpetuated the family name of the original house of Somerset.

Abergavenny

Beside the " Honour of Monmouth," which belonged to the Fitz-Baderuns, and the lands of the " Three Castles," the original Norman conquerors of Gwent had occupied the middle valley of the Usk, as far as the borders of Brecknock. Here they had established, very early, before 1100, a castle of importance at Abergavenny. Its first known occupant was Hamelin, the same man to whom the Three Castles were afterwards given. And like those fortresses, Abergavenny passed, before 1119, to the Breton Brian Fitz-Count, the supporter of Queen Matilda in the Civil Wars of 1137-54. But in the later twelfth century the lot of the two lordships became different—the Three Castles were appropriated by Henry II., but Abergavenny was allowed to pass, in 1175, to the nearest of kin of the two leper sons of Brian, the unscrupulous William of Braose, Lord of Brecon, Radnor and Builth. It was probably to him that the main work in stone of the once important Norman castle of Abergavenny may be attributed, but so little of it remains above ground that attributions are difficult. It is certain that he made the place infamous to all Welsh chroniclers by the massacre within its walls of Seisyll prince of the, as yet, unsubdued Western Gwent, whom he lured to a conference and murdered along with his son and a number of his chief followers. Yet the atrocity was futile, for Western Gwent remained unsubdued for many a year to come. Abergavenny was reckoned second in importance only to Brecon of all the many castles in the

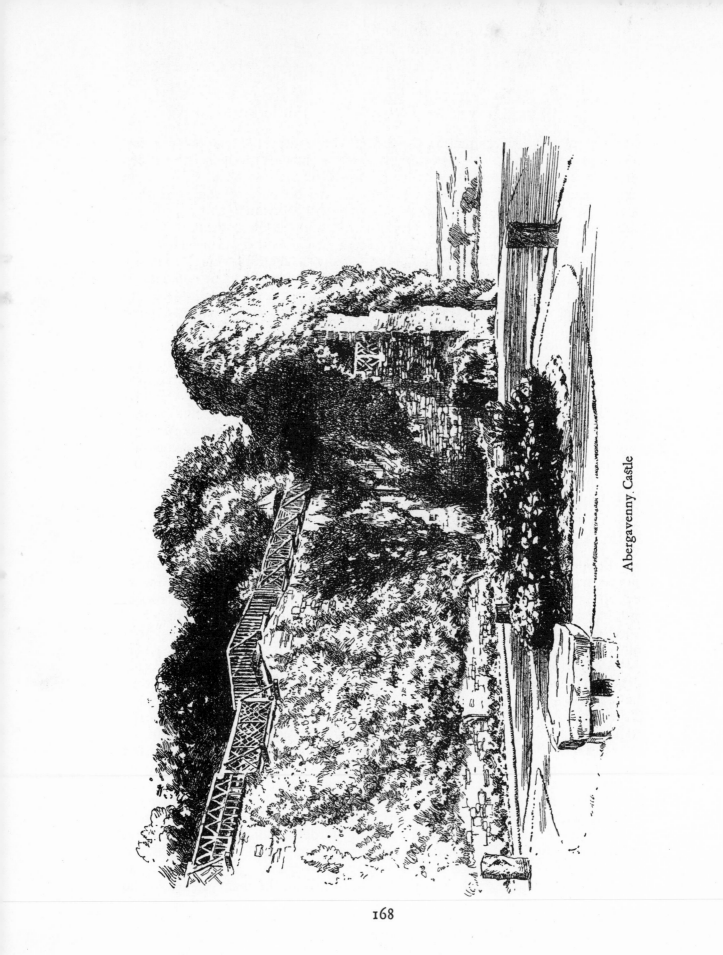

Abergavenny Castle

BRECON CASTLE

TRETOWER CASTLE : THE ROUND TOWER

Braose domains. When these were broken up in 1230, on the death of the last male of the main line, the castle went to a co-heiress, Eva de Cantilupe, ancestress through her daughter, Eva de Hastings, of the second line of Earls of Pembroke. The splendid monuments of many of the line—Braoses, Cantilupes, and Hastings, male and female—still adorn Abergavenny Church. But their castle has practically vanished : on a hill, south of the town and over the Usk, may be seen traces of Hamelin's *motte*, and some remnants of what is probably William de Braose's curtain wall, with the wrecks of a gate and two mural towers, which look somewhat later. They do not repay a visit : at Abergavenny the church and its monuments are the all-important things. As to the castle, it was taken by Owen Glendower in 1404, and by Fairfax in 1646, when, like Raglan and so many other neighbouring strongholds, it was "slighted," and never restored or inhabited again. The townsmen of the considerable town below naturally appropriated the stones one by one, and left practically nothing behind.

BRECKNOCK

There are not, in the lordships conquered by Bernard of Neufmarché and transmitted by a long series of heiresses to Milo of Gloucester, William de Braose, and Humphrey de Bohun, Earl of Hereford, nearly so many surviving castles of importance as in the somewhat smaller circuit of Gwent. Of Brecon, indeed, the centre of the lordship, there is enough remaining to make it worth while to visit a site of high historic interest. But at Builth, a very large and important castle in the thirteenth century, there remains nothing but a huge green mound and deep ditches, relics of a *motte* and bailey fortress which may go back to the first conquest of the land. There are slight traces of Edwardian walls belonging to a rebuilt castle famous in the Wars of 1277-83, but no more. Yet Leland, on his travels, saw " a fair castle of the king's " above a prosperous market town. Apparently the town has devoured the castle. Crickhowell, also a stronghold often mentioned in thirteenth century wars, is equally disappointing : there are merely some shapeless blocks of masonry standing up among

a scraggy grove of firs, on the mound which must represent the *motte* of the Turberville family. Blaen Lyfni, "ruinous almost to the hard ground" in Leland's day, is a mere site now. Bronllys, which belonged to the Cliffords, has saved a little more ; a circular tower of *circ.* 1200 stands on the original *motte*, though all outer

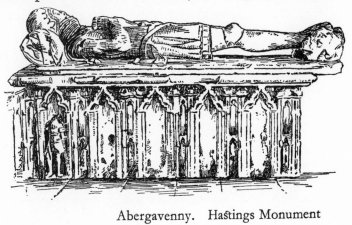

Abergavenny. Hastings Monument

169

defences are gone. The castles, indeed, belonging to the Cliffords—a great family in the March before ever they got connected with the Cumbrian North—have been singularly unlucky. Llandovery, which they conquered from the Brecknock side, and held intermittently for some generations, is as disappointing as Bronllys—showing only the knoll of a *motte* in a square bailey, with hardly any fragments of what must have been the thirteenth century castle, built when Matilda de Clifford got back the March from the Welsh in the time of Edward I. And Hay,* an earlier seat of the house, shows the outline of a *motte* and bailey, superseded by a later castle, of which a plain gateway and a tower are imbedded in a fine Jacobean manor house. Their first possession of all, before they joined Bernard of Neufmarché in the raid on Brecknock, Clifford Castle in Herefordshire, the traditional birthplace of Fair Rosamond, has a certain military interest, from its carefully chosen site, but shows only the base of a tower and some fragmentary walls. But of all the castles of Brecknock there are only two to which we need turn our serious attention—the one draws it by reason of its history, the other as a kind of curiosity of military architecture.

Brecon

When Bernard of Neufmarché surveyed his newly conquered March, he pitched his central abode above the village of Aberhonddu, where the Honddu and the Usk meet : here he set up his castle on the hill, and ere he died had founded a "*burgus*," or borough, and a Priory below it. The *motte* may still be seen, its crest ringed with the substructures of the shell-keep, which in the twelfth century superseded Bernard's original timbered house of defence. But the main and rather imposing remnants of the castle are those of the buildings reared by the Bohun Earls of Hereford in the later thirteenth century. The flanks of their great hall, and one corner tower, stand prominent on a terrace above the river, set among trees, though the greater part of the outer ward has been overrun by modern houses and gardens, including the "Castle Hotel." The hall shows fine but rather narrow "Early English" windows, and a battlemented roof-walk with slits for archery. The tower is called the Ely Tower, from the tradition that Morton Bishop of Ely was imprisoned there in 1483, but belongs to a date two hundred years earlier than that of the Lancastrian prelate.

We have already told how the lordship of Brecon passed by female descent from the line of Neufmarché to that of Milo of Gloucester, and from that of Gloucester to the Braoses, and how the eldest Braose co-heiress took it in 1250 to her husband, the Earl of Hereford. It was always a strong centre of resistance to the repeated attempts of the Welsh of Powys and Deheubarth to expel the Anglo-Norman settler. Though not quite a " virgin fortress," as Pembroke was throughout the Middle Ages, it was only once taken by the Celts, and that in

La Haie Taillée was its original name—obviously referring to some sort of palisade hedge of the primitive castle.

the very end of their long wars of independence, when Llewellyn the Last got possession of it during the Barons' War, and retained it for a few years by the Treaty of Montgomery in 1267. The late owner, the Earl of Hereford, won it back in 1276, apparently without a blow struck, as the Welsh refused to shut themselves up within walls to run the risks of siege and capture. Brecon Castle was undoubtedly restored, or even rebuilt, when its old owner came back to his own. It was by far the most important stronghold of the Bohuns, and from it as their base they carried out the stupid Marchers' Civil War with the house of Gloucester in 1290, for which Edward I. punished both parties so severely. When the last male Bohun died in 1372, and his lands were divided between his two sisters, Brecknock fell to Eleanor, the younger co-heiress, who had married Thomas of Woodstock, Earl of Buckingham, the unruly and ill-fated uncle of Richard II. Their only surviving child, Anne Plantagenet, carried Brecknock and Buckingham to Humphrey Stafford, to whom the ducal title of Buckingham was given by Henry VI. The three Stafford lords of Brecon were most unlucky—the first fell in the cause of Lancaster at the Battle of Northampton. The second was the Buckingham who did so much dirty work to put Richard III. on the throne in 1483, and suddenly repented of his activities—he drew the line at the murder of the Princes in the Tower. He it was who was persuaded to join the cause of Lancaster by his prisoner, Bishop Morton of Ely, whom Richard had placed in his care, and whom he kept in the Ely Tower at Brecon, if tradition can be trusted. Buckingham declared for the Earl of Richmond, mustered all his vassals at Brecon, and marched to the fords of the Severn, to join other malcontents. But they failed him, incessant rains made the Severn impassable, and the duke saw his army melting away, fled in disguise, and was given over to the headsman by a treacherous dependent. His son, the last lord of Brecon, perished on the block likewise—the victim of Wolsey's jealousy, of the cruel suspicion of Henry VIII., and of some un-guarded expressions of his own, which could be twisted into treason (1521). Leland going by, twenty years later, gives no detailed account of the condition of Brecon, but merely observes that " the Town of Brecknoc is well walled, and hath a fair castle joining to it : the Duke of Buckingham was, of late, lord there." Apparently, then, it was in good order about 1540 : but like so many castles which fell to the crown by attainders, and which were never visited by royalty, it started on a downward career of decay. This is said to have been brought to a climax by the townspeople of Brecon, who, during the great Civil War, wishing to side neither with King nor Parliament, took the extraordinary step of destroying their own gates, and of making great breaches in the castle, to prevent them from being seized and held as places of strength by either Royalists or Roundheads. When Charles I. passed through Brecon, after the disaster of Naseby, he lodged in the Priory and not in the castle, which suggests that the latter had been sufficiently wrecked to make it an unpleasant abode. It suffered in the end the usual fate of a royal castle situated in a thriving town— piecemeal demolition by stone-seekers. It is, perhaps, surprising that so much of the Edwardian building has survived.

171

Tretower

This little castle, the home for over two centuries of the Picards, stands a little way off the high road from Abergavenny to Brecon, in fairly level and rather damp ground. It was apparently placed to block, at its lower end, the pass over the Black Mountains, from the valley of the Wye to that of the Usk, which follows, for the greater part of the way, the ravine of the Rhingoll brook. At the other end, on the watershed, the route was watched by the high-lying Castel Dinas, of which only scraps remain. But Tretower is a good deal more than a scrap. Its situation was apparently chosen for the convenience of a low knoll of gravel, rising above the meadows about the Rhingoll, which, if wet to-day, were probably mere morasses in the twelfth century. Some one of Bernard of Neufmarché's original followers surrounded the triangular knoll with a palisade and ditch, and probably threw up a small *motte* at its south end. Later the timber was replaced by stone in the twelfth century, the northern, and lower, part of the knoll becoming a walled outer ward with a round tower at its north-eastern and north-western corners, while the south part of the knoll was covered with a rather large shell-keep, with two semi-octagonal towers at its apex, the extreme end of the castle. In some disaster of the later twelfth or earlier thirteenth century, the castle must have been taken and gutted—perhaps by Rhys ap Gruffyd of Deheubarth in 1197, or by Llewellyn the Great in 1216. The returning owner, finding his keep ruined, did not restore it, but built within it a very lofty circular tower, some 70 feet high, which rises far above the original square keep, and overlooks all the region around. The ruins of the keep became its outer defence. The puzzling thing about this circular tower is that it is not put in the middle of the old keep, but so close to its south-west corner that there is only just room for a man to scrape between them—the distance must be only five or six feet. Probably the outer ward was also restored, but it is now fragmentary, and has a modern farmyard superimposed upon it, from which the old masonry sticks up in a few places. This is apparently the only instance known of a round tower being built in the midst of an older square keep—the effect is peculiar, and the arrangement seems inconvenient.

Somewhere in the fifteenth century, when castles were growing out of favour, and manors beginning to take their place, the owners of Tretower, now the Vaughan family, transferred their dwelling to the very handsome mansion which stands a few score yards to the north of the old stronghold. It is not in the best order, being used as a farm-house: some of the original outbuildings look as if they would not stand much longer the stress of the centuries.

CARDIFF CASTLE : S.W. ANGLE : THE MAIN RESIDENCE

Facing page 172

CARDIFF CASTLE : THE *MOTTE* AND KEEP

GLAMORGAN AND GOWER

ONE of the earliest conquests of the Norman adventurers who burst into South Wales during the last ten years of the eleventh century was that of the Principality of Morganwg; and the seizure of the peninsula of Gower, which was thrown into the modern county of Glamorgan by Henry VIII., came not much, if at all, later. The invasion of Morganwg was not made, as might have been expected, by the Normans whom Fitz Osbern had already planted in Gwent, round Chepstow and Monmouth, but apparently by sea. The leader of the company was Robert Fitz-Hamon, one of a family to which the Conqueror had given wide grants in Gloucestershire. His house had a close connection with Bristol, which makes his appearance from the side of the water natural and probable. Robert seized and fortified the old Roman fortress of Cardiff, which he made the head of his lordship, and the base of his operations. He endowed his co-adventurers with fiefs all along the fertile shoreland of Morganwg. Twelve lordships, owning fealty to the head of the company at Cardiff, were founded for the Londres, Le Soers, Summerys, Umfravilles, Sullys, Grainvilles, Turbervilles and others. The remnants of their primitive " *motte* and bailey " castles, mostly overlaid by thirteenth century buildings of a more advanced architectural type, can be detected at Ogmore, Coity, Penmark, and elsewhere.

Jestyn ap Gwrgan, the last native prince of Glamorgan, was completely crushed by the invaders : he gave up the struggle and retired into a monastery, but his sons, Caradoc and Rhys, were granted, by the policy or the mercy of the conquerors, a holding in the east end of the region, the lordships of Avan, Rhondda and Meisgin, which their descendants held for many generations as vassals of the new Norman master of Morganwg. This was not the only Welsh survival within the limits of the old kingdom. Fitz-Hamon and his knights left alone all the wild and unprofitable mountain-land which overhangs the fertile shore, and here, not only in Rhondda and Meisgin, but also in Senghenydd, and the upper parts of Gwynllog, petty chiefs—those of the two last regions not connected with the line of Jestyn ap Gwrgan—were left in a condition of semi-independence. They are sometimes found doing homage to Cardiff, sometimes disowning it, but always ready to raid the shoreland in times of national effervescence. It was not till far on in the thirteenth century that the lords of Glamorgan made a final end of them, and advanced the limit of permanent occupation right up to the watershed of the Brecon Beacons, building the castle of Morlais close under their shadow. Meisgin and Rhondda were annexed in 1247, Senghenydd in 1266. The last leader in Senghenydd who raised trouble, Llewellyn Bren, was executed in Cardiff Castle as late as the time of Edward II. (1317).

Robert Fitz-Hamon's inheritance, like that of Bernard of Neufmarché, on the other side of the mountains, passed to a daughter, named Mabel ; she was married to Robert of Gloucester, the natural son of Henry I., who was far more important by reason of his wife's Welsh lands than by his English earldom. And again, as in Brecknock, after one other generation, the lordship of Glamorgan passed to another heiress, Amicia of Gloucester, who married Richard de Clare, Earl of Hertford, and was the ancestress of four de Clares, Earls of Gloucester and Hertford, and Lords of Glamorgan, the most striking figures in the baronage during the reigns of Henry III. and the first two Edwards.

The old kingdom of Morganwg had never included the long peninsula of Gower, which was always reckoned part of the realm of Deheubarth, which lay on its western flank. It was not conquered by Fitz-Hamon and his friends, or comprised in the lordship of the de Clares. This district was settled up by various adventurers, of whom Henry Earl of Warwick, a very trusted adherent of Henry I., was the patron and chief grantee. Its capital and chief stronghold was Swansea, where the castle, lying, unfortunately, in the very heart of the modern town, has been swamped by it : fragments only are visible, sticking out of modern buildings. But the picturesque Oystermouth, and Penard and Penrice, further along the peninsula, were also of early foundation, though their present representatives are obviously thirteenth century rebuildings of early Norman *motte* and bailey fortresses. Gower was like Pembrokeshire in having attracted to it not only English settlers, but part of that rather mysterious body of immigrant Flemings, who came to Wales in the time of Henry I. It does not appear to be ascertainable whether they were driven out of their own country, as some say, by inundations, or whether they were flying from the civil strife which was brought about by the disputed succession to the county of Flanders between William Clito and Dietrich of Elsass. These Flemings, visible for a generation or two as a separate element in Gower and Pembroke, were absorbed ere long in the main body of the English immigrants, and helped them to establish the "little England beyond Wales," as this western colony has long been called. They do not, for the most part, appear to have been military adventurers, but rather merchants, mechanics, and farmers : but some of them received feudal grants of land, and all seem to have turned out in arms to help, when the infant settlement was in danger of extermination.

Cardiff

It is not possible to settle the exact year in which Robert Fitz-Hamon seized the old Roman station of Cardiff, and adapted it to his own ideas of fortification. The date usually given is 1090 : but there is a puzzling entry in two chronicles, the Annals of Margam and the *Brut y Tywysogion*, to the effect that the first building fell in 1080-81, nine years before Fitz-Hamon's supposed arrival. However, the note in each may have been written up some considerable time after, and have pre-dated the settlement. It is, at any rate, clear that Robert found the old walls of the square Roman fort in a state which permitted of easy reconstruction. He took them as his outer *enceinte*, blocked up the ruined sections with earthworks, as may be supposed, and probably palisaded the crest of the whole crumbling structure. He threw up a very large *motte* in the western half of the area, cutting the eight acres of the Roman fort into two halves by a cross wall, so that the inner bailey could be defended along with the *motte*, even if the eastern bailey had fallen. The *Motte* of Cardiff still survives, not crowned by the wooden house of defence which Fitz-Hamon built, nor by the stone keep which must have followed it in the twelfth century, but by an elegant thirteenth century building of polygonal shape. This cannot, of course, be the original keep in which Henry I. held his brother, Robert of Normandy, captive for so many years. Nor can it be the building from which Ivor Bach of Senghenydd, in 1158, carried off Earl William of Gloucester, his wife and his son. This was an extraordinary feat of kidnapping : the Welshman got entry by a ladder at night, with a few followers. They caught the earl and his family asleep, gagged them, and lowered them from the window by ropes, without awaking their retainers. William was carried off to the hills, and not released till he had satisfied all Ivor's demands.

The de Clares were, no doubt, responsible for most of the older surviving buildings at Cardiff : they reconstructed the whole Roman *enceinte* in stone, set up a large gate-house, " the Black Tower of Glamorgan," in the south front, where an old Roman gate had stood, and, finding the old keep too small for their extensive household, began to erect residential buildings in the south-west angle of the western bailey (or inner ward). These gradually developed into the main block of the present castle, each family that held it in turn adding its contribution. The great Countess Isabella, the last of the Despencers, was one of the most active builders. The de Clare heritage being divided after the death of the last earl at Bannockburn, Cardiff and Glamorgan had fallen to that co-heiress who had married a Despencer. The Despencers in their turn failed in the male line in 1399, and the Countess Isabella's son by Richard Beauchamp, Earl of Warwick, became the owner. But the Beauchamp line suffered the same fate as those of Despencer and de Clare—after a tenure of little over half a century its lands went, with the hand of Anne Beauchamp, to Richard Neville—" Warwick the King-maker." His great marcher-holding in Wales was no small help to the House of York, who were already well established in the Marches through their inheritance of Ludlow, Wigmore and all the other lands of the great house of Mortimer.

When the King-maker fell at Barnet (1471) in rebellion against his cousin Edward IV., Glamorgan was one of the long list of fiefs and manors which came into the royal hands, in consequence of the late owner's manifest treason. The king, ignoring the rights of the widowed Countess Anne, gave Glamorgan to her daughter, Duchess Isabella, the wife of " false, fleeting, perjured Clarence." When the duchess died, and her husband was executed for treason against his brother, in 1478, Glamorgan once more changed hands, and was given to Richard, Duke of Gloucester, the husband of the King-maker's younger daughter, Anne. But Henry VII., on his accession to the throne, exhumed the rights of the now aged and childless Countess Anne, declared that her lands had been wrongly alienated from her, and then induced her to sell them, for a mere annuity, to the crown. After allowing his uncle, Jasper Tudor, to hold

Glamorgan for seven years, the king then annexed it permanently to the royal domain, and he and his son, Henry VIII., were " Kings of England and Lords of Glamorgan," till the Statute of Wales, in 1536, abolished all Marcher-lordships, and assimilated the local governance of Wales to that of England.

Cardiff Castle, as the head of a great lordship—to which many knights paid suit and service—owning the duty of " Castle-ward," or paying " ward-silver " in lieu of it—ceased to have its mediæval importance after 1536, and this is probably the reason why the Council of Edward VI. were content to alienate it, in 1550, to a branch of those very great acquirers of land, the Herberts, its owners in the later sixteenth and the seventeenth centuries. The present residential buildings show more of their work than of that of Isabella Beauchamp, their windows especially having been remade in Elizabethan or Jacobean days. The place twice changed hands in the Civil Wars of Charles I., but escaped " slighting " because its owner was a sound Parliamentarian. The present possessors, Marquesses of Bute, have done far more to change the face of Cardiff Castle than even the Herberts. They have recast the whole east face of the main block in a neo-Gothic style, producing effects that are sometimes majestic, sometimes merely pretty, but often inappropriate. The very high modern clock-tower, which is like nothing ever built in mediæval England, and has a distinctly Continental aspect, is decidedly to be deprecated as an insertion in a most historical Marcher castle. On the other hand the restoration of the entire Roman *enceinte*, including a new north gate, has been decidedly effective. The view of the main group of buildings, when focussed across the artificial water below it, cannot be refused the epithet of picturesque, however curious the blending of dates and styles in the long front.

Caerphilly

This is one of the largest, the most imposing, and the most scientifically constructed castles in all Wales. It must also have been one of the most striking in situation, so long as its great lake encircled it, and its vast towers seemed to rise directly from the water. But the draining of the lake in modern times has much impaired the picture, as the vast ruins now rise from a dead flat of marshy meadow ground.

Caerphilly was the earliest to be built of the last great group of Welsh castles, those of the " concentric order," in which each ward is wholly contained within that outside it. To this order belong Harlech and Beaumaris, and in a somewhat less perfect fashion, Conway, Kidwelly and Carnarvon. These castles have often been called of the " Edwardian " type, because of the great buildings of Edward I. on this plan. But the name is obviously inappropriate, as Caerphilly, the model of them all, was built not by that king, but by an Earl of Gloucester, in 1267, five years before the death of Henry III.

In 1266, the Barons' War being over, Gilbert, the Red Earl, was left as the most important subject of the crown—it was he who by deserting the cause of Simon de Montfort had restored the Plantagenets to power. He thought

CAERPHILLY CASTLE : VIEW FROM THE SOUTH

CAERPHILLY CASTLE : VIEW FROM S.W.

COITY CASTLE : THE INNER WARD

ST. DONAT'S CASTLE: STRADLING ARMS IN INNER COURT

the opportunity a good one to make an end of the last surviving Welsh princely families in his neighbourhood; they had always been a thorn in the side of the lords of Glamorgan, and joined in every Welsh insurrection started further north. Earl Gilbert, therefore, fell on Gruffyd, last lord of Senghennyd, overran all his upland valleys, and having captured him sent him as a prisoner to a castle in Ireland. To hold down the lands which he thus annexed, Gilbert planned a fortress on the most magnificent scale, placing it in the southern and more eligible tract of Gruffyd's principality, where many valleys meet.

Caerphilly was started in 1267, immediately after the conquest of Senghennyd. Its formidable beginnings roused rage and terror among the unsubdued Welsh, and ere it was far advanced Llewellyn of Gwynedd, still exalted by the memories of his successes in the Barons' War, made a descent upon it, and cast down its rising walls. But Gilbert de Clare persisted, reoccupied the ground, and finished his task by 1272. His castle, like Kenilworth, was a lake-fortress. By the skilful damming up of two streams, a large square island was produced in the middle of a broad expanse of water. The outer contour of the island was provided with a complete encircling wall, rounded at its corners into four semi-circular bastions. This formed the outer ward, which had two entrances on its east and west fronts, each protected by a strong gate-house. Rising fifty feet or more above the rather low outer ward, was the immensely strong but small central court. Its curtain was high, but much higher were the four battlemented circular towers at each corner, and the two gate-houses, east and west, which correspond to the smaller gate-houses of the outer ward. This inner ward was a magnificent pile of buildings, with large and well-lit apartments; the great hall, in the south side of the quadrangle, is 70 feet long by 35 broad, with columnar supports for its roof-arches, and windows of "Decorated" style with ball-flower ornaments.

But the special feature of Caerphilly is that outside the island fortress it has a vast fore-building, or barbican, or (if you can so call it) outermost ward, on the further side of the lake, covering its east front. This was intended to block the main approach to the island, which was over a bridge on two piers, planted where the lake is narrowest. This outer work, though it is "length without breadth," was a very important structure, with a large gate-house in its centre, mural towers along its front, and specially strong defences where its two extreme flanks fell back to the water's edge. At the southern end of this forework was a great tower, which protected the sluices of the Nant Gledyr brook, which fed the lake, and prevented enemies from drawing off the water.

It remains to speak of the west side of the outer defences. The two back gates of the inner and outer wards, on the island, looked down upon a narrow drawbridge, connecting them with a second low-lying island in the lake, which was slightly protected by a water-wall of no great height, but destitute of other defences. This "hornwork," as engineers have called it, was separated from the mainland in the western side of the lake by a broad stretch of water. Apparently it served as a sort of "outer bailey." Its lack of serious fortification was no doubt due to its complete inaccessibility save by water.

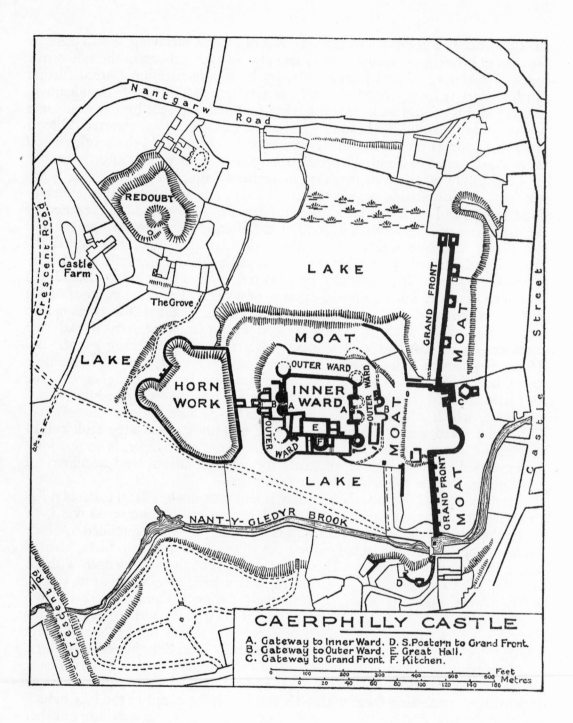

CAERPHILLY CASTLE

A. Gateway to Inner Ward. D. S. Postern to Grand Front.
B. Gateway to Outer Ward. E. Great Hall.
C. Gateway to Grand Front. F. Kitchen.

A curious spit of gravel ran across the northern lake, almost cutting it into two parts, of which the inner and narrower one served as a moat for the greater island. But it does not seem to have had any tactical meaning, being rather an accident of terrain, which the builder of the castle did not think it worth while to dig away, as it would have had no importance unless the lake were drained : and this could only have been done if the besiegers had got possession of the sluice gates in the outer work or barbican.

Caerphilly justified the expectation of its builder by its impregnability : its history is therefore comparatively uninteresting, because, though often molested, and once or twice surrendered, it was never regularly besieged, nor taken by force down to the end of the Middle Ages. It was for a moment the refuge of

Caerphilly Castle. The Leaning Tower

Edward II. when he was being hunted by his rancorous wife and Roger Mortimer. And the outermost ward was surprised and burned by Llewellyn Bren in 1315, though he failed to capture the island stronghold. But the present breaches in the massive structure, though even in Leland's time it was already beginning to show signs of decay, are in the main due to deliberate "slighting" or dismantling after the Civil Wars of 1642-46, when gunpowder was used to disrupt it. One corner tower of the inner ward, eighty feet high, which still hangs together out of the perpendicular, though its inner side has been blown away, is visible in the illustration on this page. Its persistent refusal to fall is a wonderful testimonial to thirteenth century mortar.

On what was once the north-eastern shore of the lake there is a knoll and an earth-work. This seems to date only to the Civil Wars of Charles I., and to have no connection with the tactical scheme of the castle as it stood in the Middle Ages.

179

Coity

This home of the Turbervilles for some three centuries, was one of the very first castles built by the knights who owed suit and service to Robert Fitz-Hamon. There is authentic documentary evidence of a Turberville in possession early in the reign of Henry I., and no reason to doubt that he was the first comer. Local legend will have it that on Sir Pain's first appearance on the spot, the Welsh owner displayed to him on the one hand his war-band, and on the other his not unattractive daughter, asking which way he would prefer to win the lordship, by fighting or by marriage. The Norman opted for the peaceful method, and his line of descendants were half-Welsh from the first, like the de Barrys of Manorbier. The de Clare records mention that Coity was held from the earl " by the serjeantry of hunting for him "—a curious tenure.

Coity is not a strongly-placed castle. It lies on a slight rise upon a little plateau, with several higher pieces of ground quite close. Originally, no doubt, there must have been a *motte* and a bailey, but the present castle shows two wards. A round early shell-*enceinte* forms the inner ward, with three towers in it, of which the largest might count as a small square keep. Another,

Coity Church
Gabled Coffer

of the towers, of a much later style, is the gate-house. There are apartments in all three, and continuous chambers all round the shell, some of them obviously redecorated as late as Tudor times. The earlier part of the masonry may be twelfth century, but more of it looks like thirteenth century work. The much larger square outer ward appears to be even later, and shows fourteenth century masonry. The lord, sitting on his keep in the inner ward, would have a fine view over rolling country for ten miles in each direction, though his fortress is not at all on high ground.

The lordship, where Pain de Turberville established himself, remained with his family for nearly three centuries—rather an exceptional record of descent in the

ST. DONAT'S CASTLE: INNER COURT

OYSTERMOUTH CASTLE

male line for a Marcher family. Many of its members were great fighting men, especially a Pain who did good service for Edward I. against the rebels of South Wales. The "honour" was reckoned as four knights' fees, and the owner always turned up with a stout retinue in days of trouble. The last Turberville, Sir Richard, died in the reign of Edward III., and the lordship passed to his sister Catherine, wife of Sir Roger Berkrolles, with whose descendants it remained no long time. After several changes of ownership it came by marriage to the Sydney Earls of Leicester, with whom it stayed till 1743. When it reached its present dilapidated condition is not to be known, but Leland speaks of it in 1540 or thereabouts as " still maintained— some say that it belonged once to Pain, called for his ruffellings there *le diable*. Gamage is now lord, and it is his principal house."

In the rather interesting church, hard by the castle, the visitor may note the effigies of two fourteenth century Turberville children, and a large gabled coffer of oak on legs, of the same date, showing the emblems of the Passion among much floral decoration.

St. Donat's

This lovely castle, overlooking the Bristol Channel from its series of terraced gardens, shows no trace of early buildings, yet was probably the seat of one of Robert Fitz-Hamon's original grantees, as it appears in the earliest available records, held by the service of one knight. In 1166 it was the fief of Lucas Butler [" *Pincerna Regis* "]: it passed in the next century to a family called de Hawey, who seem afterwards to have adopted the name of the Butlers, from whom they had got it through an heiress. They were holding it till the reign of Edward I., but a little later it passed to the Strad-lings, a long-lived house as marcher families went, whose tenure of the castle lasted in the male line till 1738 — over four centuries of occupancy.

The present castle appears to be a four-teenth century structure with Elizabethan additions, and some good and careful Victorian restoration, which does not (as at so many places) betray itself at

St. Donat's. Outer Gate

once and clash with its surroundings. The supposed builder was a Sir William Stradling, of the time of Edward III. It is in two wards: the outer, very narrow, has a strong gate-house with a portcullis set in its landward or northern front. The gate-house is approached by a bridge over a dry ditch. Part of this ward has been built up into solid rooms joining on to the inner ward, by some late hand of Stuart (or even Victorian ?) date.

The inner ward consists of an irregularly shaped courtyard, with three-storied buildings of good style all around it, somewhat in the fashion of a college quadrangle. The windows are, no doubt, Elizabethan or Jacobean

St. Donat's. South Front

insertions, and much of the carving in the state rooms is of even later date, belonging apparently to the school of Grinling Gibbons. Some of the medallions and armorial decoration over the doors are also of much more modern origin than the walls in which they are set. A Dr. Carne, who owned the place in late Victorian times, employed the architect Bodley to execute restorations, and Bodley's work, after a few decades, is very hard to differentiate from the original seventeenth century construction. On the west side the castle overhangs a steep ravine, at the bottom of which may be seen the little parish church. But the south side descends in a series of pleasant garden terraces to the shore of the Bristol Channel.

The Stradlings were furious royalists in the great Civil War, mainstays of the king's cause in South Wales, and not infrequently serving outside of it, in the contingents which went to join the armies of the Midlands on the West. Sir Edward Stradling, the head of the family, commanded a Welsh regiment at Edgehill, and was there wounded and taken prisoner. On his exchange (after long captivity) for Colonel Ludlow, he rejoined the king, and died at Oxford in 1644. His kinsmen, Sir Henry, and Colonels Thomas and John

Stradling, were prominent all through the first Civil War, and were seen again in the desperate rally of the " Second Civil War " of 1648, after which one of them died in prison and another was exiled to Ireland. While they were fighting, St. Donat's Castle gave a refuge to the fugitive Archbishop Usher, who abode there for more than a year after Naseby—his study is still shown, for he devoted his enforced leisure to the pen. St. Donat's was, of course, " slighted " by the Parliamentarians in 1646, but not so effectively as to prevent another Sir Edward Stradling from restoring it after 1660, when the Grinling Gibbons carving, still visible, was inserted in the state rooms, and many other interior changes were made.

The Stradlings endured till 1738, when the last male heir, while travelling on the " grand tour," was killed in a duel at Montpellier. His body was brought home, and lay in state for a day and a night. The flambeaux placed around it caught some of the funeral trappings, and set fire to the family pictures which lined the great gallery, so that the portraits of five generations of Stradlings were burned with the body of their last representative. After much litigation, St. Donat's passed through many hands—among them those of Dr. Carne, above named, a conscientious restorer of good taste. The last two owners have been American citizens. The beautiful little castle, with its glorious outlook over sea and hill, might make any inhabitant an admirer of Wales.

Oystermouth

The rather odd name of this castle on the shore of Swansea Bay does not commemorate the special richness of the neighbouring estuary in shell fish, but is simply a corruption of the Welsh Ystumllwynarth, a collocation of syllables which proved too difficult for Norman knights or English retainers. The former turned it into Ostrelaf—the latter, introducing familiar sounds, into Oystermouth. It lies close above the water, on a hill overlooking the pleasant ups and downs of the Mumbles, with a good anchorage for sailing craft below. Probably it was one of the original castles built by Henry Earl of Warwick, when he received the gift of the lordship of Gower from Henry I. It commands Swansea Bay at its entrance, and looks across the water to the castle of that town, which formed the central base of the settlement. From the Newburghs of Warwick it passed to those great getters of land the Braoses, early in the thirteenth century. The change was apparently brought about by the conquests of " the Lord Rhys," the last effective Prince of Deheubarth, who in 1189 captured it and several other strongholds. After Rhys' death, Llewellyn the Great, of Gwynedd, did not allow his sons to keep it, but made it over to John de Braose, a nephew and rival of the more famous Reginald de Braose, whom he was anxious to win over to his alliance, and to whom he gave the hand of one of his daughters (1219). From this John de Braose descended a branch of the family which outlived Reginald's stock in Brecon and Abergavenny. For the latter's broad lands had to be divided among heiresses in 1230, while the Braoses of Gower survived in the male line till the time of Edward II., when the last of them dying, in 1326, his elder daughter took their lordship to the Mowbrays. In dealing with this castle Leland, for once, gets his dates a little mixed, but proves that the place was in ruins by 1540. "A three miles from Swansey was a castle called Estwilthunarde, otherwise Ostremuth; there remain ruins there of a castle destroyed by Prince Lluelin. Mowbray was Lord of Swansey and builded the old castle there, and by likelihood Ostremuth also, for defence of the haven." The destruction in Llewellyn's time was, of course, long before the advent of the Mowbrays in 1326; Leland's informants did not have memories extending back to the Braoses or Newburghs. But the character of much of the ruins is such that they might well be Mowbray work of the middle fourteenth century, rather than Braose work of the late thirteenth century. However it is safer to attribute the buildings to the Braoses, whose principal residence this was, rather than to the Mowbrays, to whom Gower was an outlying patch of territory, very remote from their great East-Country holding. The earlier owners are much more likely to have carried out a thorough reconstruction of the place than the later.

Oystermouth Interior. Chapel Windows

Oystermouth lies on the steep side of a knoll looking toward the sea. Its one large ward slopes pronouncedly upward. Its large gatehouse is perfect, with good chambers therein, as is also its chapel on the third floor of the further side of the ward, with fine decorated windows. The hall is on the second floor in the north angle, nearly facing the gate-house. This side of the ward is much higher than that by the entrance, there being steps between them.

Though but one large ward is now visible, it is possible that there was a more slightly-fortified outer ward, or perhaps only a bailey with earthwork and palisades, in the adjacent square field to the east. There are, however, no traces of stone walls to be seen. The view over the Mumbles, Swansea Bay, and the coast of Central Glamorgan, is wide and pleasing.

Penard

This is a very desolate castle, standing far from any village on the slope above a small tidal creek, in a shallow bay. It is a melancholy relic, half filled with drifting sand; for though it stands on a rock, the wind has piled it deep with fine detritus from the neighbouring golf links—where may be seen the only signs of life in this rather depressing corner of the peninsula.

Penard is apparently a late thirteenth century castle—it is rectangular with a square tower at each corner, and a gate-house at its upper or landward end. There is a steep drop over the rock on which it stands on its western side, toward the creek. The curtain is reasonably perfect, but the battlements on it have all disappeared. This, like Oystermouth, would appear to have been an early castle, rebuilt after the raiding of Gower by " the Lord Rhys," in 1195, by some owner in the time of Henry III., possibly by the Braoses themselves, but more probably by some tenant holding under them. Apparently it went out of use when the Welsh Wars of Edward I. came to an end, as there are no traces of fifteenth or sixteenth century occupation. I have been able to find no traces of the history of the families which occupied it, but should suggest that (like the owner of Penrice, a few miles further along the peninsula) they took their name from the castle. For I find signatures of Nicholas, Robert and Thomas de Penard, as witnesses to various thirteenth and fourteenth century documents, printed in Clark's Monuments of Glamorgan. Leland, contrary to his wont, has no mention of this fairly large place, though he is duly informed as to Oystermouth and Penrice, which lie on each side of it.

Penrice

This is the largest, but not the most interesting, of the three castles of Gower. For though its *enceinte*, round keep and gate-house are standing, it is as mere masses of rubble, all the ashlar and carved stonework having been most carefully peeled off the rough cores within. It stands about a mile and a half from the sea, on a plateau at the head of a deep combe, which runs down through woods to Oxwych Bay. Its back is toward a cliff or very steep descent on the south : part of its east front is guarded in the same way. The front containing the gate-house looks north toward the inland. Like so many other castles it is not placed on the highest available spot—there is higher ground some 200 yards up the plateau, facing the great north gate.

The whole of Penrice consists of one very large ward, forming an irregular quadrangle—the west side is much shorter than the other three. All the buildings are on the north front, the other three sides consisting of no more than curtain walls. The most prominent feature of the place is the large three-storied round keep in its north-western angle. This is apparently late Norman in date, and considerably older than the other buildings on the north front, including the gate-house. It seems likely that this tower may represent the site of an original *motte*, while all the rest of the walls indicate the area of the original ditched and palisaded enclosures of the bailey: their present stones are undoubtedly much later than those of the tower. When Rhys of Deheubarth, in 1189, took Penrice, along with the other castles of Gower, the tower was probably its only stone defence. When the land got back into Norman hands, and the Braoses became lords of Gower, there was wholesale reconstruction. The old earthworks of the bailey were rebuilt as stone walls: there are small projecting bastions (only 12 feet broad) in its southern and western fronts, which should betoken early thirteenth century work. The north front was strengthened, perhaps a little later, with a large gate-house, consisting of two projecting towers with the archway and portcullis-chamber between them. They cannot be called drum-towers, as they are not circular, but square with rounded corners. Between the gate-house and the old Norman round keep were the residential buildings of the castle, but it is impossible to say where hall, chapel or kitchen may have stood, owing to the general dilapidation of the place. At two points, one adjoining the keep, the other half-way toward the gate-house, two rectangular buildings of later date have been thrown out a few feet beyond the line of the curtain: but so little even of their lower courses remains that it is impossible to say what they represent.

There is nothing in Penrice that looks Edwardian, still less fourteenth century, and no signs of Tudor residential buildings, such as so many old Welsh sites can show. It looks as if the owners had migrated to more convenient dwellings, perhaps a manor-house somewhere near the site of the present great residence below the castle, in the fourteenth century, when the old Welsh wars were over. They were called Penrice after their castle—a sure indication that they were early arrivals at the time of the conquest of Gower by Henry, Earl of Warwick. Failing at last in the male line they were succeeded by Mansels, heirs through a female descent, and now, the Mansels having also vanished, a branch of the Talbots holds the ruined castle above, and the new house below.

There are relics of many other castles in Glamorganshire—Morlais, Penmark, Dinas Powys, Llantrisant, Fonmon, Weobly-in-Gower, etc. But some are mere remains of a *motte* and bailey, others very fragmentary, others again smothered in Tudor or modern residential buildings. Of all those which we have described, Caerphilly and St. Donat's are the ones which the judicious traveller should make an endeavour to visit at all costs.

PENARD CASTLE

PENRICE CASTLE : THE GATE-HOUSE

WEST WALES

CARMARTHENSHIRE

AFTER the first rush of the Norman invaders into South Wales, which resulted in the conquest of all the more eligible lands of Gwent, Brecknock and Glamorgan, there was an attempt to reduce the whole land. It failed; the effort to build up the " March of Cardigan " ended in disaster. It resulted that a continuous belt of marcher lordships held the whole coast, from the borders of the de Clare Lordship of Glamorgan to St. David's Head and the Western Ocean, while the Inland and the rough hills of Cardigan remained in the hands of the old Welsh ruling dynasty, seldom held by one prince, on account of the incorrigible habit of heritage-partition, more often by two, three or four brothers or cousins engaged in bitter family feuds. The coastal holding of the Marchers was broad to the West—where it included nearly the whole of modern Pembrokeshire—narrow to the East—where with the royal castle and borough of Carmarthen in the centre, the marches of Llanstephan on the left, and Kidwelly on the right, extended only a few miles inland. Whenever war broke out, it was the natural aim of the Welsh to break the chain of coastal fortresses, and drive the aliens into the sea. The reconquest of the more solid blocks held by the Anglo-Normans in Pembrokeshire and Glamorgan was a very serious business, and never accomplished though often essayed. Here the castles were set too thick, and the immigrant population was too numerous to be crushed. Upper Carmarthenshire, the green vale of the Towy, and the wild hills that overhang it, was one of the two surviving *foci* of South Welsh independence after the Lords Marchers had overrun all the coast-land from Chepstow to Pembroke. The other was the tangle of mountain valleys that lie along the north side of Glamorgan, where half a dozen petty principalities lurked in the fastnesses of Rhondda and Meisgin and Senghenydd, in the rough lands now mainly covered by unsightly coal-dumps. It is odd—but perhaps more than a coincidence—that the constituencies now represented by intractable Socialist members of Parliament, should have been, in the thirteenth century, the domicile of equally impracticable Welsh hill-chieftains—the bane of their neighbours in the fertile lands along the shore.

But the princes of Ystrad Towy were much greater people than the poverty-stricken lords of the Glamorganshire border. They had a broad territory, much fertile land, and a proud pedigree that went back to the last kings of South Wales, the race of Rhodri Mawr and Howel the Good. When all their lands were united, as they were for the last time in the hands of " the Lord Rhys," the contemporary of Henry II., they were the most powerful princes of South Wales. Unfortunately for the family, heritage-partition was among its traditions, and brothers were too many and too jealous of each other. For the last century of its existence the principality, whose chief royal seat was the Palace of Dynevor, above the Church and town of Llandeilo, was always divided among wrangling kinsmen. Probably the building of the three great castles, which form its central defence, may date back to the Lord Rhys (1155-1197) who owned all the lands around them, which, after his death, were destined to be divided. For they are so strategically placed that there can be little doubt that there is system in the arrangement. Dynevor was the ancient royal seat, turned from a mere residence into a stronghold, when stone fortification was adopted by the Welsh from their Norman enemies. Drysllwyn, four miles lower down the Towy, is the blockhouse to stop the way up the river from the lowlands of Carmarthen. On a steep hill immediately above the water, at a bend where the valley closes in to a narrow passage, it is obviously designed as an outlying defence for Dynevor. Caer Cynan, on the other hand, is suited for a last refuge for the prince, if Dynevor should have fallen. Placed on a precipice overlooking a narrow side-valley, five miles south of the royal seat, it is the most inaccessible peak of the whole region. Even now it can only be approached by very poor country roads ; and when it has been reached it has only one narrow side by which the visitor can mount, the other three being sheer cliff 300 feet high. It is even more steeply placed than Harlech, and, unlike that more famous castle, it is not dominated by higher ground above, but occupies the very summit of the highest hill of the region. Mediæval siege artillery could never reach it, and as a last resort for a beaten prince it could not be bettered. Yet more than once Caer Cynan fell, taken by English from Welsh, and again retaken by Welsh from English. But this was always the result of surprise or starvation, not of regular siege operations.

Drysllwyn

This castle is only nine miles up-stream from the English castle and borough of Carmarthen, at a point where the valley of the Towy narrows down, and is easily commanded by the well-marked hill on which the fortress stands. Unlike the other two strongholds of the house of Rhys, it has unfortunately fallen into complete ruin, and only enough masonry remains standing to show what was its size and ground-plan. But it was obviously a castle of terraced wards, the lower wards running down the slope toward the river, the stronger inner ward higher up on the top of the eminence. On three sides the situation was decidedly steep, only on one was it fairly accessible.

In the last days of Welsh independence

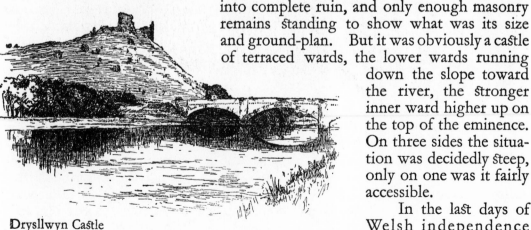

Drysllwyn Castle

DYNEVOR CASTLE

CAER CYNAN CASTLE: VIEW FROM THE SIDE OF THE PRECIPICE

Drysllwyn was the capital (if we may use the word) of one of many principalities into which Deheubarth had split itself up. Its last independent owner but one, Maredud ap Rhys, was among the few Welsh lords who struggled against the attempt of Llewellyn, the enemy of Edward I., to make himself prince of the whole land; he generally adhered to the English allegiance. And in the great campaigns of 1282-83, which saw the destruction of the principality of Gwynedd, and the death of Llewellyn, Rhys ap Maredud of Drysllwyn, last of his house, did good service to the king in resisting the incursion of the North Welsh into Dyfed, and driving them out. But it is characteristic of the inconsequence and want of practical sense in the Celtic mind, that after the fall of the northern state, Rhys flared up in 1287 into insurrection on personal grievances of his own, when all the rest of Wales was quiet. Apparently his main grievance was that Dynevor, castle and lands, which had belonged to his cousin, Rhys ap Rhys—who had sided with Llewellyn—were not made over to him. King Edward had made a half promise that he should be so rewarded, but an English garrison still held Dynevor.

On June 8th, 1287, the king being abroad in France, and absorbed in Gascon wars, Rhys most unexpectedly took arms, captured Dynevor by surprise, and also Caer Cynan, and pushed raids into Cardiganshire and Brecknock. But no one joined him save the Welsh of his own region : the recently conquered lands of the North made no stir; they even sent a contingent to join the royal levies. In short, the rising was (as so often in Wales) purely local and tribal. The regent, Edmund of Cornwall, assembled an army of almost unprecedented size ; first and last some 20,000 troops were put in motion. By August 15th he was besieging Drysllwyn with 11,000 men, while other forces under the Earls of Hereford and Gloucester were converging on the insurgent area. Drysllwyn was obstinately defended, but only held out for some fifteen or twenty days. The siege was conducted with the best engineering skill of the day—a great " engine," probably a *trebuchet*, battered the chapel, which was reckoned the weakest part of the wall, while miners pushed forward trenches and filled up the ditch. At length a great section of the wall fell forward, burying by mischance William de Montchensy and other knights who were in the advanced trench. But the breach was enormous, and about September 5 the place was captured. Rhys was not found inside—he had taken to the hills, made no great attempt to defend Dynevor or Caer Cynan, and was not heard of again till November, when he appeared on the border of Pembrokeshire and took the castle of Emlyn by surprise. To this new point of danger the great engine and miners went, and Emlyn was battered into surrender by January 20. Drysllwyn remained a royal castle with a small permanent garrison. It is probable that some of the lower wards are additions, made by the English, to the original Welsh castle—but no certainty is possible when the whole of the ruins are in such a fragmentary condition. We do not hear of any trouble in Carmarthenshire during the later Welsh risings under Madoc and Maelgwyn in 1294— probably from the point of view of insurrection it was " a burnt-out district."

Prince Rhys, after long and miserable lurking in the hills, had been captured in 1291, and sent to an obscure end. His late subjects would not rise for any other leader: and so ended the independence of Deheubarth. Only once again did Drysllwyn see the face of war—after an interval of more than a century. It was one of the castles which in 1403 were betrayed to Owen Glendower, during his first raid into South Wales. The traitors were (of course) Welshmen, who formed part of the garrison. Either Owen refused to regarrison it on principle, and dismantled it, or else his partisans made no resistance and surrendered when Henry, Prince of Wales, reconquered South Wales in 1405-06. For there is no record of any siege and recapture of Drysllwyn, which disappears from our annals in 1403.

Dynevor

This is a much better preserved castle than Drysllwyn, from which it is distant only four miles up-stream. It had also more political importance, as it had been the regular princely seat of the House of Howel the Good, long before it boasted of a castle. It lies above the town of Llandeilo, on a bold bluff projecting over the Towy, absolutely precipitous on two sides, and only to be reached by a stiff climb on the third, or landward, front. It is at present absolutely smothered in a dense wood, so that it is very hard to take any good general view of it either with pencil or camera.

A single court, roughly triangular, occupies the top of the knoll, adapting its shape to the contour of the ground. It has three very strong towers, one round and two square, the former at the south-west end of the castle looking towards the cliff and river. All three are full of apartments, those in the base of the round tower appear to be the kitchens: the position of the hall and chapel is problematical—in no part of the surviving buildings is there any chamber which looks large enough for either. The path of approach, which winds up the hill round a corner of the fortification, is commanded by some elaborate flanking defences, a sort of spur which runs out from the main front.

Dynevor Castle from the East

The surviving windows are pointed, not arched in the Norman style, so that they must be thirteenth century, not the work of the Lord Rhys, who built the original castle somewhere in the days of Henry II. They may possibly represent English repairs and alterations, made when the castle was in the hands of Edward I. There seem to be traces of a weak outer ward, or added area of defence, on the south side of the walls, with a scarped drop of 20 feet below it, and a slight ditch separating it from the main *enceinte*. This may have been merely a palisaded work—if it had battlemented walls, they have disappeared.

The possession of Dynevor was keenly contested by the princes of the house of the " Lord Rhys," last owner of the undivided principality of Ystrad Towy, as the occupation of it seemed to stamp the owner as the chief among his kindred. Its last princely owner was Rhys Windod, or Rhys ap Rhys, great-grandson of the patriarch above named. He sided with Llewellyn of North Wales in the war of 1276-7, and on the discomfiture of his ally had to submit himself and to surrender Dynevor to King Edward, who put a garrison into it. It has been already mentioned, in the paragraphs dealing with Drysllwyn, that this retention of the old royal seat in the king's hands led to the great South Welsh insurrection in 1287, when Rhys ap Maredud seized Dynevor on the first day of his rising. He apparently intended to hold it, as we are told that he put his wife and treasure within its walls ; but when the Earl of Cornwall came up in strength and began to cast trenches around the castle, both the lady and the garrison escaped by a midnight sortie, abandoning the place and taking to the hills.

Dynevor appears again in the history of the insurrection of Owen Glendower as an important strategical point. When the rebel made his great and successful inroad into South Wales in 1403, it was one of the fortresses which were not betrayed (like Drysllwyn or Llanstephan) but were surprised and taken by force of arms. Either the garrison must have been very small, or it must have been incautious or demoralized, for this is not the sort of place that can be dealt with by a *coup de main*. We have no record of its recovery by the royal forces, which certainly took place in 1405, and can only conclude that it must have been either dismantled by Owen, or surrendered without resistance, as was the case with Drysllwyn also. The castle was in sufficiently good condition in 1485 to serve as an acceptable gift by Henry VII. to Sir Rhys ap Thomas, his best Welsh supporter in the Bosworth campaign. Leland, however, wrote it down, in 1540, as "now ruinous." As a residence it has long been superseded by the modern Dynevor Castle, half a mile down the hill, and nearer to Llandeilo.

Caer Cynan

Last of the three great castles of Upper Carmarthenshire we come to this veritable eagle's nest, most picturesque of all the Welsh castles from its situation, though not vying with the somewhat less rocky Harlech in the elaboration of its architecture. The builder, presumably " the Lord Rhys," somewhere at the end years of the twelfth century, was obviously seeking for more inaccessibility, not for a strategic position. For this towering castle is on the top of a high precipitous peak, in a lovely but lonely side-valley lying far back from the broader lands on the Towy, and some five miles over steep mountain tracks from Dynevor and Llandeilo. It is surrounded on three sides by absolute

191

precipices, and even on the fourth the ascent is steep. The castle does not fill the whole of the plateau on top of the peak, but blocks the entire accessible side, leaving some unoccupied ground behind it on the edge of the precipices. Caer Cynan commands the whole of its own valley, and is not commanded from any other point, though there are hill-sides a mile away from which it could be advantageously battered by eighteenth century (not to speak of nineteenth century) artillery.

This is a square castle of a single ward, destitute of out-works—for which, indeed, there was no need. It has round towers, not exceeding the lofty curtain wall by many feet, at the corners of the side facing the ascent on the north front, with a square tower at its south-east angle, and another square tower projecting very far from the curtain in the middle of its south front. The latter, being capable of defence after the *enceinte* had been pierced, might almost be called a keep. But it does not rise far above the general height of the walls.

The castle is well-built for a native Welsh strong-hold, with larger and more regular stonework than Dynevor or Dinas Bran. And it has one feature in which it is unique, a long stepped corridor or passage cut in the face of the rock along the precipice, leading down to a well or cistern, and lighted by loopholes piercing right through the native stone. The accessible sides of the castle are well furnished with arrow slits. The few surviving windows show thirteenth and four-teenth century shapes and mouldings, and must be later than the original architecture

Caer Cynan.
Window in S.E. Tower

192

of the "Lord Rhys" in 1190. Probably they may belong to reconstructions in the time of Edward I., when the place for many years had a royal garrison.

Considering its absolute inaccessibility Caer Cynan has a most chequered history, for it changed hands several times in the Welsh wars—yet if honestly defended could have resisted any possible siege-devices of the Middle Ages. Its first appearance in the annals is in 1256, when Llewellyn, the enemy of Edward I., taking advantage of the domestic troubles of England, was using his opportunity to reduce his neighbours, the minor princes. He captured Caer Cynan, we are told, from one descendant of "the Lord Rhys," and gave it to another. But it was back in the hands of Rhys Windod, Lord of Dynevor, by the time of the later and less lucky wars of the last Prince of Gwynedd. In June, 1277, Caer Cynan was captured by the marcher baron, Pain de Chaworth, and kept as a garrison for the king at the subsequent peace. But in the last rebellion of Llewellyn (1282-83), when his brother David led a wild raid into the south, we are amazed to hear that Caer Cynan fell by surprise on April 26, 1282. The captors dismantled it, destroying all that they could, but in June the Earl of Gloucester led an expedition to recover it, patched up its gates, and threw in a small garrison. On his return march to Llandeilo he was surprised by an ambush, and his force routed, the son of the Earl of Pembroke and other knights being slain. This disaster threw the English on the defensive, and they, with difficulty, held their own in Dynevor and Carmarthen; yet Caer Cynan, hastily garrisoned by 50 men only, does not seem to have fallen back into the hands of the rebels. No doubt the warders kept better watch than their predecessors in April, till the war ended in 1283.

When, therefore, Rhys ap Maredud, in his ill-advised local rising of 1287, is recorded to have seized Dynevor and Caer Cynan on a single day, we can have no doubt that surprise or treachery settled the matter, though no details survive. Probably the captors again wrecked it, as in 1282, since there is no record of its being recovered by force, yet it was again in English hands a few weeks later.

Our latest military note on Caer Cynan is that it was maintained against Owen Glendower, when he conquered the rest of Carmarthenshire in 1403, by a castellan named John Skidmore, from whom there survives only a melancholy note that he had been blockaded for a year "so that no man may pass this way," yet was still holding out. There is no mention of its surrender, and it was back in English hands in 1405, but whether it fell by starvation in 1404, or held out till the time of recovery, seems unknown. Nothing but famine could have reduced it, if defended by a vigilant governor. Somewhere in the time of the Wars of the Roses it was haunted by outlaws, became a mere "spelunca latronum," and was dismantled and gutted by a sheriff of Carmarthenshire and a bailiff of Kidwelly [1461?].

Kidwelly

At the highest point on the estuary of the Towy to which a small mediæval vessel could push its way, lay the royal castle and the adjacent borough of

Carmarthen, the central and crucial point in the line of fortresses by which the Welsh of the South were shut up into the inland. Often sacked and often rebuilt, Carmarthen Castle had a long and chequered history. But the visitor of ancient fortresses in 1926 will not find it worth his while to linger there, for of the old Norman stronghold hardly a visible fragment remains. It is smothered up in the architecture of a large county jail of the time of the Georges. The gate-house can be detected, and considerable patches of wall, but all is built up and inaccessible.

The royal stronghold of Carmarthen, however, was flanked on each side by two first-class baronial strongholds, both of which have escaped the fate of the central fortress, and well deserve a visit. These are Kidwelly on the east and Llanstephan on the west side of the great estuary of the Towy, where it broadens into Carmarthen Bay. Each was the capital of a great marcher lordship, and associated with the name of one of the chief Anglo-Norman families of South Wales. Kidwelly boasted of the Londres and Chaworth dynasties—Llanstephan of that of the Camvilles.

At Kidwelly the founder was William de Londres, who much at the same time that William Fitz Baldwin occupied Carmarthen for the king, seized for himself a holding on the coast to the east, and built his castle, in or about the year 1106, on the muddy creek where the Gwendraeth river flows into the estuary. It was a precarious foothold for the invaders, for their numbers were small, and the castle was only a " *motte* and bailey " fortress of the earliest Norman type. The Welsh, expelled from the shore, had gone up into the hills, and were biding their time, which was to come again and again in days when civil strife in England left the marcher barons deprived of support. Kidwelly was thrice taken and thrice rebuilt, before Edward I. pacified South Wales—the last occasion was as late as 1263.

It is probable that the two epochs of building, which we can trace in the castle as it stands, represent two reconstructions, the one after the capture of the place by " the Lord Rhys " in 1190, the other after another sack by Llewellyn of Gwynedd in 1263. Kidwelly stands on a natural mound, close above the steep bank of the Gwendraeth. It shows an outer and an inner ward, the former an irregular oval following the contour of the mound, the latter completely inside the outer ward, save that on the steep front overhanging the river its wall joins with that of the exterior defence, so that for many yards the eastern wall of both is the same. The reason for this is obviously that on that side, owing to the steep slope and the water, this section of the wall is inaccessible and impregnable.

It looks as if the outer ward had been originally a big shell keep, replacing, no doubt, the palisades of the original castle of 1106. It has a strong gate-house, and four mural towers on the outer front—that not protected by the river— with a good ditch beyond. The rebuilder, presumably Patrick de Chaworth, in or about 1270, when he had recovered his ruined castle from the Welsh after the peace of Montgomery in 1267, turned it into a fortress of the newly-introduced " concentric " style. He rebuilt the earlier gate-house, making it immensely strong and lofty—it is sixty feet high—the remains of the first Norman building are imbedded in it. It shows two circular towers on each side of a recessed and machicolated archway, with two floors containing large chambers above. There was also carefully-schemed outside protection, first a small semi-circular barbican beyond the ditch, covering the drawbridge, which could be let down from the gate-house, and outside this again a second gate-house looking towards the town.

The new inner ward, completely contained within the outer ward, was a quadrangle with high circular towers at each corner, but it does not so completely overlook the outer defences as does the inner ward of Caerphilly—an almost contemporary building, of which we have spoken elsewhere as the strongest of all "concentric" fortresses. Its most curious feature is a large chapel built out from the *enceinte* toward the river—the only projection on that side.

On the north side of the castle was a postern with a small gate-house, communicating by a bridge across the moat with a slightly walled outer bailey with a separate ditch, much recalling the "hornwork" at Caerphilly. But this addition was obviously not considered very important, as it is not strongly protected. Kidwelly was refortified just too late to be of much use for the present: the old Welsh wars were nearing their end. But a century later the rebuilding was justified, when the tidal wave of Glendower's South Welsh raid of 1403, though it washed as far as Carmarthen and Llanstephan, and overwhelmed them, stopped short at the concentric walls of Kidwelly. Owen attacked them, once alone, once with the aid of some French auxiliaries who had just landed on the bay. But on each occasion the attack was short and fruitless, and the castle came safe through the years 1403-05, when so many others perished.

The history of the families which held Kidwelly, castle and march, is interesting. The original marchers of the house of Maurice de Londres ended in an heiress, Hawise, who in 1244 married Patrick of Chaworth. With their grand-daughter Maud of Chaworth, the castle again passed to a new line, for this lady married a prince of royal blood, Henry, younger son of Edmund "Crouchback," Earl of Lancaster. When Henry's turbulent elder brother, Thomas of Lancaster, went to the block in 1322, leaving no issue, the earldom devolved on Henry, and Kidwelly became swallowed up in the immense Lancastrian domains. But in 1361 the line of Lancaster, like those of Londres and Chaworth, ended in an heiress, the Duchess Blanche, wife of John of Gaunt. From Blanche and John descend almost every royal house in Europe, and the rather obscure Chaworths of Kidwelly, therefore, became ancestors in the female line of the Kings of Spain and Portugal, the Dukes of Burgundy, and the Hapsburg Emperors. The most curious memorial of this may be found at Bruges, on the magnificent tomb of Charles the Bold, which is adorned with the armorial bearings of all his house. Among the shields of Emperors and Kings of France, England and Portugal, Dukes of Brabant and Burgundy, and Counts of Flanders, may be found by the careful antiquary the paternal coat of " Mahaud de Chaworth " duly recorded.*

The castle of Kidwelly, like all those which fell first into the Duchy of Lancaster, and then, with Henry IV., to the crown, suffered the neglect which so many outlying residences of a master who never visited them were bound to undergo. In Leland's visit, in 1540, it was still " metely well kept up," having undergone repairs when Henry VII. once made a royal tour in South Wales. He saw it as "a castle very fair and doubly walled." In the Civil Wars of Charles I., though already dilapidated, it was still worthy of occupation by one party and of capture by the other in 1644. Presumably it was " slighted " by the Parliamentarians, like so many other Welsh strongholds in 1646. It was never repaired, and ultimately alienated by the administrators of the Duchy of Lancaster ; the present owner is Lord Cawdor.

Llanstephan

Facing Kidwelly across the broad estuary of the Towy lies another famous marcher stronghold, the Castle of Llanstephan, less noted in history than its pendant across the water, but far more picturesquely situated. The March of Llanstephan flanked Carmarthen on the west as Kidwelly did on the east, and as the head of a rather narrow lordship was as much exposed as its neighbour to the raids of the inland Welsh, when they were set on cutting the connection between Carmarthen and Pembrokeshire. It is said to owe its first origin to Gilbert de Clare, the first Earl of Pembroke and Lord of Cardigan, who built a castle here in 1112. No doubt it was a " *motte* and bailey " structure of a simple sort, whose site was placed on the highest point above the estuary, with the advantage of steep slopes on two sides. It was probably an affair of timber and palisades only, as our first note of it is that it was *burnt* in 1137 by Welsh raiders from the north—Owen and Cadwallader, sons of Gruffyd, Prince of North Wales. It was rebuilt, no doubt, in the same flimsy fashion, in the next year, but only to be captured again in 1145 by Cadell, Maredud and Rhys, the sons of the Prince of Deheubarth—the nearest enemy. This time Llanstephan was garrisoned by its captors, and held for several years, being only surrendered to Henry II. when all the princes of South Wales sought peace from him in 1158, because they saw that the anarchy of Stephen's reign was passed, and a strong man had arisen in his place. Henry gave the castle and march of Llanstephan to William de Camville, an adventurous knight from Devonshire, whose descendants held it for nearly two centuries—suffering many perils and tribulations as the defenders of an exposed frontier stronghold of high strategic importance. Thrice they saw their castle captured by the Welsh princes, in 1189, in 1215 and 1257. It will be noted that these three years each mark a time of trouble in English politics—the disorders of the last unhappy year of Henry II., the war that followed the sealing and repudiation of Magna Carta, and the

* But with an erroneous blazon. The real Chaworth arms were barry gules and argent, with four black martlets superimposed.

196

KIDWELLY CASTLE : VIEW FROM THE BANKS OF THE GWENDRAETH

LLANSTEPHAN CASTLE : VIEW FROM THE NORTH

commencement of the outbreak of the Montfortian party among the barons against Henry III. But the Camvilles had rooted themselves deeply into the soil, and after each disaster returned to repair once more their devastated castle. Its present aspect is no doubt that to which it was transformed by Geoffrey de Camville, when he returned to restore his home after the Welsh war had ended in 1267, at the Peace of Montgomery. Some of the details look as late as 1300, but it is possible to make deductions as to the shape of the earlier stone castles, one built probably in the time of Henry II., between 1158 and 1189, and the other soon after 1215.

The outline of Llanstephan is irregular, following the contour of the eminence on which it is built. There is a small square inner ward in the south-west corner, with its back to the steepest acclivity, of which the main surviving feature is a very strong and solid battlemented gate-house, fitted with a portcullis. The outer ward has two sides more or less straight, the third and longest curved, and narrowing to its eastern end. In the *enceinte* of the outer ward are three mural towers, and a very large and dominant gate-house in the north front, which has practically been converted into a keep. It has drum-towers on each side and a three-floored building between them, in the lowest story of which there was evidently a large arched doorway when the structure was first built. But this doorway has been completely built up, both on the inside and the outside, and on the left of the gate-house a new and much smaller door has been knocked through the *enceinte*, and has been made into the main entry to the castle. Thereby the original gate-house was turned into an isolated keep—far the strongest (though the most exposed) point of defence in the whole fortress. This keep contains a large hall with a fine fireplace supported by carved heads of ladies, and windows in "Decorated" style—their tracery is gone save that of one which has escaped complete destruction by being built up.

It would seem likely that the first stone castle, that of the reign of Henry II., may have been a building which did no more than replace the original palisades of the time of Henry I. by a walled *enceinte*, with (no doubt) some sort of a strong point where the present inner ward stands. The re-builder in the early years of Henry III. may have added the small gate-tower and other defences of the inner ward, and also the mural towers and the great gate-house

Llanstephan. Hall over Early Outer Gate-way

197

in the outer ward. These having failed to withstand the attack of Llewellyn, in 1257, the last rebuilder, Geoffrey de Camville, working somewhere in the reign of Edward I., may have turned the gate-house into a keep, and made the small new door of entry beside it. The decorations in the hall of the keep look like work of *circ.* 1300.

The last Camville, William, third of that name, died in 1338, his daughter and heiress, Eleanor, married one Robert de Penrees, three of whose descendants held the castle. The second of them, Sir John Penrees, had ill-luck, for he was captured by Owen Glendower in 1403, and (whether at the same time or subsequently) Llanstephan itself fell by treachery into the hands of the rebels. They only held it for three months, however—by December, 1403, it had been recovered, and one David Howell made its castellan. He succeeded in maintaining it for the whole of the rest of the war in South Wales.* In 1408 Sir John Penrees, having escaped from his captivity, was regranted his castle by Henry IV., but on hard terms—he obtained the place itself but only half the lordship. Apparently it was considered that by being lost, and then recovered by the royal forces, it had escheated and become the king's. On the death of the last Penrees (*circ.* 1443), this right was exercised in full, and Llanstephan was handed about between Lancastrian and Yorkist partisans for forty years, the last individual holder being Jasper Tudor, the uncle of Henry VII., to whom his nephew gave it in 1495. After his death, without issue, it became permanently crown property, and was in charge of a series of " stewards and receivers," who gradually let it fall to pieces, till in the reign of George III. it was alienated, by sale, to a private person.

PEMBROKESHIRE

This westernmost shire, " little England beyond Wales," as it has been called, was more thickly settled up by the invaders of the time of Rufus and Henry I., than any other region won from the native princes in the first rush of conquest. It received not only English settlers but a large colony of Flemings during that rather mysterious emigration from Flanders, which occurred in the first quarter of the twelfth century—whether it was due to inundations, as some allege, or to the fierce war of succession between William Clito and Dietrich of Alsace. The Flemish immigrants do not seem to have been so much military adventurers (like Gilbert of Ghent and others who followed William the Conqueror in the previous generation) but for the most part merchants and farmers. Yet they were ready to fight if attacked, and always turned out to help the Anglo-Norman lords of the marches. Visible as an alien element for some fifty years or so, they became absorbed long ere 1200 in the main body of the English settlers. They were most numerous in Pembrokeshire, but were also to be found in the peninsula of Gower.

* It is conceivable that David Howell, and not some Camville a hundred years earlier, was the person who blocked up the great gate-house as a military precaution.

198

LLANSTEPHAN CASTLE: GATE TOWER OF INNER WARD

PEMBROKE CASTLE : VIEW FROM THE WEST

The original coming of the Marcher Lords to Pembrokeshire goes back to the reign of William Rufus, and was connected with their ambitious attempts to conquer the whole of Wales, north and south. While the Earls of Chester and Shrewsbury were busy on their enterprise on the Menai Straits, which ultimately came to ruin, Arnulf of Montgomery, the younger son of the great Earl Roger of Shrewsbury, appeared at Milford Haven in 1090, and fixed his fort on a cliff overhanging one of its many creeks, where he built, as we are told, " a castle of palisading and turf "—one of the usual primitive Norman " *motte* and bailey " structures, no doubt. The situation—though not so striking as that of Harlech or Montgomery—was sufficiently strong, and unlike almost all of the other marcher-castles of Wales, Pembroke was never destined to fall back, even for a moment, into the hands of the native princes.

The geography of the region that was to depend in after years on the Castle of Pembroke, is rather abnormal. It is cut up into two unequal parts by the immense fiord of Milford Haven, and the countless muddy creeks that run out from it. The southern part of the modern county is a broad fertile low-lying peninsula between the Haven and the sea. On the other side of the Haven is the land of Rhos, much cut into by the tidal inlets : this is also fairly level and desirable land. North and east lies the other half of the county, much higher and more hilly, which was never so thickly occupied by the incoming settlers as Rhos and South Pembroke. But it was seized and overrun, and two castles, Cardigan and Cilgerran, were built to connect the Pembrokeshire settlement with the conquered districts further north, which the invaders (as it turned out) were not destined to retain.

Before the Norman attack on North Wales came to a disastrous end in 1098, with the death of Earl Hugh of Shrewsbury, in the battle on Menai Straits, the Welsh had already been rising in every direction, and endeavouring to cast out their enemies. The colony in Pembroke was saved by the fine defence made by Gerald of Windsor, the castellan left in charge by Arnulf of Montgomery in 1097-8. And when Henry I. came into South Wales and resettled matters the day of danger was past. Henry expelled the whole House of Montgomery, in consequence of the rebellion of its head, Robert of Belesme, and substituted for them the de Clares. Gilbert of Clare was the progenitor of both of the famous branches of that family. From his elder son Richard came the line which ultimately inherited Glamorgan and became Earls of Gloucester. From his younger son Gilbert, issued the family which got the title of Earl of Pembroke from King Stephen, and which produced the famous " Strongbow," the Conqueror of Ireland. Gilbert the Elder made Cardigan Castle the centre of his holding, and held most of the lands, both to the north and the south of it. On his death in 1116, he left the March of Cardigan to his elder son, but the Pembrokeshire half of his western estates, and the castle and lordship of Chepstow in the east, to the younger. Many years after, King Stephen gave the royal Castle of Pembroke and the title of earl to this second Gilbert. But in addition to the de Clare holding in this western extremity of Wales, there were other marcher lordships—Kemmes in the north-west belonged to the Martins, its castle was Nevern [Nanhyfer]. Emlyn fell to the descendants of Gerald the first castellan of Pembroke, founder of the family of Fitzgerald—from whom in the next generation came so many of the conquerors of Ireland. Wiston Castle, in the centre, was built by and named from the Fleming Wizo, whose sons held it after him, and Haverfordwest, the chief castle of Rhos, belonged to Richard Fitz-Tankard. The earl's own lands only comprised the southern half of modern Pembrokeshire, and certain enclaves in the north, surrounded by the estates of smaller men.

The March of Cardigan was lost by the de Clares during the anarchy of the reign of Stephen (1136), and the castle itself—maintained for long years after, in 1157. But Pembrokeshire (if we may use the term) remained as a whole in English hands; though at one time and another several of its outlying castles were lost in times of trouble, they were regained and generally rebuilt. No serious breach was ever made in "Little England beyond Wales" down to the days of the final annexation of the whole land by Edward I.

But the hand of time has fallen heavily on the fortresses of West Wales, and only some five or six of them still show remains which demand a visit from the intelligent antiquary. Haverfordwest, " slighted " by the Parliamentarians in 1646, shows fragments built up (like those of Carmarthen) in an eighteenth century jail. At Nevern bare traces of a *motte* and bailey castle can be discerned. Of Cardigan there are some portions of the keep visible, incorporated in a private house. Of Emlyn there is nothing in evidence but a gateway. Narberth has no vestige of its original Norman *motte* and bailey, but some drum-towers of a later stronghold, built by Sir Andrew Perrott, in the reign of Henry III. Tenby Castle, which once protected that busy little port, shows only a sad ivy-covered remnant of one small tower. Picton (Slebech) has some Edwardian work, smothered by incongruous nineteenth century sham-Norman additions, and with big Georgian windows cut everywhere. Roche is a lonely peel-tower turned into a modern residence.

Of places which contain enough evidence of their ancient splendour to make a visit advisable we can only cite first and foremost Pembroke itself, then the very interesting Carew and Manorbier, and lastly, the much smaller castles of Upton and Lamphey, Cilgerran and Lawhaden.

Pembroke

Pembroke Castle, as it now appears, is a vast empty shell, of which the outer walls are everywhere visible and imposing, while the interior fittings have almost entirely disappeared, save for the great towers of the inner ward. There is a curious feeling of vacancy and disappointment when, after entering the lofty and complicated gate-house, one finds oneself confronted with a great empty space, with a very large railed lawn-tennis ground occupying the major part of it. The proper way to appreciate the castle's magnificence is to cross the creek south of it, and view the walls and towers, rising above their

PEMBROKE CASTLE : THE KEEP AND INNER WARD

PEMBROKE CASTLE : THE GATE-HOUSE FROM THE OUTER WARD

cliff foundations, from the opposite side of the water, when the splendid shell is visible, and the inner emptiness cannot be guessed at.

Arnulf of Montgomery, coming to Milford Haven by sea in 1190, chose as his base of operations an acutely-pointed rocky peninsula between two creeks of the Haven, those now known as Pembroke River and Monkton Pill. Across the sharp projecting angle of this headland he drew a ditch from cliff to cliff, and set up a wall of turf and palisading behind it. The small space which he thus occupied now forms the inner ward of Pembroke castle. It is improbable that at the first foundation of the castle there was any " outer bailey "—if there was anything of the sort it must have been far smaller than the present very large outer ward. If there was a " *motte* " it must have been on the site of the present circular keep, but there is very little sign of earlier earth-accumulation about the base of this great tower, which is practically founded on the rock.

Arnulf of Montgomery was absent from Pembroke at the time of the general Welsh insurrection in 1096-7, and the barely-tenable castle was defended by his castellan Gerald of Windsor, who only succeeded in holding it by a combination of obstinacy and craft which moved the admiration of the chroniclers. When the place was almost starved out, the besiegers broke up the leaguer and went off despairing of success. Henry I., in 1102, confiscated all the possessions of the Montgomery brothers for their acts of rebellion, Pembroke among the rest. But after a short interval he gave it over to Gerald of Windsor, who had defended it so well in 1097, and Gerald justified his trust by long and faithful service. It is probable that it was he who first girt the inner ward with a stone *enceinte* instead of a palisade, and he may very likely have marked out the line of the future outer ward by ditch and hedge, for he held the castle for many years and was a prosperous man. Pembroke was a royal castle, but Gerald acquired many lands for himself, and built a private stronghold at Carew in the midst of them. These, his family, the Fitzgeralds, continued to hold, after Stephen, in 1138, gave over Pembroke Castle to Gilbert de Clare, and made him earl of the shire—though its limits were much less than those of the modern county. It was probably either Gilbert, or his son the famous Richard " Strongbow," the conqueror of Ireland, who built the circular Norman keep in the inner ward, which forms the most conspicuous part of Pembroke's earlier fortifications. It stands isolated, close to the outer wall of the ward, but not touching it, and was apparently intended to command the whole landward front of the *enceinte*, which was then a simple stone curtain, the semi-circular towers which now show in it being probably the work of Strongbow's successor and son-in-law, William the Marshall, to whom the earldom descended in 1189.

The keep is a big architectural experiment—some 75 feet high, circular instead of square—a rarity in this island—and vaulted with a dome of stone, which is still rarer. It has a basement and three stories above it intended for residence, though their windows are small and all look inwards toward the court. The walls are immensely thick—19 feet at the base—and the entrance is on the first story, and must have been reached by wooden steps, which have of course, disappeared long ago. If we reckon that Earl William the Marshall, recast the exposed front of the inner ward according to the improved military architecture of 1200, by furnishing it with the two semi-circular projecting towers which gave protection by flanking fire to the whole line of wall,* we shall probably not be far out in our chronology. And it may have been he, also, since he was both wealthy and a skilled soldier, who first turned the outer ward into a stone *enceinte*, quadrupling the size of the area encircled by solid defences. By this time Pembroke had grown to be a most important place, largely because it had become the regular port of embarcation for the new English possessions in Ireland; a considerable town had grown up outside the gates of the castle. This resort of merchants was protected, probably during the thirteenth century, by a wall drawn from water to water, from the Pembroke River creek on the north to the Monkton creek on the south, so that the town became a sort of outermost ward to the castle—as was the case also at Conway in North Wales.

But the development of the castle's outer ward into its present shape is, so far as architectural evidence goes, not the work of William the Marshall, but that of the two de Valence earls, William and Aymer, who held the place and earldom from 1260 to 1323, after the male line of the Marshalls had died out. William de Valence, the half-brother of Henry III., had married Joanna de Montchensy, one of the four co-heiresses among whom the Marshall lands were divided, and her share of them was Pembroke and the lands immediately around it.

The new defences of the outer ward consisted of six towers, four of them circular, and a very fine gate-house in the south-east front. The ward is, roughly speaking, an irregular hexagon, with a tower at each angle, where the curtain takes a new direction. The gate-house is its most striking feature, not only for its size and strength, but for its very elaborate outer protections, there being a barbican just outside it with a small external gate, placed not in line with the main arch of the gate-house, but at right angles to it, so that any one coming through the barbican exposed himself to flank fire from the inner building. The great door had no less than three portcullises, each requiring to be forced by an assailant in succession. It has also an inner defence of a unique sort, a battlemented flying arch connecting the two round towers in the rear-face of them. The object of this architectural freak has been much disputed. Obviously it could only be of use if the enemy had got into the outer ward and were attacking the gate-house from behind—a not very probable conjecture. The structure has two upper stories above the portcullis chamber, with good rooms therein. In one of them Henry VII. is said to have been born, and in 1540 Leland was shown the large royal coat-of-arms in this chamber, which had been inserted in his honour. The chance which brought Henry's mother to Pembroke was that his uncle Jasper Tudor (who had been presented with the castle and the earldom by his half-brother Henry VI.) was entertaining his

* One of these, the Prison Tower, is intact; of the other, called the Horse-Shoe Tower, only the foundation remains. And the old inner-ward curtain between these two towers has vanished entirely—a fact which puzzles observers at the first glance.

CAREW CASTLE: SIR JOHN PERROT'S BUILDINGS

CAREW CASTLE: GATE-WAY OF SIR RHYS AP THOMAS'S HALL

sister-in-law, Lady Margaret, who had just lost her husband in the previous November, and was delivered of the future king, a posthumous child, in January, 1457.

Jasper Tudor was the first Earl of Pembroke who had resided in the castle for many a year—the Valence line had (like the de Clares and the Marshalls) gone off into female succession in the third generation, and with the extinction in 1391 of the descendants of Isabella de Valence, who had passed the earldom to her son, John de Hastings, the title had lapsed and the castle reverted to the crown. Jasper is said to have been a builder, but the general aspect of the outer ward of Pembroke suggests late thirteenth or early fourteenth century rather than mid-fifteenth century architecture.

There are in the inner ward buildings which do not belong to the earlier Norman castle, but to reconstruction, probably by the de Valences. Such are the great hall in the north-east angle of the ward, which evidently superseded an earlier Norman hall, and the domestic buildings adjoining it, where, in the so-called Oriel, the west window may be as late as Jasper Tudor. The chancery, where the clerical business of the palatine earldom was transacted, is but a fragment, but also looks fairly late.

Pembroke possesses one curiosity unparalleled in other British castles : under the inner ward on the north side is an immense natural cavern, called the Wogan, 70 feet long and 50 broad, which was from the first utilized as a good dry storehouse. It was approachable from above by stairs, and below had an opening on to the creek, blocked by a water-gate, by which boats could communicate with the castle, and even small ships lie close in and land heavy goods. Leland saw this cave, but got neither its name nor its position quite correctly. He wrote : " In the bottom of the great strong round tower in the inner ward [the Keep] is a marvellous vault caullid the Hogan." As a matter of fact the cave is rather further north than the keep's foundations. There was another small water-gate in the outer ward, under the so-called Monkton Tower on the west side of the castle.

Pembroke Castle was so strong that throughout the Middle Ages it remained a " virgin fortress." Though Welsh rebels at one time and another captured places of such strength as Conway and Harlech, and Caer Cynan, and burnt the outer ward of the formidable Caerphilly, they never got into Pembroke—though Owen Glendower once took a sort of blackmail or danegelt out of all Pembrokeshire. In the Wars of the Roses, Jasper Tudor did not attempt to hold his own castle, but took refuge in Harlech, so that the artillery of Edward IV. had no occasion to make experiments on Milford Haven. During the Civil Wars of 1642-46 Pembroke alone of all Welsh towns not only declared for the Parliament, but held its own for years against all the attacks of the South Wales royalists. The destruction of town wall and castle wall alike was reserved for that incoherent business, the " Second Civil War " of 1648. When in that year all the discontented, not only the oppressed "Malignants," but the Scots, and many other former enemies of the king, took arms against the Parliament, the revolt in South Wales was started by Colonel Poyer,

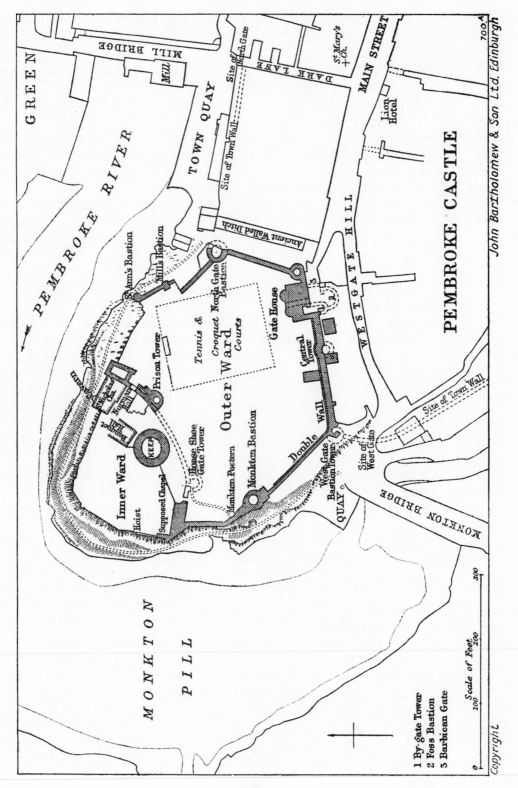

PEMBROKE CASTLE

GREEN

MILL BRIDGE

MILL

PEMBROKE RIVER

TOWN QUAY

Site of Town Wall

Site of
North Gate

DARK LANE

MAIN STREET

St Mary's
+ Ch.

Lion
Hotel

Ancient Walled Ditch

Arm's Bastion

Mills Bastion

Prison Tower

Tennis &
Croquet
Courts

North Gate
Bastion

Gate House

WESTGATE HILL

3

2

1

Hoist

Inner Ward

Supposed Chapel

Banquet Hall

Norman Hall

Michaels Old

KEEP

House Shoe
Gate Tower

Monkton Postern

Outer Ward

Central
Tower

Monkton Bastion

Double Wall

West Gate
Bastion Tower

QUAY

Site of
West Gate

Site of Town Wall

MONKTON BRIDGE

MONKTON

PILL

Scale of Feet

0   100   200   300

Copyright

John Bartholomew & Son Ltd. Edinburgh

700A

1 By-gate Tower
2 Foss Bastion
3 Barbican Gate

204

governor of Pembroke Castle, and joined by many other old Roundheads. The townsmen of Pembroke took part in the revolt, and after the rebels had been crushed in the open field, town and castle were defended against Cromwell himself from May 22 to July 11. That the siege lasted so long was due to the fact that Cromwell had only a few light field pieces with him—he sent to Gloucester for heavy guns to be forwarded by sea—but they had ill-luck by the way, and only turned up in the Haven on July 1. Meanwhile Cromwell, much enraged, tried an escalade—his stormers actually got over the town wall, and fought their way to near the castle barbican—there to be repulsed and expelled by a general rally of the garrison. On July 1 the big guns were unshipped, ten days later they began to play on both town and castle. But what was almost worse, the rebels were nearly out of food and powder. On a last summons on July 11, they surrendered—the rank and file to go free, the officers to leave the realm save five or six named men, who were to be at the mercy of the Parliament. Three, Colonel Laugharn, the head of the rebel army, Poyer, governor of Pembroke, and a Colonel Powell, were tried and condemned to death :—by a curious freak of the godly men at Westminster they were told that they should cast lots for one of them to go to death, and the other two to captivity. Poyer drew the unlucky lot, and died very handsomely before a firing party in Covent Garden.

Meanwhile the castle was " slighted "—the Barbican Gate, and five towers of the outer ward, were blown up, more or less effectively, also the curtain of the inner ward, between the two round towers. The rest of the damage at present visible was done by two centuries of stone-hunting vandals, who had houses to build in Pembroke town. The slighter and more easily demolished inner buildings gradually vanished—so, of course, did all lead and timber. And so there remains to-day little more than a magnificent shell, set here and there with the broken mediæval towers whose mortar has defied the spoiler. Only the keep, the oldest stone building of all, is practically intact, save for its inner fittings.

Carew

Soon after the first permanent settlement of the conquered lands of Pembrokeshire, when Henry I. had expelled the Montgomeries, and regulated the new holdings, he made (as we have already stated) Gerald of Windsor castellan of Pembroke Castle. This was a royal possession, not a baronial stronghold, but Gerald of Windsor was allowed to acquire for his personal enjoyment much land in the new English colony. His private seat, as opposed to his official post in Pembroke Castle, was Carew, five miles from Pembroke north-eastward, above one of the innumerable creeks of Milford Haven. Here he built a stronghold for himself, no doubt originally a " *motte* and bailey " defence of the simple Norman sort. He had other lands further to the north-east, in a separate patch, where the castle of Emlyn was afterwards built. Gerald was a great fighting man—but like Menelaus in Homer—better remembered for his matrimonial infelicities than for his exploits in war. He had married Nesta, daughter of Rhys ap Tudor, Prince of Deheubarth, and according to some authorities, Carew came to him as her dowry. Be this as it may, this first experiment in Welsh alliances was not happy : the lady was very beautiful— " the Helen of her time," say the chroniclers—and had all Helen's fatal facility. While a hostage for her father at the king's court she had become his mistress, and had borne him a son, Henry Fitz Henry. Gerald was apparently ready to ignore this slip ; but after she had been his wife some years, and had given him a daughter and several sons, she was carried off—not unwillingly as it would seem—by her cousin, Owen ap Cadogan, a prince of Powys. After she had been with him some time, Owen was expelled from his lands ; but several years after he returned to Wales and was slain on the wayside by Gerald, at a chance meeting. The castellan of Pembroke died soon after (1116 ?) and Nesta then married Stephen, the constable of Cardigan, and had a third family by him. Of the children of this prolific lady the royal bastard, whom his father endowed with the lands of Narberth, was killed in battle in 1157, but left issue— Fitz Henrys. The Fitzgeralds, who came from her first husband, and the Fitz Stephens, who came from her second, were well-endowed Pembrokeshire knights, and great allies. It is an odd fact that the first Norman invasion of Ireland was conducted in common by descendants of all three branches of Nesta's issue. Before Strongbow came over to wed the heiress of Leinster, and to claim its crown, the adventurers had been led by Robert Fitz Stephen, a son of the constable of Cardigan, and by his nephews, Meilyr Fitz Henry—the king's grandson—and Robert of Barry, son of Nesta's daughter Angharad, the child of Gerald of Windsor. And the reinforcements that joined them were under Maurice Fitzgerald, Nesta's second son by the castellan of Pembroke, and Raymond Fitzgerald, son of his elder brother William, the Lord of Carew. From this curious family party sprang the nucleus of the Anglo-Norman nobility of Ireland, where Fitz Stephens, Barrys, Fitz Henrys and, above all, Fitzgeralds, were all to be famous names. And all these founders of houses were half-Welsh or quarter-Welsh in their lineage by descent from Nesta.

The elder line of Fitzgeralds continued to hold their castle of Carew, and when patronymic surnames were superseded by local surnames in general English usage, took to calling themselves Carews. They survived for many generations as one of the most important Anglo-Norman families of Wales, and sent out a flourishing branch to the West of England where, in Tudor and Stuart times, Carews and Careys were prominent. The original castle of Gerald of Windsor has often been rebuilt : it was no doubt replaced by a stone walled building before the twelfth century was nearing its end, but the greater part of the older half of the present Carew looks like thirteenth century work, though fragments of an earlier date may lurk in it. It was evidently, by 1250, a square castle of one strong ward, with drum towers projecting at its corners, and giving some facilities for flank-fire along the *enceinte*. The two western drums were strengthened with projecting " spurs," like those to be seen at Goodrich. The eastern front, where lay the main approach, was strengthened by an outlying base-court, or slightly protected bailey, inside which was a barbican, blocking the way to the great gate. Like that of Pembroke, from which it may have been copied, it compelled anyone making for the main entrance to turn at right-angles after passing the barbican-gate.

The comparatively early date of the east front of Carew is vouched for by the smallness of its chambers, and the meagre allowance of windows, which makes them very dark. Nothing can be a greater contrast to it than the west front, which faces it across the quadrangle. This was thoroughly reconstructed in the reign of Henry VII. by Sir Rhys ap Thomas, the Welsh magnate who was the first friend to join the adventure of " Richmond " when he landed at Milford Haven. Rhys started the general defection from the cause of Richard III., which was to go so far, and Henry heaped gifts on him—Dynevor Castle (as we have seen) was among them—and made him the wealthiest man in Wales. The style of the new side of Carew is rich early Tudor, with plenty of light windows and armorial decoration. The very large banqueting hall occupies most of the west side of the court, and has at its entrance a tower over whose door appear the shields of King Henry, with the Tudor red dragon as its supporter, of Arthur, Prince of Wales, and of his bride, Catherine of Aragon. This combination fixes its date to 1501-02. We are told that Sir Rhys got possession of the castle by purchasing it from the contemporary head of the Carew family, who was a thriftless man, and was killed many years after by a cannon ball, at the siege of Térouanne in 1513. These buildings of *circ.* 1500, though mainly designed for comfort and splendour, did not wholly destroy the military efficiency of the castle. But the same cannot be said for the work of the last converter of Carew. The grandson of Sir Rhys having been attainted and executed for treason in the reign of Henry VIII., the castle fell to the crown, and was given by Queen Elizabeth to Sir John Perrott. This active and imperious person, one of the Queen's many unlucky tools in Ireland, fell to work on the surviving parts of the thirteenth century castle, and took out the whole of the two upper stories of its north side, making long handsome galleries and chambers, with broad many-mullioned windows looking outward as well as inward. In fact he made a good third of this long front of the walls into a long show of stained glass—a few cannon balls would bring it down. Perrott fell into disfavour, saw his estates confiscated and died a prisoner in the Tower. The crown was then again in possession, but for some time Carew was let on lease to the representative of the original holder, Sir John Carew, of the West Country branch—who sublet it to the Phillipses of Picton. Despite of its very unmilitary aspect in its last shape it was held for the royalists in the great Civil War—naturally to be taken with ease by the Pembrokeshire Parliamentarians in 1644. But they did not hold it for long, and the king's men were in possession in 1646, at the time of the collapse of the royal cause. The castle was left derelict in the later seventeenth century; though the family of Carew did not die out in the male line till the time of George III., when its estates were divided up among co-heiresses, they lived on their Somerset and Devon lands. Carew now makes a most satisfactory and attractive ruin—as Tudor buildings always do—Berry Pomeroy is a parallel case. The unsophisticated and ignorant eye is always pleased by the aspect of empty mullioned windows silhouetted against the sky, and of broken battlements festooned with ivy. The battered and mouldering stumps of Norman keeps and thirteenth century drum-towers, however interesting from the point of view of the student of military architecture, have no such attraction for the plain man on tour, or for the artist or photographer in search of the merely picturesque.

Upton

Situated on a narrow creek running up from Milford Haven—quite a separate one from that on which Carew lies, but only two and a half miles from that great castle, is a smaller stronghold, very typical of the solid style of building by which the minor lords of "Little England beyond Wales" maintained

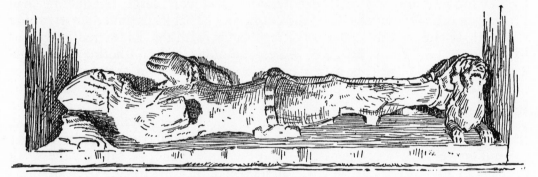

Upton. Recumbent Effigy of one of the Malefaunts

their hold on the land. This is Upton, the patrimony of the Malefaunts, one of the many knightly families who were vassals of the Earls of Pembroke. It shows a particularly fine and perfect example of a thirteenth century gate-house, with two low but strong drum-towers, and a battlemented and machicolated front between them. The narrow and acutely pointed doorway arch had a portcullis, and, no doubt, a drawbridge over a ditch, which has now been filled up. The walls to the right of the gate-house have had eighteenth century windows cut in them, and there is modern building at the back, but the gate-house alone may well attract a visitor to the little-frequented valley and creek of Upton. But in addition there is among the trees to the left of the castle, a "Decorated" style chapel, in which modern windows have been inserted—with two fine tombs bearing recumbent effigies of Malefaunts of the time of Edward III., with very pretty details. There is also a queer candle-bracket projecting from the wall, formed of a clenched hand holding a cresset in which the light would be placed. The Malefaunts survived into Tudor times, and were followed by Bowens, heirs by a female descent, who seem to have pulled the castle about, once and again, but never to have deserted it as a residence. But it has passed to many owners by purchase since their day.

UPTON CASTLE: THE GATE-HOUSE

MANORBIER CASTLE : ENTRANCE TO INNER WARD

MANORBIER CASTLE: CHAPEL STAIR

LAMPHEY : THE CHAPEL

Manorbier

Far larger than Upton, and vying in importance with Carew, is the large castle of Manorbier, close to the seashore, half-way between Tenby and Pembroke. This was the home for two centuries of the de Barrys, the family from which sprang that learned and contentious cleric, Gerald de Barry, alias Giraldus Cambrensis, to whose facile pen we owe so much information, not only about Wales but about Ireland, in the twelfth century. The first de Barry, Odo, was one of the original followers of Gerald of Windsor, and selected his place of abode obviously with reference to a convenient creek which comes up close to its walls, for the place is not built on the most commanding ground that could be got—the church on the opposite knoll is on a far more dominating site. Odo's son, William de Barry, married Angharad, daughter of Gerald of Windsor by the famous Nesta, and from her (as from so many other children of the Helen of South Wales) there sprang a very numerous family, only second to the Fitzgeralds of Carew in local importance. While the head of the house abode at Manorbier, younger scions took part in the invasion of Ireland : Robert was one of the first adventurers, who went with his uncle, Fitz Stephen, at King Dermot's first appeal ; Philip followed later. Their uncle, David, was one of the first Norman bishops of St. Davids, a place in which it was Gerald's dearest ambition to succeed him—an ambition that was never to be fulfilled.

The present Castle of Manorbier shows none of Odo's work, which was probably only a *motte* and bailey, but has some late twelfth century building, to be ascribed in all probability to the brothers of the historian, who held the castle in the reign of Henry II. The whole forms a slightly irregular rectangle, in a single ward, with no keep, but a good strong projecting gate-house, and a well-preserved drum-tower at the north-east angle, the most exposed corner. There are large traces of a barbican enclosure, covering the gate-house and tower by a shallow external work, probably one of no great height, but almost large enough to be called a base-court, or walled bailey. Much of this is now only a few feet high, it has suffered far more than the castle proper, which rises majestically behind it. The walls are all battlemented, and show very few exterior windows, all the lighting being on the side of the courtyard. There is, unfortunately, too much ivy climbing over them to allow of a satisfactory inspection of their details.

The interior buildings of the castle belong to two epochs, partly to the same age as the walls, *i.e.*, to about the time of Henry II., partly to a reconstruction in the latest years of Henry III. or the reign of Edward I. The lofty hall is upon the west side of the court, on a first floor, with barrel-vaulted cellar below, and a large living room opening out of it, with another above on the second floor. The later or Edwardian addition consists of two other great chambers one above the other, to the south end of the original hall, and at right angles to it. This multiplication of living rooms obviously shows an increased attention to domestic comfort. Adjacent to them, in the south-west angle of the court was a new chapel, built, not along the wall, but across its corner, so as to leave a triangular space between it and the *enceinte*. Access, both to hall and chapel, from this open court, is given by broad and graceful outside staircases facing each other, with doors below them opening into the ground floor, or vaults beneath. That leading up to the chapel is shown in one of our illustrations.

There does not seem to have been any addition or important reconstruction in Manorbier made since 1300. That it contains no fifteenth century or Tudor work seems to be accounted for by its history. The de Barrys held it continuously till 1399, when Sir David, a partisan of Richard II., fell under the displeasure of Henry IV., and saw his castle and lands confiscated. They were never, for two centuries, to have any long-standing owners, being handed about successively at intervals to a series of favourites of Lancaster and York, mostly non-resident magnates with interests elsewhere. There was no permanent holder till Queen Elizabeth sold Manorbier to Sir Thomas Owen of Trellwyn : as the castle shows no later Tudor or Jacobean work, it is to be presumed that the Owens preferred to live in their old manor, rather than to adapt a very old-fashioned castle to the ideas of comfort prevalent in 1580. They did not rise to the ambitious building schemes of Sir John Perrott at Carew, and let Manorbier simply crumble away.

Lamphey

The ruins of this stronghold of the bishops of St. David's are extensive and picturesque enough to demand inspection from any archæologist who has reached the neighbouring Pembroke or Manorbier. The bishop was a great landholder in this shire, owning not only a compact block of land round his cathedral, but many outlying manors. Not only was his palace under the shadow of the cathedral capable of a certain amount of defence, but he had at least two outlying fortified places. Lawhaden, near Narberth, of which more anon, was the older, and the more purely military in design, but the name of castle can hardly be denied to the more important Lamphey, half-way

Lamphey Tower

between Manorbier and Pembroke. This was a two-ward castle, with an outer bailey protected on two sides by a stream, which was, no doubt, dammed up to make a broad ditch. There is little left of the wall of this outer ward, but a good deal of the inner buildings. At the entrance was a crenellated gate-house; one side of the court was mainly occupied by a large hall with a battlemented parapet walk along it, and a barrel-vaulted cellar below. A tower shows below its battlements large arches opening to the outside, whose object is not quite clear. But the feature which first catches the eye is the beautiful Perpendicular west window of the early Tudor chapel, which has retained its tracery almost intact, though great sections of the chapel wall have fallen down. The castle is not well kept—it is overrun with pigs and poultry, who do not tend to cleanliness, and much too overgrown with ivy. But it is well worth a visit.

The bulk of the buildings would appear to be of the fourteenth century, though the chapel window is a century and a half later. Probably Bishop Gower (1328-47) a great builder also at St. David's itself, was responsible for the greater part of Lamphey. Another bishop was responsible for its wrecking— the notorious Barlow (1536-48) consoled himself for the filchings which Henry VIII. made on his see-lands, by dilapidating so much of the property of the bishopric as he could control. Not only did he strip off and sell the lead from his own palace at St. David's, but he mutilated in the same sordid way the other episcopal residences. Leland, passing by in Barlow's time, " came to Llanfith, where the Bishop of St. David's hath a place of stone, after castle fashion, standing on a brook that goeth to the salt water by Pembroke." So destruction had not yet, in 1541, got very far, for Leland is always careful to remark stripped roofs or shattered windows. But soon after Lamphey was sold in a somewhat dismantled condition to Walter Devereux, Lord Ferrers, the grandfather of the more famous Walter Devereux, Earl of Essex, the presumptuous and ill-fated favourite of Queen Elizabeth. The residential parts of the castle must still have been in habitable condition in his father's time, since the boy is said to have been bred and educated there. But the new Lamphey Court, hard by, drew away the proprietors from the old fortified buildings, and by the eighteenth century the latter were fallen into the decay in which we now see them.

Lawhaden

This other castle of the Bishops of St. Davids lay towards the eastern side of the county, in hilly ground, looking toward the lands of the unsubdued Welsh princes of Upper Carmarthenshire. It stands on a well-marked knoll, above the Cleddau River, and appears to have started as a stronghold of the normal early thirteenth century type, roughly pentagonal in shape, in order to suit the contour of the hill-top. It must have replaced an earlier " motte " castle destroyed by the Welsh in 1192. Lawhaden is surrounded by a deep-cut dry ditch, only to be passed at one point, where a drawbridge crossed it, in front of the gate-house.   There is no barbican, or outer bailey beyond the ditch. The north-western and western sides of the pentagonal castle have disappeared, but the surviving three have interesting features.   Due south is the gate-house, with the usual pair of drum-towers on each side of a rather lofty gate-arch : the size of their upper windows and the ornamental carving above the arch suggest a fifteenth century date.

In the south-east front is the chapel, of which one wall has disappeared but the others show thirteenth century " Early English " windows.   The entrance to it is by a door in the lower story of an elegant "Perpendicular" tower, so late in style that it probably belongs to Bishop Vaughan (1509-22).   The hall, of which only one side remains, would seem to have been between the chapel and the gate-house.   The north-east front of the castle, of which the greater part is still standing, contains many chambers with windows looking into the courtyard, probably of fourteenth century date.   They may have been offices below and dormitories above.

Though Lawhaden was occupied, and even had new buildings added to it, as late as the early years of Henry VIII., it was doomed to destruction by the scandalous Bishop Barlow, the same waster who alienated Lamphey and defaced his own chief palace at St. David's. The lead of its roofs is said to have gone towards making a dowry for one of his daughters.

Lawhaden Castle.   The Gate-house

Cilgerran

This is the northernmost castle of Pembrokeshire, placed in a commanding position on the south bank of the Teifi, the river which separates it from Cardiganshire. In conjunction with Cardigan on the opposite bank, three miles down-stream, it was obviously intended to dominate the lower Teifi valley, and to keep up communication with the ephemeral " March of Cardigan," which was established during the first Norman invasion of West Wales, held for a few years, and finally lost. Cilgerran was apparently built by Gerald of Windsor, the lord of Carew, and the husband of the famous Nesta, somewhere about 1110-15. No doubt his castle was but a ditched and palisaded stronghold; but it may have got a stone *enceinte* before its first destruction by the Welsh in 1165. This was the work of Rhys ap Griffith—the last prince to rule all Deheubarth—who had captured Cardigan a few weeks before. This earliest Cilgerran was completely destroyed, and it was not till 1204 that William Marshall, Earl of Pembroke, drove out Rhys's son Maelgwyn, and recovered the castle and the surrounding March of Emlyn. He must have repaired it without delay, but probably in no effective fashion, for in 1215 it was captured after one day's assault by Lewellyn the Great of Gwynedd—then at the commencement of his career. William II., the second Earl Marshall, won it back in 1223, and it was no doubt after this second recovery of the castle and its march that Cilgerran was rebuilt in its present form, though some of its detail looks like the work of the Cantilupes, who succeeded the Marshalls twenty years after, and were in possession during the later years of Henry III.

On two sides, the north-east and north-west, the fortress is on the very edge of the cliff above the Teifi, and required no further protection than a plain curtain wall of no great height or strength. The other two sides, facing landward, received strong defences. They have two lines of fortification, an outer bailey reaching from cliff to cliff, and behind this a deep dry ditch covering the front of the inner ward. The main feature of this second line of defence is not, as in so many Welsh castles, a towering gate-house, but two immense cylindrical round towers dominating the whole fortress. The gate-house (part of which is gone) seems to have been a comparatively modest structure. The two towers, in the south-east and south-west fronts of the inner ward, make the most prominent show in every view of Cilgerran. They are set into a lofty curtain, occupying the greater part of the landward front of the castle. It is probable that these great round towers may go back to William Marshall's reconstruction of 1224—they show signs of hasty construction, being built of local stones of all sizes, with no attempt at regularity of lines, and very little hewn stone "ashlar" work, even for windows. Those in the south-east tower are small Norman-style round headed openings, set in pairs. In its south-western twin they are much larger, and apparently later.

Cilgerran, thus refortified, seems to have braved successfully all later storms of Welsh insurrection, though there was a disastrous battle close to its walls in 1258, in which the allied princes of Deheubarth defeated and slew Patrick Chaworth of Kidwelly, then commanding for the king in South Wales. The castle, however, seems to have defied the attack of the victors. It passed on the death of Anselm, the last of the Earls Marshall, in 1245, to Eva, that one of the Marshall co-heiresses who had married a Cantilupe, and at the similar extinction of the line of the Cantilupes in 1272 to the House of Hastings with the hand of another Eva. The Welsh wars, having come to an end in the following generation, it does not seem that the successive Hastings owners paid much attention to Cilgerran. Their interests were at Pembroke and at Abergavenny, where so many of them lie buried. In 1387 the castle is described as in a state of decay, and as we hear nothing of it during the wars of Owen Glendower, it is possible that it may have been completely deserted before 1400. There would seem to be no building within it which need be attributed to any date later than about 1280. But the name of Cilgerran appears in all the lists of possession of successive Earls of Pembroke down to Jasper Tudor and William Herbert. Leland makes no mention of it—which suggests that as a residence was " clene gone " by 1539-40.

Cilgerran Castle, from the Teifi

CRICCIETH CASTLE : AERIAL VIEW

HARLECH CASTLE : DISTANT VIEW FROM THE SOUTH

NORTH WALES

SINCE the north coast of Wales, and the adjacent Isle of Anglesea, fall outside the scope of our inquiry, we have to deal in this section with two comparatively small groups of castles—the one containing a few of the fortresses with which Edward I. set to work to hold down the recently conquered principality of Llewellyn ap Gruffyd, after the war of 1282-3, while the other includes those castles of the old realm of Powys which lie along the Shropshire border, some of them English, others Welsh in origin.

To the former class belong Criccieth, Harlech and Aberystwyth : to the latter Chirk, Montgomery, Dinas Bran, and the Red Castle of Powys—Castel Coch—above Welshpool. The first three were built as part of a systematic plan for occupying the newly conquered lands of Gwynedd by permanent royal garrisons, and holding them as a royal domain. Edward I. had tried once and again, as many of his ancestors had tried, to secure peace in North Wales by accepting its prince as a vassal and putting him under stringent terms of vassalage. The experiment had failed once more, and the king had determined that he would not repeat it, but would simply annex the principality, which had caused such endless trouble to the House of Plantagenet. He did not distribute Llewellyn's lands among Lords Marchers, as he had done with previously annexed Welsh districts, but kept them in his own hands, perhaps opining that royal administration would be less intolerable to the high spirited North Welsh than Marcher Law. This certainly was the idea at the bottom of the curious device by which he made his heir, Edward of Carnarvon, Prince of Wales in 1301. There is no truth in the legend which makes him promise the Welsh " a prince of their own who can speak no word of English," at the time of his son's birth seventeen years before. But there is a certain appreciation of the situation in the story, since doubtless the king did hope to appease particularist sentiment by giving the recently annexed part of Wales a ruler of its own, and avoiding its partition among Lords Marchers. In 1284, immediately after the conquest, he had divided Gwynedd into the three shires of Anglesea, Carnarvon and Merioneth, after the English fashion, and had selected the sites for royal castles, of which Criccieth and Harlech were two. In South Wales the annexed lands of the rebel descendants of the old kings of Deheubarth became the nucleus of the shires of Cardigan and Carmarthen.

The main line of the princes of Powys, on the other hand, as we have already explained when dealing with the Middle Marches, had of late pursued an Anglophil policy, had done good service against their insurgent countrymen, and were left undisturbed, but with the status of great English barons, regularly summoned to Parliament, not that of vassal princes. The only annexations on this side were the lands of certain minor branches of the house of Powys, lords in the valley of the Dee, who had adhered to Llewellyn in the war of 1277, and had seen their insignificant principalities forfeited.

In this region lay Dinas Bran and Chirk, two of the castles with which we have to deal.

Criccieth

This is a castle of secondary importance, but one of those which belonged to Edward's first arrangements for the holding down of North Wales. It lies on a hill over the sea, half-way down the Peninsula of Lleyn, and dominating its coast. It is quite a small fortress : its ruins show a single lofty ward, with a

Criccieth

great gate-house on the shortest of its roughly hexagonal fronts, facing towards the small town below. If there was an outer bailey—as seems likely—the traces of it have almost disappeared, and it cannot have had an *enceinte* of any strength. Very probably there was no more than a narrow strip on the hill top enclosed by a low wall. The place, however, was formidable from the steepness of the rock on which it stands : its position is very dominant. It was one of the castles regularly provided with a royal garrison, and justified its existence by holding out through all the Welsh insurrections of the late Middle Ages. It was in a way the complement of Harlech, at which it looks at a distance of perhaps ten miles across Tremadoc Bay : beyond lies all the long sweep of the coast of Cardigan. There is a rocky knoll some 300 yards away from which the place could be conveniently bombarded after artillery came in: but it does not overtop or command the castle hill.

Harlech

Far more important than Criccieth is Harlech, the loftiest, the most precipitous, and (not even excluding Conway) the most picturesque of the castles which Edward I. built to hold down the newly-conquered principality of North Wales. Out of the flat sandy expanse of waste at the head of the estuary of the Traeth Bach, there rises suddenly a bold crag, over 200 feet of sheer rock, a projecting spur running down from the inland mountains of Merioneth. On a small plateau, upon the summit of this crag, the castle is placed. A deep artificial cut, and beyond it a small space of level ground, separate it from the mountain mass, of which the crag is an outlier. Standing at the head of the estuary, it overlooks the broad angle of Tremadoc Bay, and

HARLECH CASTLE: VIEW FROM THE S.W.

HARLECH CASTLE: THE MAIN GATE-HOUSE

from its towers there is a view of almost illimitable extent on a fine day—embracing the whole coast for twenty miles in each direction. In especial it has a most commanding prospect of the long Peninsula of Lleyn, which forms the western half of Carnarvonshire. Its aspect must have been even more picturesque in the Middle Ages, when the sea had not yet receded from the broad sandy expanse at its foot, the chosen haunt of twentieth century golfers, but washed up to the water-gate at the foot of the crag.

The main fortress, the two wards at the top of the precipice, is absolutely concentric—like Caerphilly—the lofty inner ward being entirely contained within the much lower middle ward. But in order to secure a guarded access to the sea below, the designer of Harlech drew walls downhill, right across the precipice, to give the garrison an approach to the water-gate. The space enclosed by these walls—which must be considered as forming an irregularly shaped outer ward—is in many parts inaccessible sheer rock, but the walls follow the less impossible slope, and come down to what was in Edward's day the shore, though it is now an expanse of sandy bunkers. The ascent to the castle is by a curved and angular path, cut in the face of the rocks, so steep that some of it is in steps, and much has crumbled away. Two thirds of the way up the path was barred by a cutting, a drawbridge, and a gate, and when these were passed the track curved round the foot of the middle ward, and went round to a postern at a rather unexpected point. The area of the crag-side taken in by the outer walls is so large, that it looks as if a garrison of enormous numbers would be required to defend it. But as a matter of fact this was not so: it was never seriously attacked or seriously defended. It was so steep that the only object gained by getting a footing in it would have been the cutting of the access to the water gate. The castle above would still be impregnable. Starvation might follow if the path to the sea were blocked, but it would take months to work out.

The actual castle, as apart from the irregular outside enclosure of the cliff-side, consists of two wards, absolutely concentric in arrangement. The middle ward (like that of Caerphilly) is low, narrow, and completely dominated by the lofty inner ward, with its curtain-walls 40 feet high, and its gate-house still higher. The outer defence is really a rampart-walk along the square plateau on which the castle stands, never more than 30 feet wide, and sometimes as little as ten feet. At its corners are four round bastions, too low to be called towers: on its north side is the postern to which the path from the sea creeps up.

The main entrance, on the east front, facing the mountains of the interior, is by a drawbridge across a cutting in the sheer rock, forty feet broad, which leads on to the outer gate, set between two low turrets. Like all the middle ward, this entrance is completely overlooked by the much more lofty gate-house of the inner ward, towering immediately above it. Part of the ditch outside the gateway is now filled with water, obtained by damming up a mountain stream descending from the lofty hill in front. Whether this water-defence existed in the Middle Ages is not certain.

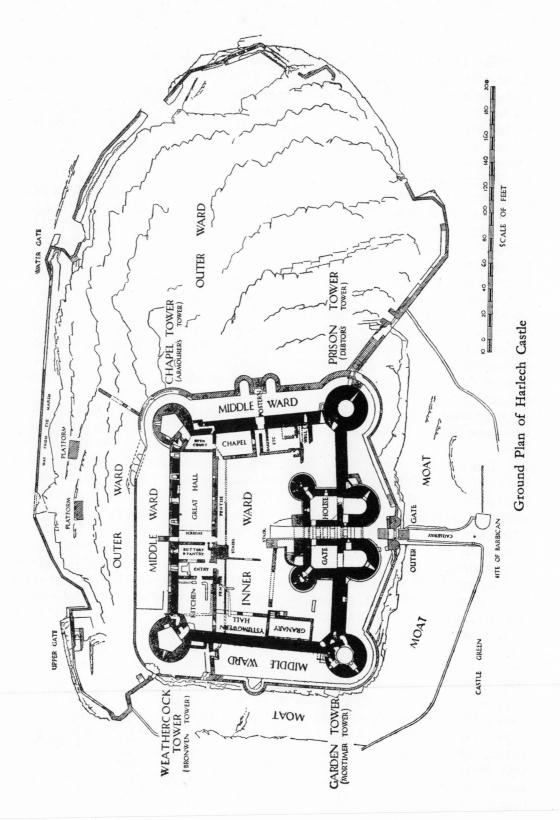

Ground Plan of Harlech Castle

WATER GATE

OUTER WARD

CHAPEL TOWER
(ARMOURER'S TOWER)

PRISON TOWER
(DEBTOR'S TOWER)

MIDDLE WARD

POSTERN

OPEN COURT

CHAPEL

ARMOURY ETC

GREAT HALL

INNER WARD

SCREENS

PENTISE

STAIRS

BUTTERY & PANTRY

ENTRY

KITCHEN

WELL

GATE HOUSE

GATE

STAIR

GRANARY

YSTUMGWERN HALL

MIDDLE WARD

MOAT

MOAT

GARDEN TOWER
(MORTIMER TOWER)

CASTLE GREEN

SITE OF BARBICAN

CAUSEWAY

OUTER GATE

MOAT

WEATHERCOCK TOWER
(BRONWEN TOWER)

UPPER GATE

PLATFORM

PLATFORM

WAY FROM THE MARSH

MIDDLE WARD

OUTER WARD

SCALE OF FEET
10 0 20 40 60 80 100 120 140 160 180 200

218

The inner ward, a marvel of lofty and solid building, is the portion of the castle which catches the eye even from eight or ten miles away. It is square, with a mighty drum-tower at each corner, and a still mightier gate-house in the centre of its eastern front, looking landward. The two western towers have turrets rising from them into the sky, while the gate-house has a third in its eastern angle: these are the high points which attract attention, when the silhouette of the castle is first discerned either from the sea or the land side. The drum-towers at the corners are sufficiently high, rising twenty feet above the forty feet of the curtain which joins them. But the solidity and height of the immense gate-house is still more striking: it is a heavy rectangle, 80 feet wide by 54 feet deep, in three stories, connected by newel staircases. The front above the portcullis swells out into two semi-circular curves, between which the recessed archway is placed. The back of the gate-house extends far into the inner court of the ward, and has also semi-circular tower-like projections jutting out from it. There are elaborate arrangements for cutting off the gate-house from the rest of the inner ward, in the last extremity of defence. This immense building is large enough to contain many spacious rooms in its upper stories: but there is, in addition, a great hall for the garrison in the middle of the west front, on the inaccessible side of the castle which looks toward the sea. When investigated closely Harlech seems a little destitute of detailed ornament—such as may be seen at Carnarvon or Raglan—it is all severely practical, with no gargoyles, shields of arms, or decorative lines of string-course. But the general effect is as impressive at a close as at a distant view.

It is surprising to find that this place of portentous strength was three times besieged and taken during the wars of the later Middle Ages: but our surprise ceases when we find that it was taken only after sieges lasting for many months —in one case for years—and that in two cases sheer exhaustion dictated the surrender. Beset for long months by Owen Glendower in 1404, and not succoured (as it should have been), for Henry IV. had other troubles to distract him, it yielded to the great rebel when the garrison had been reduced by sickness and starvation to 21 men. Owen then made it his central arsenal and store-house; there he placed his treasure, his wife, and his daughter—the consort of the pretender, Edmund Mortimer, who had put in his wild claim to the English crown—and her children. When Owen had been beaten in the open field, and had taken refuge in the hills, Edmund Mortimer, as castellan of Harlech, made a defence which lasted for some eight months, though he would get no food, because the besiegers had brought up ships to watch the bay. His father-in-law twice made desperate attempts to break the blockade from the land side, but was beaten. Though the English failed to breach the castle, either with mining or with military engines, the garrison was reduced to the utmost privations by mid-winter. Mortimer himself died of exhaustion and semi-starvation in January, 1409, and when he was gone the rebels surrendered. The ladies and children, for whom he had fought so bitterly, were sent to London, where his wife, his little son, and two out of three of his infant daughters died within a few weeks, in consequence of their long sufferings.

Desperate as was the resistance of Harlech in 1408-9, it stood a still longer, if a more intermittent siege, during the Wars of the Roses. After Towton (1461) North Wales was one of the few districts where the Lancastrians still held out. Jasper Tudor, the half-brother of Henry VI., made Harlech his headquarters, and even when the rest of the principality had quieted down, maintained from it, for several years, a guerilla warfare in the mountains of Merioneth. The castellan whom he put in charge of Harlech, Sir David ap Jevan ap Einion, held out long after Jasper had fled beyond the seas, and is said to have beaten off several spasmodic attempts of the Yorkists to deal with him. He did not finally surrender till 1468, when King Edward's Welsh champion, William Lord Herbert, sat down before the place and finally starved it out, an exploit for which he was rewarded with the forfeited earldom of Pembroke. The well-known song of the " March of the Men of Harlech," is said to recall some forgotten episode of this long defence, and Sir David is reputed by local tradition to have boasted that " he had once in his youth maintained a castle in France so long that every old woman in Wales had heard of it, and in his old age he had held a castle in Wales so long that every old woman in France had heard of it."

In the Civil Wars of Charles I., Harlech was so remote from the centres of the activity of the Parliamentary armies, that it was not assailed by Colonel Jones, Cromwell's Welsh brother-in-law, till all the other castles of the North had already submitted. It was surrendered on terms, by Colonel William Owen, the royalist governor, on March 13th, 1647. The usual " slighting " was, no doubt, carried out, but would seem to have been not very effective: at any rate there are no traces of large breaches in the walls. Perhaps the victors contented themselves with blowing in the gate, and removing the roofs. The immense solidity of the main buildings has kept them wonderfully perfect down to this day.

Aberystwyth, etc.

This castle may be described as a complete disappointment to the visitor. Knowing its eventful history, and seeing that a castle is marked upon the map, he will expect to find something that repays attention. There is nothing to be seen but a single stunted and mutilated tower, and adjacent to it a number of cellar-like substructures, representing the basement chambers of one corner of the fortress. Among them is one which is supposed to have been the mint in which Bushell coined for Charles I. the considerable amount of Welsh silver which was then coming from mines now long exhausted. The archæologist need not be tempted out of his way by these poor fragments. He might, perhaps, do better to visit after Harlech, not Aberystwyth, but a castle of less historic note but decidedly more perfect in its small way. This is Dolwyddelan —a single square keep of such primitive style that it is obviously to be ascribed to the Welsh princes of Gwynedd, rather than to their English conquerors. It stands in a small bailey, but has no notable feature save its keep. Edward I. took it by siege in 1283, and judging it sufficiently useful to be worth holding, as it blocks one of the best routes into the Snowdon Mountain-group, put a garrison into it under a Welsh castellan. He did not rebuild it—there is nothing " Edwardian " or " concentric " to be seen in it.

POWYS

The principality of Powys, as we have already said when dealing with the Shropshire Marches, was more fortunate than either Gwynedd or Deheubarth, in that the main line of its princes, dwelling in their ancestral Red Castle [Castel Coch] above the infant Severn, escaped the fate of the other Welsh royal lines, and survived the fateful year 1284—though as English barons and not Celtic chiefs. There were only two periods when the invasion pressed heavily against their borders, and thrust them back some little distance. The one was at the first coming of the Norman marchers under William the Conqueror, when Roger of Montgomery pushed his earldom up to the very foot of the mountains, and built upon their first ridge the great castle that is named after him.

Montgomery

This famous castle, overlooking from its lofty hill the little town which grew up from the *burgus* that the great earl established under its protection, is imposing but in very poor condition. What masonry there is surviving consists of large but fragmentary masses of rubble, from which the shape of the castle can be reconstructed, but little about its decoration or its successive transformations in the twelfth and thirteenth centuries. It lies on a very narrow site (like Chepstow), the crest of a spur 500 yards long and only 60 broad, with one flank, that which looks towards the town below, absolutely precipitous, partly from natural cliff, partly from scarping; the other flank, that which looks towards the west, is separated by a ravine from the neighbouring hills, and is almost as steep though not nearly so lofty. Hence, as at Chepstow, each of the wards occupies the whole breadth of the spur, and they are not contained one within another. The donjon is on the highest ground, at the point of the spur; of the other three wards, the third adheres to the keep, but is separated from it by a deep ditch, the second ward adheres to the third, and is again well shut off from it; the outer or southern ward naturally contained the gate, to which access lay from the town below, by a single steep road coming up from the south. The donjon or north ward and the third ward were both stronger and larger than the two southern or outer wards. These latter may have been additions made to a castle originally containing only the two upper lines of defence. The crest is so narrow and easily defended that there would be temptation to pile outer fortifications on to the inner ones, so as to keep the enemy at the greatest possible distance from the core of the place.

Roger of Montgomery's original castle was, no doubt, merely palisaded—as may be easily guessed from the fact that, only two years after his death, it was surprised by the Welsh during the great insurrection of 1095-6 and its garrison slaughtered.   Probably it was reoccupied when William Rufus made his retaliating expedition into North Wales a few months later.   But the next certain fact discoverable is that after the House of Montgomery had been crushed by Henry I. he gave Montgomery and much land round it to Baldwin of Bollers, a Shropshire knight who had married an illegitimate niece of his own, Sibylla of Falaise.   Bollers built some sort of a stone castle to replace the old

Montgomery.   Castle Keep

woodwork, and from him it got the name among the Welsh of Tre Faldwin—Baldwin's place.   The Bollers family held the castle from 1105 to 1207, when it passed, on the extinction of their male line, to the Fitz Urses—the one notable member of that house—Becket's murderer—being the son of a Bollers daughter. They held it but a few years, the castle and honour of Montgomery having been seized by Henry III. in 1225, and declared escheated.   From henceforth Montgomery was a royal castle, and one to which the king paid much attention, for he rebuilt it from end to end, spending nearly £3,000, a vast sum for those days, on his alterations.   The greater part of the ruins now visible must belong to his reconstruction—of the Bollers' buildings there are no certain remains. The reason for Henry's sudden energy was the long war with Llewellyn the Great of Gwynedd, who had once, or perhaps twice, been in possession of Montgomery—when the king got it back he considered it his own, by right of reconquest.   The new castle was besieged in 1231, and held out successfully, though the little town below was burnt by Llewellyn, who made another fruitless attempt to capture the fortress above in 1233.   The same thing happened some twenty years later, when Llewellyn the Last was repeating the early career of Llewellyn the Great.   He sacked the town in 1257, but failed to take the impregnable castle.   Hence the shame to Simon de Montfort, when at his very unpatriotic treaty of Pipton (June, 1265) he ceded to the Prince of Gwynedd this long-defended outpost of England, along with the castles of Hawarden, Whittington and Painscastle—all in return for the service of a Welsh contingent in his war with the royalists of the Marches. When the Montfortian cause had gone down, and the victorious Prince Edward had leisure to deal with Welsh problems, the treaty of 1267 naturally gave Llewellyn much less than he had extorted from Earl Simon, and Montgomery was restored to the king, though much land was still left to the Welshman.

The castle, therefore returned to its former rôle of outpost against Central Wales, and in the two wars which Edward waged against Llewellyn in 1277 and 1282, was in each campaign one of the regular bases from which Llewellyn's expeditions into Powys and Brecknock were crushed. But with the annexation of the land of Gwynedd after the death of its last native prince, the importance of Montgomery was much decreased. The town at its base grew in peaceful days, but the castle above had no longer an enemy to fear, or a special purpose to serve. Its Welsh neighbours, the princes of Southern Powys, had fallen into the position of simple English barons, and never gave any further trouble. There was one wild moment in 1402, when Owen Glendower descended upon the town and sacked it—about the sixth record of similar experiences—but as usual the castle maintained itself intact. When Leland passed in 1539 or 40, he notes that the little borough has been " deflourished " by Glendower; its broken walls had never been repaired, and its gates were but remnants. But he says nothing about the castle being ruinous, and apparently it was not, as a hundred years later it was used as a royalist garrison during the great Civil War. It was held till the general downfall of the king's castles in the Marches. In 1644, the old Lord Herbert of Cherbury, long past his literary and his military prime, surrendered it rather tamely. It was ordered to be " slighted " and no doubt some of its walls were blown down, but in all probability the present fragmentary condition of its lofty *enceinte* was mainly due to the stone-pilfering of the inhabitants of the town below during the next two centuries.

Powys Castle (Castel Coch)

Nine miles lower down the Severn than Montgomery lies the famous castle of the Princes of Southern Powys, which their countrymen called the Red Castle [Castel Coch], though the English generally named it the Castle of Pool, from the small town which lies a mile from its foot. It stands so close to the English border, which touched the Severn both above and below it, and runs but a few miles away, that it is surprising to find that it was never seized by any marcher, and remained the chief seat of its Celtic owners from the first to the last day of the Welsh wars. It is true that the lords of South Powys were, as often as not, adherents to the English cause, out of hatred for their rivals, the princes of Gwynedd. But they were so frequently involved, willingly or unwillingly, in rebellions, that they can only be considered lucky in escaping the fate of their kinsmen of Powys Fadoc.

The present castle would appear not to be on the site of the earliest dwelling of the princes of Powys, which was probably a sort of primitive hill-fortification which stands on a knoll in the park, a quarter of a mile from the great Red Castle. When the Welsh took to castle-building, in imitation of their Marcher neighbours, a prince of the late twelfth or early thirteenth century—it is said to have been Owen Cyfeiliog, who died in 1197, or his son Gwenwynwyn, who died in 1216—reared a strong stone fortress on a more commanding hill hard by, and here the long-lived Gruffyd ap Gwenwynwyn (1216-1289), and his son Owen, normally allies of the English against the princes of North Wales, had their usual residence, the old royal seats of Mathraval and Meifod being abandoned. A stronghold so close to the border was obviously more convenient to a prince who leaned on the English alliance than for one who nourished hopes of independence. Yet twice Castel Coch fell into the hands of the native enemy—the second time as late as 1274, when Llewellyn the Last took it, and compelled Gruffyd ap Gwenwynwyn to fly to Shrewsbury. This Gruffyd and his son, Owen, were by their ties to Edward I., more English barons than Welsh princes, and were regularly summoned to Parliaments as such. Owen's son, Griffin, died a minor in the reign of Edward II., and much litigation ensued as to whether the lands of Powys should be treated as an English feudal barony, and pass to the last owner's sister, Hawise, the wife of Sir John Cherlton, a small marcher baron, or to her uncles, who claimed them under Welsh rules of succession. The king decided in favour of the lady, and from her came a long line of half-Welsh Cherltons, lords of Powys, distinguished soldiers in the Hundred Years' War. Much dispute has arisen among genealogists and constitutional lawyers as to whether their title was more properly Cherlton or Powys—in Parliamentary rolls the territorial designation was not infrequently used instead of the family name. They failed in the male line and ended in 1422, with two co-heiresses, of whom Joan the elder married Sir John Grey, Joyce the younger Sir John Tiptoft. Oddly enough the heirs of both claimed the title of Powys—the younger Grey being summoned to Parliament as baron Grey de Powys, while the younger Tiptoft was called baron Tiptoft and Powys in his creation to be Earl of Worcester. But, what is more odd still, they apparently divided not only the estates but the castle, for when Leland went by about 1540 he noted that he found at Castel Coch " two Lords Marchers' castles within one wall." The part of the Lord Dudley, great grandson of Joyce Tiptoft, was " almost fallen down," that of Lord Grey, grandson of Joan the elder sister, was " metely good " : and Grey finally bought out the other portioner, who sold even his ancestral castle of Dudley before he died in 1553. It would appear that the outer ward had been the share of the Tiptofts and the inner ward that of the Greys.

But the Greys, too, died out in mid-Tudor times in the legitimate line, and the last baron's natural son sold the castle to Sir Edward Herbert, one of the wide-spread family that descended from Edward IV.'s Earl of Pembroke. The Herberts rebuilt the castle ; but there is much Cherlton work, and even masonry belonging to the old princes of Powys, discoverable within the

DINAS BRAN CASTLE: THE HILL-TOP

CHIRK CASTLE: THE COURTYARD

Jacobean exterior, even after further alterations in the nineteenth century. The Herbert of 1688, who had been made an earl in 1674, was a resolute follower of James II., and went into exile with him—he was outlawed and the castle was given by William III. to one of his Dutch satellites. More lucky than most of the Jacobites, the Herberts, thirty years later, not only got back their title but their castle. But their line twice died out in the male succession, and the sister of the last earl, having married the second Lord Clive, son of the victor of Plassey, the title had to be recreated for a new house, the modern but famous barony of Clive merging in the ancient name of Powys—or Powis, as modern usage spells it. The castle, majestic, if much modernized, still looks out from its lofty site over a long reach of the fertile valley of the upper Severn, which represents the core of the old Welsh principality of its lords.

Dinas Bran

This very fragmentary castle, more imposing from a distance than when seen close, is one of the few fortresses of Wales which had a Celtic—perhaps, even, a pre-Celtic origin, for it may have been a prehistoric tribal camp before any stone was laid upon it by the princes of "Powys Fadoc," the northern section of Powys, in the valley of the Dee, which got cut off permanently in the twelfth century from "Powys Gwenwynwyn," the larger and more southern section. Our first mention of it comes from the Romance of Fulk Fitzwarine—and speaks of it as a ruin in 1073. Certainly no stone now standing in it goes back to that date, but the tradition that it was pre-Norman is worth noticing. According to the wild story in the Romance, when William the Conqueror was clearing the marches from Welsh raiders, he pushed up the Dee as far as Llangollen. There one of his knights named Pain Peveril, a member of the Derbyshire house of that name, noticed ruins on the hill above and asked from the Welsh of the neighbourhood what they were. He was told that they were the remains of the abode of King Bran, a character who figures largely in Geoffrey of Monmouth, but that none dared lodge in them, or even to approach them at night, because they were haunted by evil spirits. Pain, being of an adventurous disposition, swore that he would sleep there that night, and went up the hill-side with his retinue. They encamped among the broken walls, and were for some time undisturbed, till soon before midnight a tremendous thunderstorm burst upon the mountain, with a wind so preternaturally strong that Pain's

Dinas Bran. View from below

225

knights and squires were swept to the ground, and crawled to hide themselves. Then stalking through the entry was seen a gigantic figure in rude garments, wielding a great iron mace and threatening destruction to all. Pain went to meet the fiend, trusting not to his sword but to his shield, on which was painted a cross, and to the prayers and exorcisms which he kept chanting. And they were effective, for when the fiend strove to assail him his mace was unable to strike the cross and turned aside, and when exorcised he gave ever back, till Pain was able to run in and thrust him through the breast. He fell, and the victor adjured him by the name of God to say who he was. The dying creature answered that the body which he inhabited was that of Gogmagog, one of the giants who had opposed Brutus the Trojan, when he landed in Britain. This Gogmagog's body was left intact, because he was drowned, not slain, and he, being an evil spirit wandering in waste places, had entered in and possessed it, and had been a terror for over a thousand years to all who came through the valley. King Bran, to defy him, had built a palace on the hill, but he had preyed upon the king's servants, slaying them as he pleased, and plundering their goods, so that they had fled after a time and left the place deserted. On further interrogation he said that there was a vast treasure buried below, including a golden ox of life-size, but that Pain would not find it: it was destined for others. And thereupon the evil spirit issued from the dying body with a great stench, and the night grew clear. Pain showed corpse and mace to King William next morning—his master threw the former into a deep pit, but kept the latter, which he was wont to exhibit as a marvel to his knights.

What this wild tale proves is that its writer, somewhere in the reign of Henry III., believed that beneath the existing and perfectly well-known castle of Dinas Bran, then held by the princes of Powys Fadoc, there had been pre-historic ruins, ascribed by tradition to Bran, the son of Dunwallo, a king whose name was familiar in the legends of Geoffrey of Monmouth. And very probably there may have been a Celtic hill-fort on this very prominent peak.

But what we now trace on the spot is a vast shell-keep dominating from its lofty site all the minor valleys which come down to the Dee near Llangollen. It looks like a thirteenth century or later twelfth century castle, built by no very skilful architect, probably, therefore, by a prince of Powys, rather than by a Marcher lord. It is all composed of local shale from the hill-sides around, which are full of quarries. Nothing much remains save the outer *enceinte*, but there are traces of a hall in the south front, and of two drum-towers commanding the entry on the east side. On its one accessible front the castle is cut off from the hill-side by a deep ditch: the rest of the slopes are precipitous. In the walls seven arches may be counted, some round, some slightly pointed. There are traces of a barbican or a small outer ward beyond the ditch which protects the gate of entrance.

Probably one of the princes of Northern Powys was the builder of the castle, as we see it at present, and it may well have been one of the sons of Madoc, under whom the lands of Powys on the Dee were finally alienated from the southern lands along the Severn, which were to become "Powys Gwenwynwyn." This would mean that the castle may date from about the time of King John. It is interesting to find that in 1270 no less than four princes of Northern Powys met at Dinas Bran to sign a document in common—evidently it was a central place for that much-divided house to meet in. They were the last generation destined to rule in the land or to hold the castle. They adhered to Llewellyn of Gwynedd in the war of 1277, saw Dinas Bran taken from them, but were pardoned at the peace of Aberconway which sealed the humiliation of their ally. In the great final insurrection of 1282, we find the castle again held by rebels and captured, and after this Edward made an end of the independence of the petty principalities of Northern Powys, at the same time that he annexed Gwynedd. Dinas Bran and the lands north of the Dee were given as a Marcher lordship to Warenne, Earl of Surrey; the rest of the lands, those south of the Dee, to Roger Mortimer as the March of Chirk.

It is probable that the grant of Dinas Bran to such a distant owner as the Earl of Surrey sealed its fate: it was never a residential abode again, and was allowed to sink into decay. Leland, passing by in 1540, remarks that "the castle was never a big thing, but set, all for strength, in a place half inaccessible for enemies. It is now all in ruin; and there, on the rock-side that the castle standeth on, breedeth every year an eagle." So this eagle's nest of a fortress became in very truth in its decay a real eagle's nest. It moved the sentimentality of Wordsworth, who, in his visit to Llangollen, moralized on this—
    "Relic of Kings, wreck of forgotten wars,"
as he chatted with his hostesses, the two eccentric "Ladies of Llangollen." It is incredible, I think, that he reached the summit, for his poem speaks of "Shattered Galleries," just the things which this bare site does *not* show.

Chirk

When, as we have said just above, Edward I. annexed all the minor principalities of Northern Powys, he gave the section of them which lies south of the Dee to Roger Mortimer, younger son of the then Lord of Wigmore. And Roger at once built or rebuilt a castle on the newly acquired land, some two miles from the village of Chirk, after which it has been named. But the separate March of Chirkland existed but a short time, for, on the death of Roger Mortimer, and his son John, in the reign of Edward II., the head of the house, the Lord of Wigmore got hold of it.

We have said that Roger, the grantee of 1282, built or rebuilt Chirk Castle. The phrase has to be used because there had been in the reign of Henry II. some sort of a marcher stronghold here, but in 1166 it had passed into the hands of Jorwerth the Red, a prince of Northern Powys, to whom the king confirmed it, in order to win him to an alliance against Owen, the rebellious Lord of Gwynedd. It is quite uncertain whether Jorwerth and his successors kept up the castle, or let it fall into decay, for in 1166 it had not yet become usual for the Welsh princes to maintain fortresses, and its site may not have been that of the present building, but one near the village, where there are traces of a *motte* and ditch. Probably Roger Mortimer went to new ground, for the earliest parts of the present castle indicate work of the time of Edward I., and no earlier.

Chirk is a perfectly square Edwardian castle with four drum-towers at its four corners. Two of its sides, those toward west and south, have a steep descent behind them ; to the others, there is access up an easy slope. There are no visible traces either of a ditch or of an outer bailey—but such may have existed, and have been swept away when the castle was modernized.

The effect of the single square ward is somewhat like that of a college quadrangle, as all the four sides are composed of domestic buildings, looking into the court. There is a tower at a corner of one of the sides, but it is not a high one—nothing approaching a keep in character. The effect of the whole is somewhat squat, owing to there being no high dominating building in any part. All the windows have been modernized, and are many-mullioned and large : the mediæval aspect of the place is particularly impaired by big windows having been inserted in the four drum-towers at the four angles.

All the Mortimer estates, as we had occasion to mention in other places, went to the House of York, and then to the crown. The castle was sold in the time of Elizabeth to Sir Thomas Myddleton, Lord Mayor of London, the founder of a long line of owners, who still possess Chirk, though it is let on a long lease to Lord Howard de Walden. It was undoubtedly Sir Thomas who knocked out all the mediæval windows of the inner court, and replaced them by the broad and handsome Elizabethan ones now visible. His son, another Sir Thomas, was a prominent personage in the great Civil War, started as a lukewarm royalist, but changed over and became a hot Parliamentarian. His consequent experiences were unfortunate, as he saw his castle seized by the Royalists and failed to recover it himself, but afterwards as unsuccessfully defended it when chance had thrown it into his hands. Chirk was, however, taken by Cromwell in 1645, after the third siege which it had undergone in three years. It is said to have been sadly battered, but its owner repaired it when it was returned to him by his victorious friends, and it was not "slighted" like so many other castles of the March. Its present appearance would seem to show that it has not been much pulled about since 1650. Approached by a curling woodland path for nearly two miles from the park gates, it is a pleasant enough specimen of an occupied Edwardian castle, a thing not too common in the Marches.

ENVOI

The last words of this book shall be devoted to the praise of John Leland, my predecessor in so many devious journeys, who toiled on his nag over countless miles which I traversed in train or car. He studied in my own College of All Souls, though he was never apparently either a Fellow or a Bible-Clerk therein. For several years on each side of the central date, 1540, he was compiling his *Itinerary*, the most precious record existing of the state of castles, towns, and churches, at the end of the reign of Henry VIII. I have had to quote him a hundred times, always with gratitude, for he had a specially watchful eye for castles, always noting which were " metely kept," which " half ruinate," and which " clene gone to the very ground." A never-tiring investigator, a patient recorder of every observed fact, he may truly be called the first English Antiquary : and to the spiritual ancestor of the whole tribe his latest descendant pays his homage of admiration.

FINIS

Goodrich Castle : South Front.

229

ACKNOWLEDGMENTS

The Photographs and Plans herein are reproduced by permission as shewn:

WINDSOR CASTLE: Aerial View	*Surrey Flying Services*
WINDSOR CASTLE: Exterior of St. George's Chapel	*G.W.R.*
WINDSOR CASTLE: Interior of St. George's Chapel	*Photochrom Co.*
DONNINGTON CASTLE: The Gate-house	*G.W.R.*
WELLS: Interior of Bishop's Fortified Palace	*Phillip's City Studio, Wells, Som.*
WELLS: The Gate-house and Moat	*Phillip's City Studio, Wells, Som.*
FARLEIGH HUNGERFORD CASTLE	*G.W.R.*
BERKELEY CASTLE: Aerial View	*Surrey Flying Services.*
POWDERHAM CASTLE: Aerial View	*Surrey Flying Services.*
BERRY POMEROY CASTLE: Seymour's Buildings and Inner Ward	*G.W.R.*
FOWEY: Battery and Polruan Tower	*G.W.R.*
ST. MAWES CASTLE: View from the Land Side	*Valentine & Sons, Ltd.*
ST. MICHAEL'S MOUNT: Aerial View	*Surrey Flying Services.*
ST. MICHAEL'S MOUNT: View from the Shore	*G.W.R.*
GOODRICH CASTLE: Corner Tower	*G.W.R.*
WHITECASTLE: The Gate-house	*W. A. Call, Monmouth.*
CALDICOT CASTLE: Aerial View	*Surrey Flying Services.*
CAER CYNAN CASTLE: View from the Side of the Precipice	*W. A. Call, Monmouth.*
GROUND PLAN OF KENILWORTH CASTLE	*Author.*
GROUND PLAN OF LUDLOW CASTLE	*George Woolley, Ludlow.*
GROUND PLAN OF CAERPHILLY CASTLE	*Muirhead's Guide Books, Ltd.*
GROUND PLAN OF PEMBROKE CASTLE	*J. Bartholomew & Son, Ltd.*
GROUND PLAN OF HARLECH CASTLE	*H.M. Office of Works.*

Those marked with an asterisk (*) are from the negatives of C. C. OMAN, ESQ. *The remaining photographs are by permission of* MESSRS. FRITH & CO., *Reigate.*

INDEX

N.B.—*Names of Castles of which a description is given are in Capitals: those only mentioned are in small type*